D1860591

THIRTY FIVE YEARS IN THE EAST

In the treasury of Nature there are many Gems; but those only are worth carrying away, which we know how to set.

Honigberger.

THIRTY FIVE YEARS IN THE EAST

ADVENTURES, DISCOVERIES, EXPERIMENTS, AND HISTORICAL SKETCHES

RELATING TO

THE PUNJAB AND KASHMIR

IN CONNECTION WITH

MEDICINE, BOTANY, PHARMACY & C.

JOHN MARTIN HONIGBERGER

ILLUSTRATED WITH NUMEROUS ENGRAVINGS,
CONTAINING PORTAITS, FAC-SIMILES

GYAN

Published by

Gyan Publishing House
5, Ansari Road
Daryaganj, New Delhi-110002
Phone: 011-47034999, 9811692060
E-mail: books@gyanbooks.com

Distribution Network
gyanbooks.com
India, USA, Canada, UK, Australia, France

© Publisher

All rights reserved. No part of this work may be reproduced, stored, adapted, or transmitted in any form or by any means, electronic, mechanical, photocopying, micro-filming, recording or otherwise, or translated in any language, without the prior written permission of the copyright owner and the publisher.

ISBN : 978-81-212-4097-0 (PB)
First Published, London, 1852

2nd Impression 2020

Printed at: Gyan Press, Delhi.

The book is sold subject to the condition that it shall not, by way of trade or otherwise, be lent, resold, hired out, or otherwise circulated without the prior publisher's written consent.

Thirty Five Years in the East
Author: John Martin Honigberger

THIRTY-FIVE YEARS

IN

THE EAST.

ADVENTURES, DISCOVERIES, EXPERIMENTS,

AND

HISTORICAL SKETCHES,

RELATING TO

THE PUNJAB AND CASHMERE;

IN CONNECTION WITH

MEDICINE, BOTANY, PHARMACY, &c.

BY

JOHN MARTIN HONIGBERGER,

LATE PHYSICIAN TO THE COURT OF LAHORE.

Illustrated with numerous Engravings, containing Portraits, Fac-similes, &c.

LONDON:

H. BAILLIERE, 219, REGENT ST. & 290, BROADWAY, NEW YORK (U.S.) R. C. LEPAGE & Co. CALCUTTA.

1852.

मिनश्शर्कि तलअत बकुदरतुरहमानि।
अनवारुद्दीन वलइल्म वलउमरान॥

Min-as-shark talata ba kudrat ar-rahman,
Anwar-ud-din wa al-ilm, wa al-umran.

From the East, by the power of the merciful One,
Lights of Science, Religion and Culture have shone.

PUBLISHER'S NOTICE.

JOHN Martin Honigberger was a physician in the Court of Lahore when Maharajah Runjeet Singh, the Lion of the Punjab, was ruling the country. On the death of the Maharajah, Honigberger stayed long in Lahore to thoroughly understand the people and the Court, the intrigues and the conspiracies which brought about the downfall of the Khalsa Power. Honigberger was not only a man of science, but he knew politics and could follow the trend of public affairs and forecast the future. He commanded a happy narrative style of writing and related the stories of the Court of Lahore with a felicity of diction and a charming *tète-á-tetè* fashion, which rivet the attention of the readers to the subjects of narration.

"THIRTY-FIVE YEARS IN THE EAST" is divided into two volumes. The first is full of historical sketches and personal reminescences, the second deals with medicines and medicinal plants. The second volume is too technical for the general reader now, besides the great progress, that the modern Medical Science has made during recent years, Honigberger's theories have all become more or less antiquated or exploded. We have therefore left out the second volume and published the first.

It is said that India has effected a complete "turn round" during the last half of the nineteenth century, under British guidance and having the impulse of English education. Honigberger's historical sketches will distinctly show that the Punjab of 1848 is no more,—so great have been the changes effected. When we think that it is but sixty years that the Punjab has come under the British domination and when we contemplate of the marvellous material and moral changes effected, we cannot but be filled with wonder and amazement. Honigberger's book deleneates the half-forgotten past and accentuates the sense of wonder and admiration.

This book is a good and useful companion to Cunningham's "History of the Sikhs". Cunningham is rigid and matter of fact, Honigberger is amusing, and informing. Cunningham deals with high politics and affairs of State, Honigberger exults in Court gossips and personal stories, domestic incidents and dark conspiracies. We have already published Cunningham's history and we now offer Honigberger's book with the hope that it will form a fit complement to the "History of the Sikhs."

It is needless to say that "Thirty-five years in the East" is now out of print and almost forgotten. Though a neglected gem, it will, in its new garb attract sufficient public attention and patronage. Almost all the wood-engravings of the features of all the leading notabilities of Lahore during the Khalsa rule and before, have been reproduced in this edition. These engravings, we are told, are all faithful likenesses.

THE BANGABASI OFFICE,
Calcutta, September, 1905. } THE PUBLISHER,

INTRODUCTION.

---o:o---

On presenting this work to the English public, in an English dress, I would state, that notwithstanding much has of late been written, by travellers and physicians, on the important countries of the East, they have not exhausted their topics; and I have been induced to publish the results of my experience, from a conviction that this work may form a valuable addition to the publications already extant.

Thirty-five years spent in Asia—travelling from my native country (Transylvania) by way of the Levant, Egypt, Arabia, and Persia, to India, residing several years in the Punjab, and returning by Affghanistan, Bokhara, and Russia, at a period when these countries were but little known to Europeans—afforded me ample opportunities for satisfying my ardent desires for research, and for obtaining an acquaintance with some of those secrets of nature which had so long been concealed in that quarter of the globe—the cradle of humanity and the birthplace of science.

The prosecution of my researches was considerably aided by my influential position, during many years, as Physician to the late Sikh Court of Lahore.

Those who take an interest in the history of the Punjab, may find, in this, the first volume, many sketches of oriental character, and illustrations of Eastern manners, customs, and intrigues; also, a faithful summary of recent events.

The second volume, although a medical work, has not been written for physicians only; it is apprehensible and may be useful to all readers. To render it the more acceptable to those in the East, in addition to the Flora Medica of Cashmere, with its properties and uses, as also those of many other oriental plants and drugs, I have superadded a Medical Vocabulary, in nine languages.

A variety of discoveries, curious experiments, and remarkable incidents, may be found in these volumes, collected during a sojourn of many years—useful, I hope, to both naturalists and historians.

During my fifteen years' residence at Lahore, as well as on my frequent journeys, I embraced every opportunity of devoting my attention to the examination of the various medical systems of the day, and to the experimenting on the qualities of numerous medicines, whether known or unknown to practitioners. Freed from every selfish motive, I now ingenuously present to the British public, the results of these researches, which were carried on with unwearied perseverance. I am not under the influence of the mania of *system-making*; my object is, simply, to aid the alleviation of the sufferings of humanity and to enrich science, as far as my abilities may permit. I have been guided solely by the proverb, "*Nulla re homo proprius accedit ad Deum, quam salute hominibus danda;*" *i. e.*, "Nothing brings man nearer to God, than man's helping his suffering fellow-creatures."

It is no easy matter to eradicate systems which have been deeply rooted for centuries. Who will take upon himself the responsibility of a *change* affecting the existence and welfare of myriads of human beings? Accurately expressed, my System can scarcely be called a *new* one; it is, more properly, a *medium* between two extremes; a system grounded on experiments, which I advisedly adopted, and which success impelled me to pursue. I am persuaded, that any one who may be guided by the instructions I now give, and who may follow a like course, cannot fail to obtain similarly happy results.

Notwithstanding I spared no pains, endured much fatigue, and deemed not any sacrifice too great, particularly during the last ten years I abode at Lahore, to accomplish my object, I am far from supposing the subject to be exhausted. On the contrary, I feel, that though much has been done, much remains still to be done; and I trust that others may assist in bringing the work which I have commenced, to that degree of perfection, of which I am convinced it is susceptible.

It is impossible to entertain any high opinion of the healing-art of the Mahomedan doctors, derived from the ancient Greeks and Egyptians (Thababet-junany of the Hakims) or, of that of the Hindoos; for, they have made but little progress beyond that defective medical science which is found in their old manuscripts. Their directions for the treatment of patients, contain little else than extravagances and superstitions—to which the Hindoos, whose system is the most ancient, add *astrology*. As their religion stands in the way of every attempt at improvement, there is but little hope that they will ever make much progress in medicine, or, relinquish their absurd theories; and nothing remains for us, but to pity those who are doomed still to continue in darkness. Yet, we ought not entirely to disregard old works, but to select, as I have done, such portions as appear useful. I have tested some of the simple remedies mentioned in their books, which, having been injudiciously administered, had fallen into disuse (their real utility being misunderstood, or, overlooked) and, in some cases, I found them very efficacious. In prosecuting my experiments, I principally consulted the Persian works, *Tohfet Khany*, and *Tohfet al Mominin*. And to these I shall refer, as often as the special cases I relate, may require.

At present, there are *two* different systems of medical treatment practised in Europe, *viz.*, *Allœopathia* and *Homœopathia* ; both of which have been contending for supremacy, during the last half-century. The former is the ancient method, and is universally recognised and taught in all the universities of Europe ; but, as both of these systems have their *pro.* and *con.* I shall, for the sake of the general reader, give a concise account of each ; which accounts may, at the same time, serve as an introduction to the *medium-system* I have adopted.

Allœopathia contains remedies which operate so violently, that, if the doses administered are not very nicely adjusted to the disease, or, if a mistake occur (which too often happens) the effect, instead of being salutary, proves injurious, if not fatal ; and the patient then dies, not of disease, but, from the improper means used for its removal. In such cases, it would have been better to have left the patient to the fostering care of nature. The number of those who are sent (some of them in the prime of life) prematurely to their graves, through injudicious treatment, is by no means inconsiderable ;

neither is the number small of those unfortunates, who, from the too violent operations of medicine, live only to wander about as cripples or phantoms, weak and disabled, a burden to themselves and others, some of them longing for death, as the only deliverance from their miseries.

Girtanner, in his *Therapeutics*, Vol. II., p. 600, acknowledges, that " The *apparatus medicaminum* is nothing more than a careful collection of all the sophisms which have been invented by the medical practitioners of former times. It is true, some valuable experience may be found among this immense heap of verbosity ; but, who would spend his time in selecting a few grains of pure metal from such an enormous heap of rubbish as that which has been accumulating for 2,000 years. In the worse than Egyptian darkness in which the physician has to grope his way, he scarcely perceives a ray of light to guide him through the ' palpable obscure.' When two physicians meet at a sick-bed, it is with difficulty they refrain from laughing—like two augurs of Rome."

Lemiere is quite right in saying—

Lorsque la fievre et ses brulantes crises
Ont de notre machine attaqueles ressorts,
Le corps humain est un champ-clos alors,
Ou la nature et le mal sont aux prises,
Il parvint un aveugle, appelle medecin
Tout au travers, il frappe a l'aventure :
S'il attrappe le mal, il fait un homme sain,
Et du malade un mort, s'il frappe la nature.

In the *Heidelberg Clinical Annal*, Vol. V. Part 3, it is stated, " More individuals perish through the interference of physicians, than are saved by their assistance."

Hence, many have lost all confidence in medicine; for, the dark side (the defects of the art) cannot be concealed from even the uninitiated. Lord Bacon says—" I will not deny that physicians of the present day are indifferently well acquainted with the general symptoms of a disease ; but, either they do not rightly understand, or, have not sufficiently examined the medicines which they prescribe in particular cases. The addition, diminution, and alteration of medicines, in the most arbitrary manner, so that usually one medicine is substituted for another, is quite a common proceeding."

Peter Frank, in his *System of Medical Police*, Vol. I. says, "It is strange that the government should interfere only in time of epidemics and against charlatans, whilst it takes no notice of the thousands who are daily sacrificed in their solitary chambers. Governments should determine either to banish all physicians and their art, or, take measures to render men's lives more secure than they are at present."

Confessions like these, by physicians themselves, are so numerous and so well known, as to render more quotations unnecessary ; those which I have given affording the most conclusive evidence of the defectiveness and uncertainty of *Allœopathic* medical science.

It was, without doubt, the defects of the science of healing as practised by the Allœopathists, which induced the immortal Hahnemann to embrace and propagate the doctrine of *similia similibus curantur.*

There cannot be anything more irrational, than an implicit adherence to a system, without a previous examination of it; without having tested it, and satisfactorily proved it ("*Jurare in verba magistri*") consequently, I do not profess myself a votary of Hahnemann's system. In the course of this work, I shall have to cite cases wherein it will appear, that the most minute doses of a medicine have, sometimes, proved efficacious; whilst, in other instances, they did not produce any effect whatever; and I am bound to confess, that, in the majority of cases, the results I obtained from Homœopathy, were not favorable; I felt persuaded, that larger doses would have been better. I have also found it injudicious to wait too long in order to discover, by the operation of a medicine, if it were well-chosen; and I consider it erroneous to prescribe for a patient the strictest diet, prohibiting the use of such things as the body has been accustomed to—particulary *tea* and *coffee*, which have a stimulating influence on the nerves and blood vessels. I do not deny the *antipsoric* theory in several chronic diseases; nor do I, like Hahnemann, reject the use of external *adjuvantia*—such as bleeding, blistering, &c.

The disciples of Hahnemann are of opinion, that, as tea and coffee exercise a peculiar influence on the nervous system, and are *therefore* good and certain remedies for persons unaccustomed to the use of them, they should be used medicinally only. But let me urge, amongst the substances which constitute our usual nourishment, or things which we consume as articles of luxury, there are many which affect the nerves even more strongly than tea or coffee; therefore, by parity of reason, we ought to debar ourselves of them also.

Hahnemann, who daily enjoyed his glass of beer and his pipe, took both these favorites under his protection, declaring them less obnoxious than tea and coffee; but, who can blame me for having inclinations of an opposite cast? I cannot endure strong beer, and smoking produces nausea, whilst I find tea and coffee very agreeable, never experiencing the slightest injurious effect from either of them, for, I am accustomed to both. Similar results will necessarily occur to every one who habitually uses certain special articles of diet. We daily consume a considerable quantity of common salt, in our various dishes. Many would be surprised, could they see the yearly amount collected into one mass; and would be inclined to think, that our stomachs, and, perhaps, our intestines, also, would finally become crusted with a coat of salt: yet, whilst in combination with our diet, it does not produce any striking, or sensible effects, it, nevertheless, proves a very efficacious remedy, when administered as a medicament, in proper doses.

On attentively considering what I have just stated, the reader cannot think it extraordinary that I regard the *two* medical systems, *Allœopathia* and *Homœopathia*, as two opposite poles. The first rushes into the field, armed with enormous pills, and bottles of all sizes, containing the most powerful mixtures, striking at the foe with wild and deadly force; the other, with less martial display, attacks the enemy in a manner which seems the quintessence of feebleness and inertia—a small case, containing pygmean flasks, filled with lillpiutian pills which the least breeze would scatter to the winds, and a few minute drops, are all the direful weapons. The drops are not always the pure extract of the medicinal plants, but are sometimes diluted to a *decillionth* of their strength; and even the smelling at some of these substances is said to be occasionally sufficient to work miracles.

All our medical knowledge is the result of experience; and the reason why we have made so little progress in medicine is, that its professors have not divested themselves of that narrow-minded adherence to ancient maxims, which rejects all experimental results that are not recognised in their dogmas.

I look upon the immeasurable realms of medicine as a republic, founded for the welfare and prosperity of mankind. There should be neither exclusive authority, nor respect of persons. The members of this commonwealth, in wandering with measured tread about its sometimes gloomy precincts, will, by careful research find some untrodden paths, which lead to undiscovered treasures. It is thus that I have spent the greater part of my life, and I am desirous of pointing out to others the road which I found most agreeable and safe. It is unlike that followed by many of our contemporaries, who, infatuated by their own system, drag their patients over gulfs and precipices. Mine is a smooth and middle course; following so much only of every other as I have, by the observation of many years, proved useful. Moreover, this new path is easier, less perilous, more agreeable, and less expensive.

During the latter years of my residence at Lahore, my *practice* was corwned with the greatest success; and after having scrutinized my *theory*, I became convinced that this *medium-system* was the best, and I now confidently recommned it as the most efficient.

"Magna est veritas et prævalebit."
"Truth is mighty, and must prevail."

Besides other advantages which this system possesses, the remedies are administered in so agreeable a form, that they may be taken without the consciousness of their being medicinal. This is worthy of attention, as it removes one of the many difficulties which obstruct the way of the physician, in the exercise of his profession. He has often to contend with prejudices and notions imbibed in early infancy, and to attend to idiosyncrasies, lest he should increase instead of removing evils. In children, he has to struggle with obstinacy, ill-humor caused by pain, &c. In the treatment of females, he must never lose sight of their nervous mobility (natural or affected) which often becomes constitutional; their greater sensitiveness, their stronger irritability, and their more delicate organisation; and if, eventually, he is fortunate enough to conquer all these difficulties, still he may not cry *victory*, until he has acquired the art of removing from his prescriptions all that is nauseous or disagreeable.

It is a palpable act of cruelty in mothers to force their infants to swallow remedies which are repugnant to their taste, in the mistaken notion that bitter pains must be removed by bitter medicines. Nature, in placing at our disposal such vast stores of medicinal treasures, surely never conceived the revengeful notion of punishing those who had recourse to their aid. It is more consonant with reason to suppose, that they were benevolently endowed by nature with their nauseous flavor to warn us against the danger of using them too freely.

A physician might as rationally assert, that it is possible for him to give to the rotation of the earth any direction he *wills*, as that the remedies he administers in accordance with the mere custom of the profession, must infallibly prove beneficial. He cannot dictate laws to Nature in either case ; experience alone is the teacher and arbiter, and on experience must we ground our hopes. But, as hope often deceives us ; and as even the most skilful physician is not infallible ; the grand rule to be adopted is—"*all strong doses to be avoided, and such only to be administered as, though they may not benefit, yet, cannot do any harm.*" This rule may easily be followed, if we acquaint ourselves with the effects of medicines both in large and minute doses ; and I think, that without this knowledge, no physician can prescribe any remedy whatever, with a clear conscience. The point to which I devoted the greatest attention in my investigations, was—observing the effects produced by various medicines ; and it was not until the operation of a prescription had been thoroughly tested, that I felt confidence in prescribing it in similar cases—*similia similibus.*

The ancients, without being acquainted with the natural law of *similia similibus curantur* (according to which small doses are required) were well aware of the injurious effects of large doses, and recommended the greatest caution—*Praestat pauca dosi, et per intervalla remedia exhibere, quam uno impetu ventriculum remediorum moleste obruere* ; *i. e.*, "it is better to give a medicine in small doses, and at intervals, than to load the stomach with it in large quantities at once." If they thus spoke and acted in the days when remedies were mild, and had but little influence on the patient ; if they then said—*Salvia cum ruta faciunt tibi pocula tuta*, how much more should this golden rule be observed by us, now that the progress of chemistry has unfolded the powers of those simple remedies.

I have no great opinion of the so-called *nostrums* ; but, as we are recommended to " prove all things, and hold fast that which is good," I tried some of them, out of curiosity. The celebrated Morrison's and also Holloway's pills, I found, as I expected, violent purgatives, which may, however, be employed with advantage (?) by a judicious physician. I need scarcely observe, that they do not deserve the name of *panacea* ; neither can I advise any one, to take either of them in the beginning of a violent fever, having witnessed bad consequences from so doing, I have administered the above-mentioned pills, in small doses ; also Warburg's fever drops, which are reputed good ; and the reader may find a description of their effects and composition in the second volume. I was pleased to see in a Report in the *Bengal Pharmacopœia* (1844, p. 147) that *arsenic* in very minute doses, recommended as a diuretic, which is driven off with the urine, may be again easily detected in it. It is highly probable, that if we were as well acquainted with the re-agents of other medicines as we are with those of arsenic, and if we know where to look for their action, *i. e.*, whether in the blood-vessels or in the nerves, in the lymphatic system or in the cellular tissue, in the gall or in the bladder, in the spleen, in the liver, in the kidneys, in the stomach, or even in the intestinal canal, we might then be able to detect their *modus operandi* also.

In the *Bengal Dispensatory*, p. 162, it is said of Ranunculeæ—" They are extremely acrid and corrosive; and so unmanageable, as to be excluded from medical use by all modern practitioners." It would, indeed, be much better to desist from using such strong medicaments altogether, when they are employed in undiluted doses only. It is really pitiable when all other arts and sciences have made such important progress, that medicine alone should continue stationary; that its professors, from an unwillingness to investigate the nature, virtue, or proper use of medicinal substances, should fancy themselves bound to condemn simple yet efficacious plants to oblivion, as things which providence has created for the delight of our eyes only, and which are sure to injure us, should we attempt to use them! Almost all the plants which were employed formerly, have met with this fate. Where are the Salvia, the Ruta, Euphrasia, Imperatoria? As for the deadly poisons, Calomel and Opium! these glitter as fatally brilliant in the East Indian medicinal horizon, as they do among English physicians. How beautiful and true are the lines of Shakespeare—

> O, mickle is the powerful grace, that lies
> In plants, herbs, stones, and their true qualities:
> For naught so vile, that on the earth doth live,
> But to the earth some special good doth give;
> Nor aught so good, but strained from that fair use,
> Revolts from true birth, stumbling on abuse.

If the bee can suck nectar from poisonous plants, why should not man discover their properties, and derive benefit by employing them as remedies for ills ? "*In formica non modo sensus, sed etiam mens, ratio, et memoria.*" What vast medicinal treasures do the varied productions of the Himalaya Mountains offer to the inhabitants of India ! Could they be made to appreciate their value, how readily would they employ them.

As the efficacy of a medicine depends upon its being properly prepared, I advise physicians in India to keep such plants as the Ranunculaceæ (which grow abundantly in the Himalaya Mountains and in the valley of Cashmere, and which contain volatile substances) in well-closed vessels. They ought to be prepared on the spot, either as an essence, or, as as a conserve, and kept in a temperate place, secure from the decomposing rays of the sun. The supply should also be renewed once a year, at least. Such precautions are absolutely necessary, if we really desire to attain our object. Dried herbs, from the apothecary or druggist, are often ineffectual, from being old and spoiled. It must not, however, be inferred, that the volatile parts alone are valuable ; brewers, from long experience, consider old *hops* more powerful than new ; and *asarabacca* acts in its fresh state as an emetic, and when old as a purgative.

Much depends upon the soil in which plants grow, as also on the climate. "*Differe quoque pro natura locorum genera medicinae.*" *Celsus Med. Libr. præfat.*

Thus, *Cannabis Indica* grows higher, stronger, and more luxuriantly in Cashmere than in the plains of India, and has been monopolized by the Cashmerean government. The *churrus* is prepared from it, and sold in India, where it is mixed with *tomakoo* (tobacco), and used for the purpose of producing intoxication, principally by the faqueers, who smoke it through the hooka. Besides the hemp-plant, two other valuable productions of the country, saffron (*Crocus sat.*) and the putchuk-root (*Costis nigr. Cashm.*) have also been monopolized by the government. Notwithstanding this fact, and the proximity of the country, it is stated in the *Bengal Dispensatory*, p. 692, "Putchuk-root is brought from Lahore, where it is called *koot*, it is of unknown origin; it is chiefly exported to China, where it is used as incense," &c. (!)

Twenty years ago, when I was still ignorant of what drugs were to be obtained in the Bazaar at Lahore, I sent to an apothecary in Calcutta, for *Strychnos faba St. Ignatii*, and *succus sepiœ;* instead of the first, I received *Strychnos nux vomica*, which belongs to the family of the *Strychnos!* and instead of the latter (the *tint* of the cuttle-fish) I received *cuttle-fish shells*, although, as the reader may be aware, the latter have a different color and a different effect. All these species of *Strychnos* and *ossa sepiœ* can, however, be procured in any quantity at the Lahore Bazaar.

My long residence in "the land of the five rivers" afforded me the opportunity of becoming well acquainted not only with the country and its productions, but, also with its endemical and epidemical diseases; its medicinal substances, and the vernacular names both of diseases and medicaments; all of which are less known to English physicians than those of the lower provinces, that part of Hindostan being a newly-conquered country. In order to render the work more acceptable to the English faculty, I have introduced these particulars in the second volume, where, besides a description of the new method of treatment I adopted, may be found (as already stated) the Flora Cashmerean, which, though not perfect, contains many of the principal qualities and hitherto unknown effects of those plants, which, by experiment, I discovered.

The illustrative plates have been drawn with accuracy.

My object is, to place the work within the reach of every one whose health is dear to him, and to render it useful to all. It will be found more especially valuable to those, who, living in the interior of the country, are shut out from immediate medical assistance; also to travellers, who are much exposed to noxious influences, and who may not have a physician near them. With the aid of this work, and a family medicine-chest (which can be prepared, at a trifling expense, at any pharmacopolist's, where the purity of the articles and the exactness of their preparation may be depended upon) my advice can be followed, as easily and certainly, as if I were consulted personally.

Every rational being ought to possess at least some slight acquaintance with the structure of the human body, and also of its functions ; and should acquire a knowledge of so much of the healing-art as may be necessary to maintain a healthy action under ordinary circumstances. The celebrated Delphic inscription—*i. e. Know Thyself*, which sentence of the Oracle greeted every one who entered the Temple of Wisdom, teaches us, plainly, that the sages of antiquity were well aware of the importance of this study. It often happens, that he who has even but a slight knowledge of medicine, and understands the peculiarities of his own constitution, is able, by the timely application of a suitable remedy, entirely to remove, or lessen, any illness with which he may be attacked.

English physicians residing in the East, and more especially those in the Punjab, may derive great advantage from the *Flora Medica Cashmereana.* I should recommend them to apply to the Secretary of the Medical Club at Lahore, that he may send them, *annually*, a small but fresh supply of herbs, and to use them according to the System I lay down in this work.

It would, indeed, be desirable for physicians who intend to establish themselves in any country, to make themselves acquainted with the productions of the locality, and to try the qualities of indigonous plants on healthy as well as on diseased individuals, that they may be ablo to use them advantageously. Such a course would not only render the physician independent of the supplies of medicines from foreign countries, and furnish him with remedial agents on the qualities of which he could depend, but he would, at the same time, be rendering a service to mankind, by the occasional discoveries with which he might enrich medical science. It was thus, that I discovered the healing properties of nearly all the plants which are mentioned in my *Materia Medica*, in the second volume.

If this advice were generally acted upon, a considerable saving would be ensured to the

Government in India, which is now at much expense, in importing costly medicines, for the use of the troops, &c., an expense which might be almost entirely avoided, if the physicians there were acquainted with the properties of the native plants and drugs.

When I went to Lahore the second time, I was, as before, appointed Physician to the Court, and also Superintendent of the gunpowder-mill and gun-manufactory. The *Dar-ul-Shefa* (hospital) in the city, was under the direction of two brothers, Azeez-oo-Deen and Noor-oo-Deen, both rich faqueers, and the government paid for the medicines which were daily distributed there; but, although I made some experiments on my new system, at my own expense, yet, my opportunities were very limited, as it was not within my province to attend the *Dar-ul-Shefa* of the faqueers. When the English came, however, they shut up the gun and powder manufactories, and ordered the Durbar to erect a public hospital outside the city. The management of this establishment was entrusted to me, and I then obtained the long-desired opportunity of continuing my experiments, uncontrolled, in the new method of treatment, and on a large scale, until the annexation of the country, in May 1849; the results of which surpassed my most sanguine anticipations.

My waiting-room was constantly filled with patients, attracted not only by the inviting appearance and sweet taste of the medicines (lozenges), and the (to them) pretty wooden boxes in which they were delivered; but also, by the efficacy which they found these *bonbons* to possess. The establishment presented a curious aspect. My department, more resembling, in its adjuncts, a confectioner's shop than a repository of drugs, was on one side of the building, and the other side was occupied by the *Hakim* (Mahomedan doctor) appointed by the Durbar to assist me, and who was at liberty to treat patients according to his own system ; so that applicants could employ native or European remedies, as they felt disposed. But, what a difference ! what a wide gulf between the two methods ! On the one hand, my hitherto unknown *medium-system* (which then still slumbered like an embryo), the principles of which I have already mentioned, and, on the other, the obsolete *Junanian* (Grecian) or *Arabic system*, which, with many of its medicaments, has long been banished European practice.

In this hospital, also, I was entrusted with the care and treatment of lunatics ; and, in the interior, sat three *Jerahs* or native surgeons, also appointed by the Durbar, who were occupied in the administration of ointment, plasters, &c., for external healing ; so that, with those patients who came to avail themselves of the services of these *Jerahs*, those who came to consult with the *Hakim*, and those who preferred my advice, the hospital was a complete *mile* (fair) from morning till night.

It was with difficulty that I could satisfy the demands of the multitudes who came from the neighbouring towns and villages for medicines, notwithstanding I was provided with several assistants besides those already mentioned.

One day, a man, who, in passing, had heard that the *Dakter Saheb* (Gentleman Doctor) distributed such good medicines, in boxes, was desirous to obtain some for himself and friends. A few months afterwards, the same man returned, bringing back the box I had given him, and asked for some more of the lozenges, for one of his friends, as the previous supply had been of much service. The paper on which I had written the symptoms of the disease, the remedy *(lens)*, and the date when I had given it, was still in the box. The man assured me that he came from Loodiana, a distance of 140 miles, that he had no other business in Lahore, and that he intended to return immediately. A long journey, thought I, to take for a few lentils which I had that day prepared.

To avoid mistakes in the application of remedies (one messenger often applying for medicines for three or four patients), I made use of larger and smaller boxes of different colors; each of which contained a paper, whereon was noted the principal symptoms of the disease, the name of the remedy, the quantity, how to be taken, and the date on which it was delivered. It may easily be conceived, that, as I sometimes did not see the patients, it was difficult to form a *diagnosis*, especially in such cases as cutaneous diseases and affections of the eye. For instance, I once sent a remedy for blindness, and received the agreeable intelligence that the patient had recovered his sight ; but, I confess, to this day, I am not aware *what* the disease of the eye was ; probably, *Amaurosis*. Besides the afore-mentioned occupations, I received an order from the Durbar to establish an hospital in the jail of Lahore also; which was on the same spot whereon, a short time before, I had erected the powder-mill. During the last two years of my office (1848 and 1849) out of 800 prisoners, only twenty-one patients died in the space of twelve months, and they, of severe wounds, marasmus, or dysentery. The jail, with its hospital, is situated outside the city, in one of the filthiest quarters, where all the wells of the neighbourhood contain briny or bitter water ; and notwithstanding all my endeavours and remonstrances, I could not obtain from the government any better nourishment for my patients, than the usual jail diet, so that I was obliged, in several cases, to have recourse to a part of the unemployed funds of the public hospital of the Durbar, in order to provide such comforts as were necessary. Taking these circumstances into consideration, my management was peculiarly fortunate ; for, during a period of two years from the foundation of that hospital, not a single patient died of an acute disease—such as inflammation, fever, cholera, serpent bites, &c., of which I had many cases ; some of them so dangerous, that I had to visit the patients three or four times a-day. My successor was less fortunate ; for, during the first six months after the annexation (from May till October 1849) while I was still in the country, he lost upwards of sixty patients out of 1,000, not to mention those who were dismissed as incurable. I may state, with regard to the latter, that the experiments I made on similar diseases had often been crowned with success. It was thought that the great mortality during these six months was caused by the small and unhealthy situation of the hospital, in consequence of which a larger was built, on the opposite side of the jail. The prisoners received better nourishment, were not so oppressed by hard labor, and were permitted to use tobacco, opium, poppy-heads, hemp, churrus, &c., which had been prohibited. I afterwards learned, that these changes had not been of much use ; and I believe the mortality is still greater than that of the first two years.

Among my papers, I have met with the following letter, which I received at Lahore, and which may serve as a proof to unbelievers in the efficacy of my minute doses—

Residency, 2nd December, 1847.

Dear and respected Sir,

I may appear seemingly to have neglected your prescriptions, but I assure you, I have not. The reason of my not doing myself the pleasure to call on you, has been owing principally to heavy business, consequent on Col. Lawrence's leaving this, and some little to the distance of your present residence. The *lozenges*, however, last supplied, being over, I come before you again a beggar ; but, before you comply with my petition, permit me to mention the effect of your medicine. The largest sore in my gums is nearly filled up with fresh flesh, while the discharge generally from the gums is greatly lessened. My general health is improved so much, that I fear I am becoming almost as stout again as I was at Simla, and when it is considered that I had but lately recovered from a violent attack of the liver, it must be confessed that my present improved health is to be ascribed to your valuable medicines for the last month and half. While I thus express my most grateful obligations, I trust you will continue your kind favors for a little longer, and therefore beg a fresh supply, to be sent in an envelope, the box being at home. Allow me to subscribe myself, with high respect,

Dear Sir,
Your obedient humble Servant,
WM. SKINNER,

I might produce many such testimonials, but they are unnecessary ; as I have not any desire to obtrude my System on the public. I simply call attention to that which I have experienced, and leave it to every reader to examine and judge for himself. I wish to avoid self-praise, and honestly to give the impartial reader an opportunity of judging from this work, whether the happy results, herein described, are to be attributed to good-fortune, or, to the excellence of the system, and my peculiar mode of treatment.

We have continually to combat with deeply rooted habits and prejudices ; and it requires no little patience, constancy, and perseverance to come off triumphant. Habit exercises a powerful influence on the mental faculties, as well as on the physical organisation. It is a very difficult task, and one which requires indomitable resolution, to forget what we have once learned, and to apply ourselves to the study of things which may have appeared impossible. Yet, men of sense often *change* their opinions—blockheads, never. This is especially the case with persons who are strongly prejudiced in favor of Systems to which they are indebted for their reputation, extensive practice, and good income. It can scarcely be expected that men should abandon their lengthy prescriptions and familiar methods, to study new ones ; or, that they should be persuaded that minute doses could produce effects more salutary and rapidly than larger ones. Above all, those who prefer gain to conscientiousness, may be expected to raise an outcry against this publication. To those who may attempt to decry my System, whether from pecuniary interest, ignorance, or a lack of power to relinquish prejudices,

I say, with Cicero—*Tacere præstat philosophis, quam loqui.* To those who may ingenuously desire to correct errors, and who possess manliness sufficient to offer judicious advice, I shall give my cordial thanks, knowing how to appreciate an impartial critique. *Palmam qui meruit ferat.*—"Be his the palm who merits it."

If my work meets with a favorable reception, and is considered useful, I shall feel happy in having attained my most ardent wishes; I shall forget the toils, dangers, and sacrifices I have undergone, and, moreover, escape the lot of many, who, after having spent the greater portion of their lives and fortune, and, not unfrequently, ruined their health, in rendering themselves useful to mankind, have too often met with ingratitude, and, sometimes, with persecution. Many benefactors of the human species have experienced such treatment, and analogy almost prepares us to expect it. If we turn to the histories of important discoveries and inventions, we shall find, that, on their first announcement, they were contemned and ridiculed, while the inventors and discoverers were laughed at, misrepresented, and vilified. Sydenham, whose memory we must revere, was, by several of his contemporaries, stigmatized with the name of *quack*, and *murderer.* Many now celebrated men, who, in the fourteenth century distinguished themselves by their knowledge of physical science, were burned as sorcerers. Galileo was imprisoned in his seventieth year, for maintaining the rotation of the earth; and posterity may, perhaps, admire some of our cotemporaries, who having done much for the advancement of arts and sciences, have not enjoyed the esteem they merit.

We daily observe what extraordinary things can be achieved by persevering practice, and what strange facts are brought to light by scientific investigation ; nevertheless, there are men of our day, who will not even admit the truth of *animal magnetism* ; still less will they give credence to that remarkable power of suspending existence, as illustrated in the account of the *Faqueer Haridas*, who could place himself in a state of *asphyxia*, and, after remaining buried in the earth for months, could, by pursuing his instructions, again be restored to life. This fact is already known to the reading world, and appears in a detailed form, in this volume, page 127.

We may perceive from what is passing around us, that nature works destructively on one side, and productively on the other; incessantly striving, as it were, to preserve a balance. In this continual change of matter, subtile elements are generated which sometimes have pernicious influences on living beings, and occasion various diseases. We know, that the preserving and healing power of nature (*viz., conservatrix et viz medicatrix naturae*) may go hand in hand with medical assistance, although we do not know by what agency they operate ; nor do we know anything of the formation and constituent parts of any disease, epidemical or endemical. Do we know the nature of mineral, or, animal magnetism? electricity, attraction, or repulsion? Who can say, how aerolites are formed in the higher atmospheric regions? The book of nature lies open before us ; but, who can decipher it?

The different qualities of a medicament can be determined only by careful and reiterated trials on healthy as well as on diseased individuals. Experience teaches us, that the effects of remedies are manifold; that the same medicine operates very differently, according to the quantity of the dose, or the intervals at which it is administered. Thus, minute doses of certain medicines remove nausea and arrest vomiting; whilst the same medicines given in larger doses, produce a contrary effect; others, when taken in large quantities, act as purgatives; but, when administered in minute portions, check diarrhœa. *Therefore, since we are aware that medicines in minute doses possess peculiar qualities and powers, it is our bounden duty to make ourselves acquainted with this mode of using them, and it is imperative on us to forego such notions and principles (hereditary or acquired) as are founded on prejudice. Minute doses alone can produce real medicinal action.* Properly employed, they operate beneficially; because, their action is confined to that part of the body which is the seat of disease, while the remainder of the system is not attacked or weakened; if improperly employed, they cannot, from their minuteness, be very injurious. Large quantities of any materials, whether from the kitchen or the apothecary's shop, whether prepared by cooks or prescribed by Greek, Arab, Indian, or European physicians, are not entitled to the name of *medicines*; they are to be considered *nutriments*, when properly used—when abused, they are *poisons*.

Instances frequently occur, wherein large doses of so-called *medicine*, appear to produce curative effects upon the patients; but, it is probable, that, in some cases, the recovery is attributable to the healing power of nature alone, which often repairs what bunglers have injured.

Many persons cannot conceive, how minute doses, which are so small that they are supposed to be lost before they can reach the stomach, can produce any effect. They argue thus—As the stomach is the medium through which we obtain everything we require to preserve life, and by means of which those substances are assimilated that serve to compensate for the loss caused by the action of the vital functions, it requires to be deluged with medicines, in order to produce any effect on the system. But, experience teaches us, that this is not necessary. Small particles of medicaments, dissolved on the tongue by the saliva, on entering the stomach, mix with the chyle; and their effect is then conveyed by the electric or magnetic action of the nerves, to the remote parts on which they are destined specifically to operate.

I advise every medical man to extract from the *Materia Medica* (in the second volume), a list of such remedies as he can procure; and to arrange them alphabetically (with the diseases and symptoms to which they are applicable), that he may be able to refer to them readily. A pocket-book so arranged, would be useful to families as well as physicians. The remedies for different diseases (which are suggested in the first part of the second volume) are intended for those physicians only, who, having time and opportunity, desire to continue the train of my experiments. I have arranged the various diseases or symptoms in groups, many of them being closely allied. I have noticed in which cases the remedies proved beneficial, and, in short, I have pointed out effects of any kind. I have also retained several *untried* remedies, and have marked them as such. Not knowing how long I might enjoy so favorable an opportunity of prosecuting my experiments, I was assiduous to determine, in the shortest possible time, the qualities of most of the substances I have mentioned; consequently, I treated many of them superficially, not occupying myself long with any particular medicine. I preferred making a large collection of such substances as had been either long disused, or which were so new, that their qualities and effects were unknown or unappreciated.

Be it observed, most of my informations regarding the *effects* of the medicines were gathered from the uncivilized natives of Asia, whose statements cannot always be relied on; and that, notwithstanding my circumspection, mistakes may have occurred, for which I can hardly be held answerable. Many ignorant persons took different remedies at the same time (several different kinds of lozenges, which were of the same form and color)—in such cases I could not decide which medicines had produced the desired effect. I have stated the effect as attributable to different medicines, that they may be further tested.

It also often happened, in the public hospital at Lahore, that people took medicine from me and from the Hakim at the same time, for the same patient; simply because both were gratis: and they took my medicines whilst they were under treatment by the Jerahs for abscess, ulcer, scrofula, &c., as if the interior had no connection with the exterior.

In a hasty perusal of the *Bengal Dispensatory*, *Bengal Pharmacopœia*, *Ainslie's Materia-Medica Indica*, and the summary of East Indian drugs contained in the *Great Exhibition Catalogue*, I observed a few inaccuracies and deficiencies, which I have taken the liberty of correcting and supplying, in an Appendix to the second volume; which I trust may not be found a useless Supplement.

In closing this Introduction, I feel it incumbent on me to express my thanks to the Governor-General of India and the Board of Administration in the Punjab, for the Pension they have honored me with, in consideration of my long medical services to the Maharajh Runjeet Sing and his successors.

This Pension, added to the savings of a laborious life, secures me a moderate income in my retirement; and enables me to devote the profits of this work, be they great or small, to the Educational establishments of the Saxon colony in Transylvania— my native country.

JOHN MARTIN HONIGBERGER.

London, January, 1852.

There is a land, of every land the pride,
Beloved by Heaven, o'er all the world beside;
And in that land of Heaven's peculiar grace,
The heritage of nature's noblest race,
There is a Spot of earth supremely blessed,
A dearer, sweeter spot than all the rest.
Where may *that* Land, *that* Spot of earth be found?
Art thou a Man? a Patriot? look around—
O thou shalt find, howe'er thy footsteps roam,
That land THY COUNTRY, and *that Spot* THY HOME!

MONTGOMERY.

ADVENTURES, DISCOVERIES, EXPERIMENTS.

AND

HISTORICAL SKETCHES.

HOWEVER agreeable it may be to return home after an absence of many years, and after having escaped many dangers and endured many toils, to tread again the soil of one's native country, enriched with knowledge and experience; still, it is not without a feeling of emotion, that we recall those scenes of danger and fatigue to our recollection. They flit past us like dissolving views, which appear only to vanish, yet still leave behind them deep traces of the past.

It was a secret impulse, an inward voice, which urged me towards the East, where the first man lived of whom history makes mention, where culture was first practised, and where arts and sciences flourished; where religion—that heavenly light—began to spread its rays. *Patriam fugere, peregre proficisci.*

I left my native town of Kronstadt, in Transylvania, in the spring of 1815. After having crossed Bukovina, Moldavia, and Walachia (where I remained above a year), I arrived, in the autumn of 1816, at Varna, on the Black Sea, whence I embarked for Constantinople. This was my first voyage. Being aware that the distance from Varna to Constantinople was short, I did not apprehend it could be attended with danger. On arriving at Varna, I was informed that several Turkish vessels were bound for Constantinople, on one of which I embarked. Besides seventeen Arnauts (Albanian-Turkish soldiers) a pretty French lady (from Jassy) was on board, with whom I conversed in Moldavian. On the approach of evening, we sailed from Varna, with a favorable wind, in company with a Turkish fleet of about twenty small vessels. Fatigued by travelling, and lulled to sleep by the soothing motion of the vessel, I sank into the most charming reveries of the future ; when, towards midnight, I was aroused by the noise of the crew and passengers. A dreadful tempest from the north had overtaken us so suddenly, that there was not time to haul down the sails, which, in a few minutes, were shivered to pieces, and continued flapping and whistling in the storm. The mast itself did not escape the violence of the elements, but fell overboard with a crashing noise ; and the foaming waves gushed into the open vessel. The night was profoundly dark, illumined occasionally by flashes of lightning, accompanied with peals of thunder ; hail and rain fell tempestuously ; the elements seemed to have conspired against us. Too late, I became aware of my error, and regretted having embarked in a heavily laden open vessel ; but, as all the other ships were of a like size, and similarly laden, I had no choice. By the lightning we could, now and then, perceive some of the vessels belonging to our squadron exerting their efforts to get through the foaming waves, sometimes riding on the watery mountains, at other times plunging between the gaping billows. We felt some consolation so long as we held them in sight ; but, they soon disappeared altogether.

As our vessel had shipped a great deal of water, the sailors (few in number) were obliged to bail without intermission, in which they were assisted by the passengers, while standing up to their knees in ice-cold water. Every exertion was made to save the vessel ; and, at the commencement of the tempest, when the mast went by the board, it was found advisable to lighten the vessel by throwing the cargo into the deep. Notwithstanding thirty-five years have elapsed, I vividly recollect their beginning with a large earthenware-stove which stood on the poop. They then threw overboard barrels of honey, bags of walnuts, &c., so that there remained only a quantity of burduffes (ox hides, containing tallow) which could not be removed in consequence of their great weight. They were, therefore, obliged to cut the tallow with axes and large knives, and throw it piecemeal into the sea. This required hard labour, as the tallow was frozen. In this operation, our Greek captain (we had also a Turkish one) broke his yatagan (a large Turkish knife); and upon seeing that the water in the hold continued to increase, he gave up all hope, and retired to his little cabin in despair. There he fell on the knees before the image of his *Havayia* (the Virgin), and left the vessel to the care of heaven and the Turkish captain. Happily the tempest did not last long; the storm, which had come on so suddenly, left us with the same rapidity. Filled with hope, the day dawned upon us, when we descried the high mountains of Greece in the distance. The first rays of the sun, whose appearance infused new life and fresh courage into our breasts, arose majestically from the horizon, and beaming brightly, diffused warmth through our limbs, previously benumbed with cold. With the aid of the mizen-mast, and favoured by a gentle breeze, towards the evening of the same day we approached the shore, where we cast anchor. At the break of day on the following morning we disembarked, and thanked heaven for our deliverance. From thence we walked up about ten miles, and arrived at Apollonia, a city once celebrated among the Greeks, but now of little importance, and bearing the name of Sissopoli, to which place the vessel was brought to be refitted. I here found my companions, the Arnauts, who had taken up their quarters in a large coffee-house, where they literally roasted their frozen feet at a coal fire. Although they discontinued this in consequence of my warnings, it was too late; and I afterwards learned that several of them died in Constantinople of mortification. It was so hot in the coffee-house that I could not stay there long, and although I kept aloof from the stove, which was heated to redness, in order to avoid the sudden transition from cold to heat, I nevertheless caught a severe rheumatism in my feet, which tormented me for four months during the winter; with the approach of spring, however, it was radically cured. Amongst the many remedies which I applied, *Lawsonia inermis* proved the most effective. Every evening, before going to bed, I applied to the affected part the pulverized herb, with as much water as was sufficient to make a soft poultice. In the morning I washed it off, but the place continued red ; it is the same herb, indeed, with which the fair sex in the East stain their hands and feet. To strengthen my body, and especially my feet, I also used sea-bathing, which had a very good effect. From Sissopolis, we arrived, after a voyage of two days, at Constantinople. The view of the panorama of the Turkish capital and its environs, which we had on entering the Bosphorus, was so fine, and so imposing, that I felt compensated for all the dangers and troubles hitherto endured, and completely forgot them for the time. In winter (the middle of December, 1816) nature was still arrayed in green. This, however, did not last long ; for in the beginning of January a heavy fall of snow, three feet deep, took place, and it grew much colder than I expected to find it in Stambul.

Before the expiration of the year 1817, I had an opportunity of continuing my journey towards Jerusalem, a city I was desirous of visiting. I was engaged as physician in ordinary to the Governor of Tocat, with whom I travelled into the interior of Asia Minor. However agreeable this journey might have been during the summer, it was very fatiguing during the winter, as almost every step cost us an effort, and we made our way with difficulty through the snow which covered the high mountains of Asia Minor. The caravan of the new governor, which whom I travelled, consisted of sixty horses and mules. One day we lost our way during a violent snow-storm in the mountains of Anatolia, and we had to pass a very bad night, till at last we got out of the deep snow, and found a village. On this journey I began to make a collection of antiques (ancient Greek coins and engraved stones), which at that time were easily obtained at the silversmiths, at a low price. I regret I did not then so well understand the value of them. From Tocat I travelled to Aleppo, passing through Kaisari,

Tharsus, Adana, Alexandretta, and Antiochia. At Aleppo I found many Germans among the numerous Europeans, and on that account would willingly have practised there for some time. Unhappily I fell sick on the road, as between Adana and Alexandretta I had to cross an unhealthy, low and marshy country, where malaria and marsh-fever were prevalent. In consequence I was attacked with a disorder called sub-acute inflammation in the spleen, which afterwards turned into an obstinate quartan ague, of which I got cured only when I had left Aleppo; and that, I suppose, was the reason why I could not get an extensive medical practice. A physician (was the saying) who is not able to cure himself, can never cure others.

After a two months' stay on the Syrian coast, during which time I enjoyed the best health, I tried to get back again to Aleppo; but at the last station before reaching Aleppo I caught the fever, on the same spot where it left me, and curious enough I found, in my journal, it happened on the same day it would have befallen me had I not left Aleppo at all. Thus it continued to be my constant companion during all my stay there; but as soon as I took my leave of that place, it deserted me, without having been expelled by any remedy. I had full ten months to suffer by that tiresome guest. The experience I had myself, agrees with that sentence, "Febris autumnalis est longa non lethalis." During these ten months I got but few cessations of my illness, and then only at short intervals. One may infer from this, that obstinate diseases, defying every medical assistance, can only be cured by travelling, I mean to say (change of air) by removing from the country where the disease is caught.

Subsequently I had the opportunity of effecting several cures in Tripoli—where these marshy fevers are endemical—with a compound mentioned in the second volume of my work, containing arsenic and bitter almonds (prussic acid) in minute doses, which was eminently efficacious where sulphate of quinine failed.

I quitted Aleppo before the fatal catastrophe of the

earthquake, which caused so many disasters; the village called Jisershol, on the river (between Latachia and Aleppo), was entirely destroyed. Following the Syrian coast, I crossed Latachia, Tripoli, Beyrout, Seida, Sur, Acre, Nazareth, Jerusalem, and Bethlehem, and visited the Holy Sepulchre, &c., in the autumn of the year 1819. From Jaffa I embarked for Damietta and went up the Nile as far as Cairo. At that period an Armenian from Tocat, named Giovanni Bozzari, enjoyed the title of First Physician, under the superintendence of whom I obtained employment in the fortress. Giovanni Bozzari pursued his medical studies at Constantinople, in the house of a Venetian doctor named Bozzari. Availing himself of the name of his professor, when in Egypt, Mahomed Ali, at that time a Binbashi (chief of 1,000 men), protected him, as he had been well advised by Bozzari when he applied for his assistance. Subsequently, when Mahomed Ali was promoted to the dignity of a Pasha, Bozzari was invested with the title of privy counsellor, and occupied at the same time the post of physician in ordinary: Cui fortuna favet, sponsa petita manet!

At that period (1820—1821) Mahomed Ali despatched an army to Upper Egypt, under the command of his second son, Ismail Pasha; his elder son, Tossoon Pasha, having died by the plague some years previous. I was one of the first among the physicians engaged for that expedition; but whilst they were preparing for the march, the plague broke out, which induced me to give up that fatiguing and perilous journey, cede my post to another, and go back to Syria. Some time after, I learned that the expedition miscarried, that none of those ten or twelve physicians who accompanied the army had returned, and that Ismail Pasha himself had been massacred.

At Cairo I was so fortunate as to be very successful in my cures. Among others, I attended a merchant of Constantinople, a Greek, who was greatly afflicted with the stone during a period of forty years, so that he was willing to undergo an operation. I cured him of his complaint by administering to him (for a period of six weeks) diluted muriatic acid. More recently I tried the same remedy with other patients for the malady, but without any success. I deduce from this, that the substances of the stones in the latter cases were not the same as with my patient at Cairo, and that muriatic acid has not always the quality of dissolving stony concretions. Not finding any dissolving medicine that would act universally, I was obliged to effect the cure of stone in the bladder by an operation with the instrument. In Syria there were also Arabs, known as stone-operators, who adhered to the old method of Celsus, *i.e.*, to bring the stone down by introducing the fingers into the rectum, and cutting it out through the perinœum ; but I preferred the apparatus altus, where the stone is cut out from the bladder, through the pyramidal muscle of the belly, which produced a very great sensation, and obtained for me the name of a skilful operator. The first operation for the stone I made was on Mount Lebanon. Afterwards I performed similar operations at Damascus, Bagdad, Persia, India, and even at Bokhara, as the reader will find.

In the year 1822, I began to vaccinate in Syria, with a lymph received from Aleppo, which acted well. Two particular cases which occurred at the villages in the neighbourhood of Tripoli (Syria) deserve especially to be mentioned here. The small-pox raged epidemically in those places, in a horrible manner, killing adults as well as infants, without any distinction. The use of vaccination was as little known in Syria, as it was in Europe before the time of Jenner, and I was just in the centre, or rather in the focus of that epidemical disease. A widow having two children, one son and a daughter, the latter of whom she loved and idolized, insisted upon only permitting the male to be inoculated, and if it should prove successful she would allow the operation to be performed on her fondled darling, the daughter. Accordingly I only vaccinated the son. When I visited him, after a lapse of eight days, I found the mother in despair, her daughter having during the interval died of the small-pox, whilst the boy was quite well, with large pustules like pearls on his arms ; she regretted, but too late, not having followed my advice, and looked upon the event as a punishment from heaven. In another village, not far from the above-mentioned, I had to attend a whole family of eight persons, old and young, who were vaccinated all at the same time. After eight days, upon calling on them, I found a young man of about twenty years of age, in agony, in consequence of confluent small-pox, which eruption had taken place on the evening of the vaccination. He was the only person in the house on whom the vaccination had failed, on account of the man having carried on his shoulders a dead body that was infected with the natural small-pox ; thus the lymph failed, by the counter-agency of the contagion. The rest of the family enjoyed excellent health, and were saved through the medium of vaccination.

There is an opinion prevalent, that vaccination will only keep off the small-pox for a period of twenty years. I was (if I am not mistaken) vaccinated in my native country, in the year 1800, with such an excellent lymph (not crust), that I treated a great many cases of small-pox, such as lately occurred in the years 1848 and 1849, at Lahore, without being affected by the disease myself, and that without having been a second time vaccinated. Nevertheless, if the second or third vaccination is of no use, it does no injury to the constitution. In one year I got from English physicians, lymph of quite different qualities, some from Umbala, and some from Delhi ; the former was of a good quality, but the latter was of a very bad one, as the pustules sprang rapidly up and vanished in a very short time ; neither was the areola of them red enough, which accounted for many of those whom I vaccinated catching the small-pox. I therefore discontinued to vaccinate with the matter from Delhi, after I had received some of a better quality from Umbala.

At Tripoli, I met with the then new Governor Barber, who although of very low birth, had managed to get possession of the fortress, and afterwards of the town itself, by fraud and cunning. He was a short-necked man, thickset, inclined to apoplexy (Habitus apoplecticus), and, in consequence of his sedentary life, was troubled with hemorrhoids and obstructions. He consulted me, and when I ordered him to apply a clyster, he measured me wildly with his eyes, as if I had ordered him some dangerous remedy; I repented having done so. I remembered afterwards, that the Arabian physicians, although aware of the efficacy of clysters, as they are recommended in their medical books, seldom apply them, and only in cases where all other remedies fail, as they consider it as a last resource; in a country where pederasty is in vogue, it is disgraceful to acknowledge that fact. At his request for a proper remedy to be taken by the mouth, I prepared for him the well known aloetic dinner-pills, mentioned in the second volume of this work, from which he found great benefit.

Besides these pills, I ordered him to observe the following rules: Post coenam stabis, vel possus mille meabis, or—

"After dinner, sit a while,
After supper, walk a mile."

For several years I spent the cold seasons in the maritime towns on the Syrian coast, at Tripoli or Beyrout, where the winters are only rainy; but I passed the hot summer-months in the most agreeable regions of Mount Lebanon. At Araba, not far from Seyda, I made the acquaintance of that original person, Lady Hester Stanhope, who called herself Queen of Palmyra. I was told that she ordered a herd of goats to be killed, and buried, and paid the people who did so, well, only because a few of them were scabby, and she thought by that expedient to prevent epidemical diseases, which might occur by their eating the flesh, or drinking the milk. Not far from Tripoli, there lay at the foot of the Lebanon, in a very romantic valley, a village called Mesrut-ul-Toofah (apple-district), where I was requested to attend some fever patients. My friends advised me not to go there, as in their opinion an epidemical disease was raging at that place; but I did not listen to their warnings as I wished to be useful to those people who had implored my assistance, and at the same time to extend my experience. When I was near the village, I saw a great many Maronite girls (Christians), coming back from the well, with pitchers on their heads, each of them holding an onion in their hands, at which they frequently smelled.

The epidemical disease had the character of a Synochus, and several persons had died suddenly, which caused great alarm among the inhabitants. The silk gathering was just ended, and I found the diseased were located in miserable, low houses, deprived of fresh air; I thought it advisable to cause them to be removed from their habitations, and brought into the manufactories, where previously the silk worms had been; and the result of my treatment was, that none of my patients died of that disease, I was conducted from Mesrut-ul-Toofah, to a place a little farther up the Lebanon, to Aito, where the former French interpreter, Isaac Torbei, was confined to his bed with Angina, and was unable to articulate, in spite of all his efforts to do so. I examined his throat, and found an abscess therein, which I opened immediately; by which operation my patient was able to talk instantly, and after a few days he entirely recovered.

From Aito, I was brought to Kannobin, to the residence of the Maronitan patriarch, where the Bishop Mootran Seman lay very ill. Kannobin is situated on a declivity, from whence a beautiful view is obtained of the valley. It is by no means a town, as the Dictionnaire Encyclopedique Ferancaise (second edition) erroneously asserts, it being merely a convent. There is a curious custom attached to this country, and in most places of Asia. A physician being called on to attend a sick person, it is first arranged as to how much he will require for curing the same; upon that arrangement being completed, the physician receives one moity of the sum agreed upon, and upon the recovery of the patient, he receives the balance, which includes the cost of medicine.

Having arrived at Kannobin, I found the bishop suffering from nervous fever, in a state of insensibility. After a strict examination, I entertained but little hopes of his recovery. His numerous relatives, standing round his bed, appeared to have resigned all hope previous to my arrival. I agreed with the brothers of the bishop as to the amount they were to pay me for my attendance, the half of which I received in advance, for the medicines to be delivered, the other half to be paid after the recovery of the patient, from whose own hands I should receive it, according to the above-mentioned custom. All was legally signed by the parties and witnesses. I caused the troublesome spectators to withdraw, as by their thronging around the bed they occasioned disturbance and confusion, and only permitted four of them to remain as attendants. Then I was able to reflect, and found that the patient had been wrongly treated by his former physicians, and so reduced to a most pitiable condition.

They had copiously bled him unnecessarily, and, led by a false diagnosis, they had prescribed him a quantity of decoctions and purgatives. I learned from the attendants, that four days previously the patient was constipated, which occasioned him to fall into a state of insensibility. I found it necessary to commence my treatment with a lenitive clyster, which did not fail to have its good effect; I afterwards ordered the room to be aired, sprinkled the patient's face with vinegar mixed with rose-water, and ordered his feet to be warmed by friction.

At ten in the evening I applied a blister on the nape, and administered a compound opiate powder, which was given in a strong dose. I put it into his mouth, rinsed it from his tongue, after which he began to perspire, and passed a tolerably quiet night. The beneficial result was owing to the properly proportioned mixture of the opium, as I afterwards experienced in many cases, whilst a lesser dose (1—2 grains opium) made the malady worse. By this process the patient was saved. On the day of the recovery of the bishop, I had an opportunity to cure another patient, which occasioned a great sensation. The sexton of the patriarch was troubled with a tertian-ague. It was the fever day, and the patient complained of feeling dizzy, want of appetite, a bitter taste in his mouth; he looked very ill, and the white of his eyes was rather of a yellow colour. I ordered him an emetic, he vomited, and a long tape-worm was expelled, which I drew until it broke. On giving him a second dose of solution of tartar-emetic, it operated, and caused the ejection of the rest of the worm by an evacuation. I ordered the pieces of the ejected worm to be washed. I measured them afterwards, and they were fifty-two yards long. I found among them three heads, and I concluded that three tape-worms were there, consequently the denomination of solitaris is a wrong one. It was the broad tape-worm. I kept the pieces in spirit; but it was no extraordinary novelty for those people, as the disease of the tape-worm is very common on the Lebanon. Whilst I was measuring the tape-worm, the old patriarch Hanna stepped in, and asked me, with a smile, if I knew Bonaparte? I answered that I knew him by name only. He continued; people arriving just now from Tripoli, bring the news, that Bonaparte has died in the English prison. Then that great genius has come to an end, said I, whose memory will for ever be revered in France!

The inhabitants of the Lebanon are of opinion that the frequent disease of tape-worm in their country is caused by their eating raw flesh, and afterwards drinking brandy immoderately, which may indeed be considered as a secondary cause. I ascribe the principal cause of the frequent appearance of this disease on the Lebanon, to the fact, that the poor people of that country, who are mostly affected with it, are living in rooms where they are breeding silk worms, also sleeping in the same apartments, and breathing the noxious air of the rotten substances and putrefied mulberry leaves which serve as food to these worms. I cherish this opinion so much the more, as the root of the white mulberry-tree is considered, according to the Homœopathic principle, as a worm-destroying substance (anthelminticum). Those people have a particular method of curing the tape-worm when it becomes annoying by unpleasant symptoms. They take, early in the morning, before breakfast, a small piece of common soap, enveloped in the skin of a fig; afterwards, they roast a piece of fat meat on a fire of charcoal, in order to coax the worm (as they believe) to come up from the intestines to the stomach; they chew the roast meat, without swallowing the spittle or the juice. Believing the worm to be in the stomach, which they think they feel afterwards, they drink a good draught of vinegar, or even strong spirits, stopping their nostrils, which is supposed to affect the worm (perhaps also the man) with intoxication, by means of which the worm is driven to the lower parts of the intestines, and ultimately ejected by a brisk purge, such as in a civilized country would only be employed by a veterinary surgeon. If the worm is in the stomach, then the next process is that of administering tartar-emetic (as I have previously alluded to), and thus preventing the necessity of using spirits, and the drastic purgative. But if it is probable that the purgative will, together with the worm, eject also the mucus, then it is advisable to administer, a few days after the ejection of the worm, the purgative, but without the assistance of spirits, or vinegar.

Not far from Kannobin, below the highest summits of the Lebanon, covered with eternal snow, beneath which the well-known cedar-trees grow, are the villages of Eden and Besherri, where I succeeded in effecting many cures in the summer of 1821.

The chiefs of the Maronites and Druses (Emir Beshir and Sheikh Beshir) on arriving at Besherri to meet the rebels, applied to me for medical assistance; and at a later period I was invited to their residences (Tidin and Muktara), where I practised for some time, so that I lived for several years very agreeably, enjoying the most beautiful and romantic views of the Holy Land (Palestine).

At Besherri I tried vaccination, but I found that the inhabitants were not affected by the operation, the vaccine matter producing no pustules, and I was told that none of them caught the small-pox, because their cows have sometimes the cow-pox, the origin of which is caused by the change of climate. The inhabitants of the higher regions pass the winter, together with their cattle, in the plains of Sgorta, not far from Tripoli. Hence I infer that the inhabitants of Besherri, through being in continual contact with their cattle, as cows, &c., become infected with the disease, and are thus preserved from human contagion. A quite distinct disease, occurring frequently on the Lebanon, is the so-called habbet-ul-kei, which is a sort of gangrenous ulcer, but very different from the endemic sore at Aleppo and Bagdad called Butone d' Aleppo, an ulcer which seems to have a preference for the cheeks of fair young ladies, lasting twelve months, and leaving an ugly scar, but not dangerous. The habbet-ul-kei, on the contrary, appears as a small pustule, is very acute, and endangers life; it occurs in the interior as well as on the exterior parts of the body, for which reason it is often difficult to be recognized; but as soon as it is recognized, the healing of it may instantly be effected with the cautery, be it internal or external. That is the reason why, on the Lebanon, so many children are seen on whose forehead the cauterium actuale was applied as a preventive. If this ulcer appears on the surface, for instance on the face, where an inflamed pimple arises, which is at the beginning of a red or bluish color, and afterwards becomes black, like a carbuncle, then life is in danger, if not attended to betimes, *i e.*, by burning and destroying it with a red-hot iron; for that reason it is called habbet-ul-kei, that is to say—" ulcer to be burned." It is said, that the bursting of the pimple being heard at the moment of the operation, is a good omen of the success of the cure.

In the Agosta, in the province of Kesroan, there occurred a case, which rendered me really ashamed of our imperfect medical knowledge.

I was called on to give my assistance on the commencement of an acute inflammation of the eyes to a lady of the first family, called the Sheikh Khoasni (nobility of ancient descent), where I tried the antiphlogistic plan in its full extent, namely :—bleeding, blistering, leeches, calomel, emetic tartar (in minute doses), purgatives (*viz.*, senna, manna, salt, &c.), Dover's powders, different colly-riums prepared from corrosive sublimate, plumbi acet., laudanum, camphor, rosewater, &c., without any positive result. One morning I found the lady a great deal better which I naturally ascribed to the good effects of my treatment. "No," said my patient, "I do not owe my convalescence to your remedies, but to the shoemaker Ibrahim; he called on us yesterday evening, and on viewing my sore eyes, he recognized it to be the habbet-ul-kei. He applied immediately the red-hot iron; and since that moment I am a great deal better and have enjoyed also a quiet night." I requested her to send for the *ustad* (master) Ibrahim, which she accordingly did. I asked him how he could know that the inflammation of the eyes was caused by the habbet-ul-kei? He answered me, that it could be recognised by the following circumstances :—

1 Bleeding and all other treatments remain useless.
2. The patient has offensive breath, the spittle is tough and stringy.
3. There is a local burning pain, tormenting the patient day and night, which (according to his assertion) is the surest symptom of the kei (burning).

Beside this, Ibrahim understood but little of other diseases; nevertheless, no one should apply to him the Latin proverb, Ne sutor ultra crepidam (Let not the shoemaker go beyond his last).

The cauterium actuale was applied also to this lady, on the forehead, her hair having been previously cut very short. There is no doubt, that the effect of the red-hot iron is more violent and efficacious than that of a blister, and cannot be replaced by the latter, wherefore the Arabs apply it to men and animals, very often at the present day, as in ancient times; our contemporary medical men in Europe make but little use of it, probably because they are afraid of the violent pains inseparable from such operation; but this only produces the healing effect.

At Tripoli (Syria) I met with a very disagreeable incident by my improvidence, from which I learned some experience, and for that reason I will give the reader some account of it. Being an enthusiastic sportsman from my earliest age, I pursued some ducks in a marshy ground, where I remained for a couple of hours. It was in the winter season, on a lonely and desert place, about five miles from the town, and not far from the sea-coast.

I was quite alone, and so intent on the pursuit, that I observed, only a short time before sunset, that it was high time to return to my abode. I left the marsh, sat down on its border to dress myself; but to my astonishment my feet were motionless, stiff, and paralysed so that it was impossible, without assistance, to get on my pantaloons and boots. But my terror increased, when I reflected that I was in the desert, far from every human being! What will become of me, thought I? Must I perish by the frost of the night; or must I become a prey to the wild beasts on their nightly wanderings? Similar ideas rose in my imagination, and I was in a desperate situation.

But sometimes, at the moment when our calamity is highest, our delivery is nearest. Having committed that imprudent step of going into the marsh when I was fatigued and excited, I felt nothing as long as I was wading about; but now, as the sharp air came in contact with my body, I felt the consequences of the evil I had brought on myself. Against that paraplegy, there was only one remedy, namely:—to produce a perspiration on the whole body. But how was I to effect this? "Necessity is the mother of invention." I grasped my cloth pantaloons, and began to rub my feet with all my strength, until my hands got weary, and in the meantime my whole body became covered with perspiration. To my great satisfaction, I perceived that my feet began to become flexible, and so I continued the operation, and succeeded so far as to be able to put on my pantaloons and boots, and walk slowly towards my abode. There I arrived very late, ordered a warm bath to be prepared, and after half-an-hour's bathing went to bed, having previously drunk a glass of punch prepared with tea, which produced a good effect, and thus I fell asleep. In the morning, when I awoke, my legs were restored to their former activity.

At the same period, while I was private physician to the English consul at Tripoli, there happened an extraordinary case. An organic defect of a young woman in labor required a Cæsarian operation to be made on her body, and I was appointed to perform it ; but the Greek bishop refused to give his consent thereto, because that operation was an uncommon one, and I could not guarantee her life. Even after the death of the poor woman, wife of Georgius Jani, the bishop again opposed the operation, by which the infant might have been saved. I and my friends, the twin brothers Katzifliss (scarcely twenty years of age, one of whom was Austrian, the other English consul) often regretted the circumstance. At Bagdad there happened the following case :—the wife of an Armenian curate having been for eight months with child, had died in consequence of a scald. On both sides of the belly of the deceased a certain motion was visible for a long time, which caused some people to believe that she was about to bring forth twins, which they wished to save. They sent for me, but, to my grief, they came when all assistance was too late. I cite this unhappy accident of the poor woman, that it my serve as an example to those people who deal in spirits and other combustible articles, and as a warning to them to be cautious in their management. The above-mentioned woman went upstairs late in the night, with a candle in her hand, and entered a room, to pour some brandy from a damejane (a large glass jar, covered with straw). Keeping the light too near to the spirits, they caught fire. Instead of covering the mouth of the jar, to extinguish the flame, she permitted the damejane to fall on the ground, and, sprinkled as she was with the burning spirits, she fell a victim to the flames. Some time afterwards, she was found in the dark room, in a fainting state, amidst the ashes of her clothes.

From Tripoli I went, by order, to Akar, in the mountains, to attend the Prince Ali Essat, who, together with his numerous family (wife, brother, children, and slaves) were infected with the venereal disease, which, although appearing under different forms and complications, may be ranged in the class of syphilis secundaria. At that time I knew no better remedy for that complaint than corrosive sublimate combined with salmiac, accompanied by decoctions of sarsaparilla, china-root, gujac wood, &c.

Whilst I was at Akar, it was reported that Abdula, Pasha of Acre, had commenced war against the Pasha of Damascus, in consequence of a dispute, and that he had sent troops, the greater part of them Christians (Maronites from the Lebanon) and Druses, under the command of Emir Beshir, towards the holy city of Damascus (Bab-ul-Kaba, or entrance to the Sanctuary of Mecca), and that the inhabitants of Damascus had been defeated. The Sultan despatched immediately five pashas to Acre, in order to bring the heads of Abdula Pasha, of Emir Beshir, and of the new governor at Tripoli, the above-mentioned Barber, for having taken part in the war, by sending his own troops to join the main army. Ali Essat Bek took advantage of the moment, having his partisans at Tripoli; he came down from Akar, blockaded and bombarded that town, and forced it to capitulate. Meanwhile, Barber betook himself to the citadel, in which he surrendered under certain conditions. The five pashas arrived so suddenly, that Emir Beshir had only time to escape, and embark between Seida and Berout, in a French vessel, which conveyed him to Egypt, where, by the interference of Mahomet Ali Pasha, he obtained from the Sultan his own pardon and that of Barber and his superior, Abdula Pasha, which, by the by, cost each of them an immense sum of gold. At London

I was recently told, by the missionary, Dr. J. Wolf, that Abdula Pasha and the Emir Beshir were residing at Constantinople, but since then the public journals have announced the death of the latter, and that one of his sons had embraced Mahomedanism.

I was present at the siege of Acre, and found an opportunity of employing myself in surgical attendance and operations; as the garrison used to make nightly sallies, and do a great deal of mischief. I had a dozen native surgeons, or rather barbers (jerahs), as assistants, to whom I gave theoretical and practical information.

Tigers are rarely to be met with on Mount Lebanon, yet during my stay an order was issued by Emir Beshir, that the muzzle of every slain tiger should be sent to the government, in order to prevent the use of it as a poisonous drug. This strange order induced me, when at Lahore, to examine its virtue, the results of which I refer to in the second volume of this work, under the denomination of Tigrineum.

My passion for antiquities prompted me to undertake a voyage to Alexandria; accordingly I made a trip, which was attended with a very fortunate result. I went on to Damascus, *via* Haspeye and Rasheye, from whence I continued my journey to Homs and Hama, in Syria, with the caravan of hajjees (pilgrims). At the latter places I purchased a considerable collection of old coins, in gold, silver and copper, as also several engraved gems. I made my way back to Beyrout, *via* Akar and Tripoli, where I embarked on board an English vessel for Alexandria. This short journey had also its peculiar adventures; for it happened in a period when, after the revolution in Greece, the Mediterranean was infested by numerous pirates. In the evening of the same day on which we lost sight of the snowy summits of the Lebanon, we discovered, by the light of the moon, that we were surrounded by five ships-of-war. Our captain was, in insulting language, summoned by the respective captains of these vessels to come on board their ships, so that he was at a loss which of them to choose. He therefore remained in his own vessel, until some soldiers were sent on board our ship to fetch him. The visitors, who were but little acquainted with politeness, set about carrying away some purses filled with crowns (dollars), during which operation a quarrel arose among them, and we saw them on the point of beginning a fight, as their swords, knives, and pistols were already held forth for the assault ; but happily, no blood was shed. It was the patrol of Mahomed Ali making the round. They took our captain with them, and examined his papers, conveying him from one ship to another, which operation lasted four hours. As this happened in the vicinity of Cyprus, the captain made his complaint there to the British consul, and, on arriving at Alexandria, he immediately received satisfaction, as an imperative mandate was forwarded, and the patrol recalled.

At Cyprus, I called on my friend the French ex-Consul of Tripoli, Mr. Reynold, where I met with a kind reception, as he required my medical assistance. I had also, during my short stay at Alexandria, the opportunity of curing a countryman of mine, a Hungarian, who had been many years afflicted with ulcers on his legs. As a testimony of his gratitude, he sent me a letter, from which I copy the following lines :—

"May this serve you as a proof of my gratitude and sincerest thanks, for the complete restoration of my health; with the request that you will not, when far distant, forget your true and affectionate friend,

"ATTANAS KEPTENAK."

Alexandria in Egypt,
April 1, 1823.

At this time the plague was raging dreadfully at Alexandria. The direction of the hospital was committed to a Jewish doctor, whose name was Marpurgo. Among the infected, there was an Italian, named Bellmondo, an apothecary by profession, who died the day after he was attacked with the plague. The people, on this occasion, said: "*Il povero Bellmondo, è nell' altro mondo.*" Here also I had an opportunity of observing the course of the plague. I did not, however, remain long in this place, but returned to Syria. Unfortunately, the vessel I embarked in was an old Danish one, leaky in every corner, so that the crew were obliged to pump day and night. After my return from Alexandria, I fixed my abode on the eastern side of the Lebanon, and began to practise in a little town named Sahli, beautifully situated in the proximity of the valley of Balbeck, where the famous ruins of the temple of the sun (Heliopolis), notwithstanding the attacks of time, rise from the ground like rocks, and are admired by travellers, as one of the most remarkable monuments of antiquity. As I was living in the neighbourhood, I accompanied the two Prussian naturalists, Drs. Hemprich and Ehrenberg, at that time on their way towards Balbeck. The latter is the celebrated naturalist at present in Berlin. From Sahli I went to Damascus (which I had formerly passed through), in order to pursue there the practice of my profession. At that period there was living in the Capuchin convent, a monk, named Padre Tomaso, who used to perform vaccination; and besides that, professed the medical art. But the following amusing story may serve as an illustration of the system he adopted. A goldsmith of middle age, a Catholic, came to me one day, asking for an Aphrodisiacum; he confessed he had impaired his bodily strength by improper indulgences, to such a degree that he could not perform his conjugal duty; and he added, that he was in a very distressing situation, for his nuptials were to be celebrated on the following Sunday. I expressed my willingness to comply with his wishes, but finding probably the price of my medicine too high, he left me, and repaired to Padre Tomaso, hoping to get his medicine *gratis*. On Monday, after the wedding, at the break of day, Father Tomaso entered my room quite embarrassed, and asked me for my advice, as the goldsmith was constipated, and in great pain, in consequence of the large doses of Cantharides which he had administered to him on the eve of his nuptials. Although somewhat moved with compassion, I could not help laughing at this account and I desired tc see the patient, whereupon he told me that, after having read mass, he would come and conduct me to him. My lodgings being opposite the convent, he very soon returned, and we repaired to the residence of the newly-married pair. It was one of the largest Christian houses in Damascus, and the family of the goldsmith was one of the richest of that country. In the large court-yard and in the saloon through which I had to pass, I saw a great many handsome ladies, and not being shy, they displayed their jewels and other ornaments, because I was come with a priest, and consequently appeared to be also a Christian, in spite of my Turkish costume. In a corner of a large room, I found the unfortunate bridegroom cowering and lamenting over his pains; he had only one servant with him. He told me he had taken only a third part of the majoon (electuary) which Padre Tomaso had given him, but that, instead of its producing the desired effect, he was tormented with pains that were no longer supportable. I immediately gave him a few pills (a compound of opium, camphor, and ipecacuanha), and also ordered him to take almond-milk, *ad libitum*, which did him a great deal of good, and I afterwards effected the cure of his original complaint.

The aforesaid Father Tomaso (a Piedmontese, I believe) is the same individual who created a great sensation in Europe, some years ago, by his sudden disappearance from his monastery, where it was supposed he was murdered by the Jews, on which occasion some hundreds were massacred at Damascus.

According to the annual custom, there came from Constantinople, the Surra-Emini (leader of the pilgrims), with thousands of Musselmans, who united themselves at Damascus with the pilgrims coming from Bagdad and Persia. At the expiration of the Ramazan (Lent), the Pasha of Damascus set off for the desert, where a great fair is held at an insignificant fortress (Muzerib), at which a large quantity of articles are sold and purchased, and whither also the Arab chiefs, of different tribes, from the desert, bring their goods, principally horses, for sale. At that time, the Pasha and the Surra-Emini pay them money, and distribute state dresses among them, for which they undertake to provide the pilgrims, going to and coming from Mecca, with the required number of camels, without which the road through the desert would be impracticable.

I accompanied the Pasha both going and returning. On my arrival in Damascus, I found a medical man, Mr. H. I. De Turck, now at Ghent, who was come from Paris, where he had studied medicine, and the Arabic language. Shortly after, I received a letter from Bagdad, from Mr. Anton Swoboda, a native of Hungary, who had a warehouse there for Bohemian glass, under the firm of Ign. Zahn and Company, of Pesth and Aleppo; it was in the latter place that I made his acquaintance.

He informed me in that letter, that Dohud-Pasha wished to engage a European physician and surgeon, and advised me to accept his offers. I communicated the contents of this letter to Mr. Henri De Turck, proposing to him to undertake the journey with me, to which he agreed. At that time there were two caravans, a great and a small one (galat), the latter of only ten camels, ready to start immediately for Bagdad. But as the former, for the sake of food and water, was obliged to take a roundabout way, lasting full six weeks, whilst the latter, by following the direct road through the desert, would occupy only two weeks in the journey, we sent our luggage by the greater caravan, and went, with our two camels, with the galat, which consisted now of twelve camels. We were obliged to take with us provisions for about ten or twelve days—some clothes, and a few medicines. Each camel was provided with two goat-skins, to carry water, as we arrived only every third or fourth day at watering-places. Each camel had also its driver, who sat behind, and his furs, by the way, were full of vermin.

Kirkor, an Armenian merchant, from Bagdad, who led

this galat, advised us to leave behind every kind of weapon, as he suspected that the journey would be a dangerous one, undertaken thus at random. He added, that if we met, by accident, the Arabs in the desert, and they found us to be armed, they might become suspicious; whilst if we passed them as poor hajjees (pilgrims), saluting them with "Selam alekim," we might be saluted with their "We alekim selam," and be allowed to continue our route unmolested. We made forced marches by day and night; at noon we looked about for low ground, to light our fire on without being observed, and where we could take our mid-day meal, which consisted of rice with butter, biscuits and dried fruits. In the evening we were not allowed to light a fire, nor to whistle or sing. At a distance of about twelve or fifteen miles, on our left, we saw the famous ruins of Palmyra. Up to the ninth day we saw neither men, nor birds, nor wild beasts; when on a sudden, in the darkness of night, we happened to light on a place situated between some low hills, where we perceived some Arabs and their tents. Fortunately, and to our great joy, they were all women, whose husbands, as they said, were absent, hunting, that being their means of subsistence. They manifested no hostile intentions, and offered us a liberal portion of black dried meat, which had not an unpleasant taste, but I do not know what kind it was. The next day I cooked it with my rice, for my camel driver put it into my pot without my knowledge.

To deceive the women, we told them that we were coming from Bagdad and going to Damascus, after having provided ourselves with water, we retraced our steps, but only to make them believe so; for we had hardly got out of their sight, when we struck into an opposite direction, and marched the whole night, for fear of being overtaken by their husbands. On the eleventh day, we arrived at Quoise, a village where we rested for one day, waiting for the escort from Hit, which was to bring us to the banks of the Euphrates. On the journey, I was told how the Arabs of the desert heal their wounds. They make a hole in the ground, in the form of a grave, which they heat with fire, the patient is placed therein, and covered, and he remains there until he is either cured or dies, a matter which takes but a very short time to decide. In the case of death, they have only to fill up the grave with earth; while, if the patient recover, he has to mount his camel and meet the enemy. Their wounds are either spear-thrusts or sword-cuts, as they very seldom use guns in the desert.

The caution with which the camel-drivers carried us through the desert is not to be described. On the third or fourth day, on our arrival at the wells, in order to give water to the camels, and to fill our leather-bags, the most sharp-sighted among them placed himself on an elevation, to ascertain whether there were any men discernible in the distance. If they found embers or ashes, they examined the place strictly. The excrement of the camels also underwent a scrutiny as to whether it was new or old, which way the animals passed, &c. We were brought from the banks of the Euphrates into Hit, as they told us that the place we were in was not perfectly secure. The governor ordered us to appear before him, and he demanded a certain sum from the two Armenians, our fellow travellers, but not from us nor the pilgrims, as we were provided with a letter of recommendation from the Pasha of Damascus to Dohud Pasha of Bagdad. This letter, which served us in the meantime as a passport, was so much respected by the Agha of Hit, that he placed it on his forehead as a token of respect.

At midnight, we were alarmed by a great noise and uproar in the town. Upon asking for an explanation, they told us that the Arabs of the desert were in pursuit of the pilgrims. This information filled us with fear and anxiety, for we were all assembled in the same house, and firmly believed that it was the husbands of the women we had met with previously, and that their intention was to plunder us; but we were mistaken. A short time afterwards the people informed us that they were the Agha's enemies, the Agelis, who were come to take revenge on him, and it was rumoured that they had forced the palace, and killed the Agha.

However much we regretted the murder of that poor man, by whom we had been recieved only the evening before with such kindness, we could not forbear rejoicing at not having been ourselves the destined victims. We were told that the Agelis (an Arab tribe) had been settled for fifty years at Hit, and having paid the same taxes as the other inhabitants, had been forced by the new Agha (regent), the greedy Kurde (wolf), to pay a certain sum with which they, as true subjects, should not have been charged, and they accordingly obstinately refused to pay. But the governor obtained troops from the Pasha of Bagdad, with whose assistance the Agelis were driven out of Hit, and their goods were confiscated, for which treatment they swore to take revenge on the Agha.

With the break of day, a soldier came to inform us that the two innocent sons of the Agha, and his brother-in-law, had had their throats cut while asleep, but the Agha himself was only wounded, and had escaped from the grasp of the Agelis, and desired us to visit him. We found him outside of the town, not far from the city gate, sorrounded by about fifty horsemen, with whom he had been pursuing his enemies, who had taken possession of all his moveable property; but his pursuit had been in vain, as he could not overtake them. He was wounded in one of his legs, and he escaped death only by throwing himself from the high verandah of the palace into the neighbouring yard. He requested us to prolong our stay with him, in order to cure his wounds, promising, as soon as he should be well, to escort us to Bagdad. We could not resist this application, partly owing to our gratitude for his kind reception, and partly because we thought by curing him, which seemed an easy matter, we should render a service to the Pasha of Bagdad, which might be of greater advantage to us than the letter we had from the Pasha of Damascus. Accordingly, we separated ourselves from our travelling companions, who on the same day went down the Euphrates on their way to Bagdad. We committed, however, a very great blunder, for which we had to suffer, by quitting the house of the pilgrim, where we were living so comfortably, and establishing ourselves in the miserable palace of our patient, the Agha, who was reduced to such a miserable state of poverty by the robbery, that he could hardly provide for his most urgent necessities, and was very glad to see us order our victuals to be brought from the bazaar. On the third or fourth night of our stay in our new abode, we were alarmed by the same tumults as before, and awakened by a lamentable cry from the women, of "Lilililili," proceeding from the terraces, where they slept in the open air. We soon saw armed Arabs filling the yard, quarrelling and disputing, and we took them for the Agelis. As our room was on the ground-floor, and had only one door and two windows looking into the yard, we imagined ourselves prisoners and lost, till I got to a corner of the window, through the wooden lattice of which I perceived the long tshibuck (pipe) of the Agha, which encouraged me to venture out. He was sitting among a great crowd of his people, quietly smoking his pipe, so drawing nearer to him and saluting him, I inquired about the cause of the tumult. He told me that the mother of the unhappy slain children, having passed a sleepless night, was frightened by the report of a musket, which appeared to proceed from outside the town, and she imagined that the Agelis had come back to attack the palace. She began to scream, and the neighbouring women joined in chorus, crying for help, which awoke all the population of the city. By a strict inquiry, however, it was ascertained that the gun had been fired by the watchman of a garden, to frighten the wild beasts, which resorted to the place for the purpose of devouring the melons. Although the whole affair ended with our fright, we nevertheless desired heartily to depart as soon as possible from that miserable place, where robbery was the order of the day.

At mid-day we witnessed the owner of an ass being forcibly deprived of his beast; the deed was effected before the gates of the city, and the ass was driven away into the desert. In fact, the Arabs in general may with justice be looked upon as robbers of the worst description.

In the course of a week the Agha was perfectly cured upon which we requested him to despatch us without any further delay to Bagdad, according to his promise. He replied, that his gratitude towards us for the important services we had rendered him, would not allow him to expose our lives to his enemies the Agelis, who had by this time pitched their camp on the banks of the river, and he advised us to wait for a caravan, and join it when passing. But we so urged upon him the necessity of our departure, that he despatched us in a boat, in which we descended the river. We were escorted only by one soldier, so that with the owner of the boat, and his man, our party consisted of five persons.

On the evening of our departure, we got wet through by a violent shower of rain ; and owing to that, and the fear of being attacked by the Arabs, who were supposed to be on the banks of the river, we could not sleep. That night and the ensuing day, which by the bye was a delightful one, we passed down the river through lonely and desert regions, where not a man was to be seen ; nor, indeed, had we any great wish to see anyone. But on the following evening, when it had become quite dark, we were aroused from our slumbers by hearing from the right bank, where the Agelis (as we were told) had their camp, an imperious voice, crying " jedem ! jedem !" (come on, come on.) Here they are, thought we, and to prevent their firing on us, we obeyed the call, and approached the shore. We could perceive none of them till we came to land, where we met eight naked fellows armed with sticks, whose first business was to moor our boat, jump in, and plunder our luggage. Whilst this gang of robbers were busy plundering the bow of our boat, and searching the pockets of my companion, the servant of the owner of the boat, who was sitting on the poop, whispered me in a low voice, " I am a native of Quoise (a village before mentioned, near Hit), and have nothing to fear from the Agelis, I may save your purse, if you trust it to me." I did so ; but a small bunch of keys, belonging to the luggage, which we had sent by the caravan, being attached to the purse, and rattling when I handed it to the man, betrayed us, and they seized the servant, laid hold of the purse, and struggled to get it. The obstinate resistance of the poor man was in vain, for the rascals kicked him into the river, and succeeded in getting possession of the purse. But the owner of the boat, when all the robbers were out of it, profited by the circumstance, cut the ropes by which it was fastened, left his man behind, and made an effort to gain the opposite bank of the river.

Scarcely were we in the middle, when we heard them vociferating, and calling us back, with a promise to return all they had taken, swearing, even by the name of their prophet, that they had a patient among them whom they wished to be cured by us. But we could not rely on their oaths, as we believed them to be Agelis, and so we rowed towards the opposite bank. Scarcely, however, had we arrived there, when one of them came swimming upon an inflated goat-skin, in order to persuade us to come back to the patient, who was his brother, and we were so embarrassed, and driven to such extremes, that we felt ourselves obliged to soothe him with the promise that we would come to them early in the morning. As he remained with us, we passed another sleepless night. At break of day, we perceived a few black tents, not far from the place where we were, which gave us some consolation. Accompanied by the soldier, whom the Agha of Hit had sent with us, my companion went into one of these Arab tents, to convince himself of the truth of the man's statement. He soon came back, and told me that the robber was the Sheikh Dendal, the chief of the country on the other side of the river ; that he was assured that the elder brother had been for some time sick and swollen, and he added that he was ready to go there on horseback to see the patient. They then led him to a fordable part of the river, and I remained with the boat ; and whilst I was musing on this barren, but still somewhat cultivated ground of the desert, calculating what day of the week we were in, and guessing that it might be Sunday of the second week of November, probably St. Martin's day

(when in my native country it is deep winter), I saw two men coming up the river, armed *cap-a-pie*. They passed by without saluting me with their Selam, which surprised me, and they went straight to the boat, inquiring for my companion. They then loaded me with abuse, asking who had brought us from Constantinople to cure the wounds of the Agha at Hit, and adding that they would punish me immediately for having done so, if it were not for the Khater (favor) and for their regard for their friend, the Sheikh Dendal, and they finished, by assuring me that we must not expect to escape from the grasp of their brethren, as one hundred and fifty Agelis were hunting after us.

After this menace, they left the boat and crossed the river, at the same spot where my friend had crossed on horseback, with as much ease as if they had been walking on land, carrying their clothes and their weapons on their heads. When I lost sight of them, the owner of the boat came up to me, asking whether I understood what they had said to me. " But too well," replied I ; then I asked him, what was now the best to be done ? He advised me, first of all, to put off my new richly decorated and gold embroidered cloak (Aba), and to take his old worn-out striped one. He concealed mine, and led me to a neighbouring field, covered with high Indian corn (maize), and desired me to sit down and remain quiet, until he should come to me. I followed his advice, and after an hour had elapsed he came back, with a smiling and contented countenance, telling me that the man of Quoise, to whom I had given my purse, and who remained the previous evening on the opposite bank, had arrived, and reported that all the stolen luggage had been restored to my companion, and that he had administered some medicine to the sick sheikh ; so that we might now safely go over the river to fetch him, and then continue our journey. He added that the sheikh, although dropsical, and dangerously ill, after some consoling words from my companion, entertained hopes of being again restored to health, and my companion had promised to send him still better remedies from Bagdad, by the man he should send with us. We then crossed the river, and having met my friend, we all embarked, together with the restored luggage, accompanied by a messenger from the sheikh, and left that place about three or four in the afternoon. On the same night we were again disturbed, a great noise on the shore rousing us from our first slumber ; the owner stopped the boat, and on our asking the cause, he told us that a caravan was on its way to Bagdad. No news could be more agreeable to us ; elevated with joy, we jumped on shore, and found that they were carrying corn to Bagdad ; the caravan consisted of about forty asses, two of which we hired for our accommodation ; and then joined them. The messenger of the sheikh accompanied us on foot, the other three persons from Hit we sent back, rewarding them for their services. Although we felt extremely happy at having escaped from the Agelis, nevertheless, we were not completely at our ease, for we observed our drivers bending their bodies almost to the ground all the night long, listening, and looking first to the right, then to the left, in order to ascertain whether the steps of the pursuing robbers were on their heels ; and this they continued doing till dawn. About that time they stopped, and proceeded to unload their beasts, and we then lay down on the hard ground to enjoy a couple of hours' rest.

At sunrise we were aroused to resume our journey, and when we opened our eyes and looked about, we observed some ancient ruins on an elevated site, which they called Boorj-Nimroud. At a greater distance we saw the golden cupolas and minarets of Kerbela, the holy tombs which the Shias (Persians) had consecrated to their martyrs, the Imams Hassan and Hussain, which are situated on the right bank of the Tigris, above Bagdad. At noon, our procession entered that famous city, where we met with a kind reception, in the house of Mr. Swoboda. The French consul, who was a bishop, presented us to the Pasha, and as our reputation had already reached the ears of the inhabitants, we soon had plenty of professional occupation. My companion, as acting physician, only cured the internal diseases, whilst I occupied myself with surgical cases.

Dohud Pasha was a native of Georgia, who had killed his master, the former Pasha of Bagdad, and usurped his dignity and place. As long as he paid the Porte the required subsidies, he enjoyed the protection of the Sultan; but when he began to organize his troops, by putting them under the command of French officers, he found himself in difficulties, as he had exhausted his treasury in the equipment of his army. Even the expedient of manufacturing base coin, did not suffice to raise the sum required to be sent to Stambul. Besides that, he had ordered a Kapoojee-Bashi (dispatched by the Sultan, probably to bring him his head) to be murdered; for that reason the Porte made war against him, which ended in his captivity; he was brought to Constantinople, where he was pardoned, and I saw him there in the years 1836--1838.

The first patient the Pâsha requested me to attend, was a peasant-lad, belonging to a silk-manufactory of the Pasha's whose case had been treated without success by almost all the physicians of Bagdad. The lad was about twelve years of age, and was tormented by insects in his ear, which caused such pain that he was continually crying; sometimes the vermin crept out of his ear. After having tried some injections with a syringe, containing substances calculated to destroy insects, a few of them died, and I was now fully satisfied as to the cause of his complaint, of which I had doubted at the commencement. After the lapse of a few days, I placed the patient in the rays of the sun at mid-day, lifted the ear-lap in such a manner that the rays of the sun could enter it, and then I discovered some black object, which I extracted with a forceps, and found it to be a nest of insects. Almost distracted with joy, the boy fell on his knees, and expressed his gratitude, for having been restored to his sense of hearing. The nest was two-thirds of an inch in length, and half-an-inch in diameter. I put it into a vial filled with spirits, and went with it, accompanied by the boy to the minister, Masraf Effendi, who introduced us to the Pasha.

He examined the nest in the vial, and asked the boy whether he was really cured? "Yes, my Pasha," was his answer, whereupon he said to me, "Afferim," (well done); and I received 1,000 piastres, besides a Tshokha (cloak of honour).

Many readers will ask, how did these insects come into the ear? I questioned the boy, and was told that he slept in a stable where cows were kept. I therefore considered the insects to be cow-lice, which had crept into his ear and bred there.

At the suggestion of the minister, the Pasha requested me to attend an Arab, who was lame, in consequence of a gun-shot wound which he had received a few years before in his hip. Although the man felt no pain, and no foreign body was perceptible in any part of his limb, he nevertheless persisted in stating that the ball was sticking somewhere in his hip. The surgeons endeavoured to convince him, that if such had been the case, they could never have succeeded in healing the wound. The question with me was, whether or not I ought to re-open the cicatrix, and search for the extraneous substance in the hip. I thought this operation was needless, and yet I felt compelled to do something, in consequence of the order of the Pasha.

It occurred to me that exercise was necessary, so I ordered him to walk a great deal, to beat the ground firmly, and caused the hip to be tapped on that part where I presumed the ball to be, rubbing it frequently with the hand downwards, and I gave him also an emollient ointment, &c. After three weeks the man felt a pain in the hollow of his knee caused by the presence of an extraneous substance. I examined the part and felt a protruding body, which was easily moved from one part to another. It was, in fact, the ball which I immediately cut out, and the patient was very soon cured of his lameness. Thus the mystery of this case was solved, my fame was established, and the Arab surgeons, or more properly barbers, were cast into the shade.

Pasha Dohud was at this time waging war with the Arabs, between the Euphrates and the Tigris, and I was sent, at the request of the minister, to Hilla, where I had the opportunity of seeing the ruins of ancient Babylon. On the road, between Bagdad and the camp, I beheld a horrid spectacle, namely, a pyramid of some hundreds of the heads of Arab rebels. I had only followed the expedition from Hilla to Sugeshuck (Schuka-Shu), when the Pasha ordered me, by a Tartar express, to return to Bagdad. The same messenger brought me a letter from my companion, from which I learned that a princess of the Pasha's had been delivered of a deformed child, where indeed no surgical assistance was required, but he had seized the opportunity to send for me, under the pretext of consulting me about the state of the patient; while his real motive was, to draw me out of my disagreeable situation. I wrote to him, stating that in this campaign we were feeding on sand rather than on bread, which made such an impression on his feelings that he caused me to be recalled. On my return, I had only the Tartar and one servant with me. By the Pasha's orders, we made forced marches, changed horses, crossed the Tigris, and arrived one evening very late at a small town named Mumilla, situated on the left bank of that river. There I met with the inspector of the provisions for the army, who was afflicted with an inflammation of the eyes, and requested my medical assistance. I bled him, and prepared a collyrium of acetate of lead, laud. liqu. Sydenh., camphor, and mucilage of quinceseeds, which caused a burning pain at the commencement, but effected in the meanwhile a visible amelioration. In his joy for the happy result, he ordered a sheep to be killed as an offering (kurban), and accompanied the feast with musicians and dancers, and he made me a present of fifty piastres in small Para pieces. Fatigued as we were, we wished rather to rest ourselves, than to be amused, and accordingly dismissed the assembled people, a proceeding which we thought excusable, and then continued our journey. At our request, an Agoo (guide) on horseback was ordered to lead us through the desert. Accordingly, we started at two o'clock after midnight, entrusting our Agoo with our wallet, in which our provisions (roast meat and bread) were packed ; we put also the horses' provender under his care, and left the place, hoping to reach a watering-place about nine or ten in the morning, where we might likewise meet with some Arab tents, and breakfast, and allow our horses to rest ; but the Agoo missed the road, and it was not till the afternoon that we became aware of the fact, when we observed him deviating first to the right and then to the left. The Tartar, in a rage, menaced the guide continually, and added that he would cut off his nose and ears. I did my best to appease him, making him understand that the guide, who was already perplexed, would get still more puzzled by his continued threats, and that he ought to consider that he had not intentionally misled us ; but my admonitions were of no avail. The evening was now drawing near, and in the darkness of the night our guide decamped. Imagine our state ! in a desert, without a guide, not knowing the way, even by daylight, no human being visible, forsaken by all the world, riding hungry, thirsty and exhausted horses, without nutriment for either man or beast, and, above all, the anxiety as to whether we should ever get out of that maze. The sky was clouded, it was raining, and we were chilled by the cold, it being the end of the year. In the heavens not a star was visible, to guide us ; we were like blind men, not knowing whither to direct our steps. We left the horses to their own instinct, but, like ourselves, they did not know the way. In this desperate dilemma, my happy star, beneath whose influence, perhaps, I was born, and which has often guided me in difficulties, shone again. We observed at some distance, a small fire, towards which we directed our steps with renewed courage ; but it appeared and disappeared, as the rain and wind either extinguished or revived it. We heard, also, in the stillness of the desert, the barking of a dog. We followed the sound till we arrived at a thicket, which we had some trouble in getting through, found a river, and perceiving that the fire and the barking came from the opposite bank, to which we could not pass. From the course of the river, however, we had known in what direction Bagdad was situated ; and, travelling upwards, we very soon reached a few black tents ; but the people were so poor that they could not offer us any hospitality, as they had food neither for us nor our horses. The only service they proffered was to give us a guide, who brought us, after half-an-hour's walk, to the tent of the sheikh, where we met with a very kind reception. The sheikh himself was at this time in Bagdad, but in his absence his wife performed the duties of hospitality. She ordered the servants to light a fire under the large tent, where we dried and warmed ourselves, and were served with fresh coffee and rice-pilaw. The servants took charge of our horses, and after having taken my meal, I went to sleep. A corner of the tent served me for my bed, and my saddle-bags as a pillow. Before dawn, the Tartar awoke me, saying : " We must proceed on our journey." I drowsily arose, and at the same time my servant showed me that they had cut through my saddle-bags on one side, and extracted the bundle containing my best clothes. I remembered having heard, during the night, some goats bleating outside the tent ; and probably the thief had brought them there, that he might perform his exploit with more security. The Tartar began to make a noise, threatening to arrest the sheikh at Bagdad, and to make him pay ten times the value of the stolen property, if they did not find out the thief. They made researches, it is true, but without any good result. On the same day, towards evening, we arrived at Bagdad, where I was informed that my intended patient required no more medical assistance, as he was reposing quietly in his grave.

At Bagdad I also performed several operations for the stone, but I did not vaccinate, in consequence of being informed, to my great astonishment, that several Christian ladies obtained their livelihood by vaccinating. Provisions were at this time so cheap at Bagdad, and the coin so bad, that one shilling was valued at about five grush (piaster); consequently, little was to be obtained there. We were told that there were four French military officers in the service of Runjeet Sing at Lahore, in India (Allard, Ventura, Court, and Avitabile) who, after the defeat of Napoleon, having served in Persia, were about to organize a regular army at Lahore, and that no European physicians or surgeons had been yet engaged. We therefore, thinking it better to accelerate our departure, requested our dismissal, which was granted, and we thus left Bagdad. Our friend, Mr. Swoboda, furnished us with letters of introduction to the aforesaid French officers, and we went down the Tigris to Bassora, and embarked there for Bender Bushir, in Persia. At Bushir we met, at the British consul's, with six English officers (one of whom was a medical man, coming from Bombay), who were on their way to England overland. We sold them our two Arabian horses, and becoming acquainted through that transaction, we went with them as far as Shiras, where we visited the ruins of Persepolis, and then separated. On the journey we had an opportunity of rendering a special service to our companions, namely, that of saving their luggage, and at the same time of witnessing the cowardice of the Persians. The fact was, that a fortress in the mountains, between Bushir and Shiras, having capitulated, the garrison, which consisted of a couple of hundred robber-like looking fellows, had met us in a forest, and fallen on the luggage-train of the English officers, who, together with their numerous servants, were considerably in advance. When I saw the miscreants dragging about by the hair our men, I fired a pistol, partly to give a signal to the Englishmen to come to our assistance, and partly to frighten the assailants, which had the desired effect ; for they fled right and left among the trees. We then pursued our journey without further molestation, and received the thanks of the Englishmen, who were coolly taking snuff, and waiting for us at the top of the hill, near the fortress that had previously capitulated.

As it was too late for us now to proceed to India by sea, we preferred staying a few months at Shiras, following our profession, and waiting for the winter season, which is more convenient for travelling to Lahore. We employed that time in studying the Persian language, as the knowledge of it would facilitate our getting an engagement. But we could not remain there long, being continually ill-treated and robbed, and we therefore thought it preferable to go overland to Lahore, by the way of Hispahan, Heirat, and Cabul. On this journey we had again to endure a great deal of annoyance from the Persians, who being defeated by the Russians in war, were anxious to revenge themselves on us ; they treated us, in fact, worse than their dogs, cheating, robbing, and insulting us to such a degree, that M. De Turk on one occasion cocked his pistol to fire at a radar (road-keeper) who was very insolent ; but I prevented him from executing his design. Arriving at Hispahan, we found there a gallant governor, Hosruff Khan, from whom we met with a kind reception, and who gave us some medical practice, by appointing us to attend about forty Russian prisoners, some of whom were suffering from wounds and others from fevers. At this time we learned that the Russians were at Tabris, that Abbas Mirza had taken flight, together with his wives, to Hamedan, and that the latter had upbraided the Molla (high priest) for having induced the Shah to wage war with the Russians, by assuring him that the Persians would remain unhurt by the fiery balls of the Russian guns, as his prayers would render them invulnerable. The priest took their reproof so much to heart, that he soon afterwards died. It is commonly said, that Abbas Mirza exclaimed, on that occasion " Pul bigirend, we pes birovend "—" The Russians shall take money, and go back to their country." In consequence of the fatigues and toils which we had to endure at Shiras, as well as on our journey to Hispahan, my companion caught a nervous fever, which weakened his mind and body to such a degree, that he no longer wished to go on to Lahore, and he persuaded me to return with him to Bagdad At Hispahan, a conspiracy was formed by the native doctors against our lives, of which we were informed by an Armenian, and, by the interference of the governor, we were preserved. I availed myself of my influence with Hosruff Khan, to procure from him some genuine Persian *mumiai*, for the wounded Russians. In Turkey and Arabia they highly praised the wonderful effects of this medicine, and I was therefore eager to convince myself of its efficacy. But as the cases I had to treat rather required the use of instruments, I postponed the trial.

Our return to Bagdad was *via* Urugurd and Kermansha. At Urugurd we were detained for several days by the Shazadah (the reigning prince), who requested us to attend to a few patients belonging to his household, the healing of whom brought us a tolerable little sum of money, and a few handsome presents. Here again we had an opportunity of witnessing the manners and customs of the Persians. It was then Muharem (time of mourning), and the tenor of the Shazadah's order ran thus, "during the time of the mourning, all merchants are summoned to appear in the Meidan (a square in front of his palace) at three in the afternoon, in order to shed their tears for the martyrs, Hassain and Hussain." On one occasion we saw the Faratshes (Shazadah's servants) dragging a tradesman by force out of his shop, which was at the caravansary where we lived, and driving him to the Meidan. The plea of necessity was urged, to make those people weep by blows, whose feelings did not afford them tears freely. But we witnessed other atrocities, on the last days of the Muharem. We saw fakirs and dervishes, with tiger-skins round their bodies, their long black hair hanging down and covering their faces and backs, beating themselves with iron-headed clubs, till the blood flowed down their bodies. They ran like savage beasts, or maniacs, through the streets and bazaars, howling, "Ya Ali!" One of our friends, a native of Bagdad, told us, that if any of the Sunits, to which sect he belonged, should venture that day to acknowledge his religion, he would run the risk of being immolated by the fanatical Persians ; so inveterate is the hatred between these two sects, though they are both Mahomedan ; and this is not the case in Persia alone, but in every place where Shias and Sunits are living together. Great animosity prevails between these two sects in India, also on the day on which the Shias expose the Tabut (coffin) in procession. In Cashmere, on these occasions, the Mahomedans burn each others' houses and shawl manufactories. From Kermansha we went to Bagdad, with a caravan carrying several embalmed dead bodies of Persians to Kerbela, their sanctuary.

Persia is a high plain, diversified by ranges of hills and deserts. It was in the month of August that we were on our journey, and the air was so bitterly cold on the morning of our setting out, that our very teeth chattered; I recollected that at home they call these the dog-days. We arrived at Bagdad, where M. De Turk left me, as he was resolved to return to Paris by land *viâ* Tocat and Constantinople, in order to take with him some Arabian horses; a speculation, by the way, which proved by no means lucrative. A short time after his leaving me, I received some good news from Lahore, through a Persian who had been in the service of General Avitabile, which induced me again to attempt going there at the commencement of the favourable season, *i. e.*, the early part of the winter (1829). I felt the more inclined to do so, as the plague was already raging at Mosul, and the inhabitants of Bagdad were fearful that it might extend as far as their own city, a thing which occurred soon after. In the year 1828, there had been at Mosul and its environs, a famine, in consequence of the crops failing, and numerous families went down the Tigris to settle at Bagdad, selling their children for a mere trifle, owing to the want of means to support them. I myself saw a beautiful Christian girl purchased for twenty grush (four shillings). Scarcely had I left Bagdad when the plague broke out, and this scourge was followed by an inundation. A war, previously noticed, also broke out, during which Dohud Pasha was conducted as a prisoner to Constantinople.

My only companion was a faithful servant, called Antun, a Christian, whom I brought with me from Bagdad, and with whom, after having passed through Bassora, and Moscat, I arrived at Bender-Karatshi in Sind. From Karatshi, we pursued our journey to Hyderabad, with a camel caravan. At that town I stayed for a few days, and made the acquaintance of a Persian Emir, who gave me some letters of introduction to one of the most respectable houses at Heirpore, which I had to pass on my journey from Hyderabad to Moultan. At the former place I hired two camels. The road was always at a distance from the river, and we were therefore frequently obliged to drink stagnant and stinking water, and on account of the heat; at this time being the month of February, we travelled by night only, and rest during the day. In consequence of this, I was tormented with costiveness, an internal burning, and an excessive longing for acid drinks. I accordingly prepared some tamarind whey, but it operated on me like poison; for after much vomiting, I discharged a quantity of blood, and fainted away, falling down beneath a tree in the forest, in which state I was found by the people, who had been for a long time in search of me. They brought me to the camp, where the camels stood ready for our departure, as this happened only a short time before sun-set. My tongue was parched, and I felt an acute pain in my right side, which led me to believe that I had an inflammation of the liver; besides which, I had become very weak, in consequence of the loss of blood, so that I was unable to walk without assistance.

I desired my camel-driver to procure some leeches, but he could only console me with the hope of getting them on the following morning, at Heirpore. As I was quite exhausted, and unable to mount the camel without assistance, I ordered my servant to place himself behind me on the animal to prevent my falling off. But as he was soon asleep, and the slightest accident would have caused us both to fall, I ordered him to mount his own camel, and to bind me safely on mine, where I passed a sleepless night, being unable to articulate a word without having previously moistened my tongue with water, which I had always near me. At break of day, on our arrival at Heirpore, I was conducted to the house to which I had my letter of introduction already mentioned, and the first favour I asked was, a quiet retreat, that I might have rest, and recover myself. The people, seeing the difficulty with which I dragged myself along, called in a Hakim (a Persian physician) who lived in their house, and he offered me his assistance. I thanked him very heartily, and requested some leeches. "We have not any," was his reply; upon which, as my only resource, I applied a blister; after which I became senseless, and remained in that state until the evening of the following day. On my revival, my tongue was still so parched, that I was unable even to ask for water to moisten it, and I only obtained it by making signs. My feet were excessively cold, and besides the above-mentioned internal pains, I also felt the effects of the blister, although it had risen but very slightly. I examined my pulse, but the pulsation was imperceptible, from which I concluded that my last moments were near at hand. My servant told me that, during my stupor, I had had some discharges of blood; I ordered him to fetch the Mirza (scribe) of the establishment, that he might make my will; and he came with his paper and kalemdan (writing stand), and placed himself at a respectable distance, the hakim having told him that my disease was dangerous and contagious. I felt so weak and debilitated, that I was scarcely able to sign my name. I told my servant that I had but little hopes of living over the night, and desired him, should it be the will of God that I must die on the banks of the Indus, to bury me and convey my effects to Lahore, and deliver them, with my papers, to the Generals, Court and Avitabile, to whom there was a letter of introduction, sent by Mr. Swoboda. For the services he himself had rendered me, I gave him a liberal remuneration, that I might secure his executing my wishes, upon which he wept and promised obedience. In this deplorable state, considering myself at death's door, like many other medical men, I began to think that, in spite of the numerous remedies, there was no chance of my recovering from the effects of the poison I had taken, and that the medical art was but a fallacious one. I began to recollect that I had always avoided bleeding in my own case, so as, a last resource, in spite of my previous loss of blood, I resolved upon trying the experiment, it being considered by many that the first operation of that kind, in dangerous cases, is usually beneficial.

I summoned all my resolution, and was determined to use the lancet ; and having no one to perform the operation, I ventured to do it myself. I ordered warm water, put my hands and afterwards my feet into it, and tried to bleed myself, but neither I nor my servant, Antun, could succeed, as no blood came. Nevertheless, my courage did not abandon me, for I thought that if I spared my body to-day, it might be put to-morrow into the grave. In a fit of desperation, I cut through the median vein of the left arm, upon which the blood began to trickle, but to the amount only of about two ounces. After my wounds had been dressed, I lay down exhausted, and recommending my soul to God, I soon fell asleep. I passed a tranquil night, and on awaking in the morning, I found my feet warm, my pulse beating, although but faintly, and the internal pain somewhat abated ; but the external pain was more acute, as the erysipelatous inflammation had extended from the back to the navel, and from the arm to the hip, and owing to my excessive debility, I was afraid of mortification. Nevertheless, I had more hopes of my recovery, relying on the efficacy of the bleeding and blistering. To free myself from the troublesome dryness of my tongue, I sent for some quince kernels, which, enveloped in a small piece of linen, I put into some water, and with this little pad I frequently moistened my tongue, which produced a very good effect. In the course of the day I began also to chew some monaka (large raisins), which refreshed me. To arrest the farther extension of local inflammation, I sent my servant to the bazaar, to endeavour to procure some leeches, and in case he could not obtain them, he was to bring a barber or some other person to cup me. He came back, accompanied by a woman provided with a quantity of leeches, by which I ascertained that the Persian physician, who told me that no leeches were to be obtained, was a rogue. I caused twelve of them to be applied around the blistered part, and requested the woman to return in the evening, when I ordered her again to apply the same number of leeches to the place where, a few years before, I had been afflicted with piles. The next morning I applied six leeches to my side, and in the evening, the same number behind, by which means I completed my cure without having had recourse to any other remedy. Keeping the blistered part in a state of suppuration, and treating the external inflammation with cold water, I made such an improvement in my health, that my restored appetite soon enabled me to digest solid food. At the expiration of five days I felt sufficiently strong to resume my journey to Lahore, to the astonishment of those who witnessed my departure, wondering whether I was really recovered, or in a state of delirium, as only three days had elapsed since I made my will, and their hakim had asserted that there was no chance of my recovery. At the commencement I made but very short journeys. I shortly afterwards had several abscesses where the leeches had been applied, one of them as large as a hen's egg, so that it was difficult for me to maintain a sitting posture, and, notwithstanding my good appetite, and the salubrious air I afterwards breathed in the mountains, the weakness, produced by only five days' illness, continued for a space of six months. What contributed greatly to my illness, may perhaps have been the circumstance that I had not been seasick, on our voyage to Bassora *via* Moscat to Bender-Karatshi, as was the case with my servant Antun, who inhaled the same atmosphere, ate and drank the same kind of food and stinking water, &c., without suffering any inconvenience. At that period, the Sindians were not yet acquainted with the English, although they were their neighbours, and accordingly we passed villages, where the people were not inclined to furnish us with provisions, even for payment. Our camel-driver advised us to lodge in the mosques, in order to be taken for Mahomedans. By so doing, we were provided with food gratis, by the hospitable musselmans. I and my servant were dressed in the costume of the inhabitants of

Bagdad ; we could speak the Persian, Arabic, and Turkish languages, had long beards, and addressed each other as Hajee, *i. e.*, pilgrim. Our carpets, which constituted our beds, were quite similar, and were placed close to one another. We ate together, according to the eastern custom, using our fingers instead of knives and forks ; in fact, we played our parts so well, that none recognised us as Christians. Having our quarters in the mosque, it was very annoying for us to see the musselmans come five times in twenty-four hours, to offer up their prayers. They thought it strange that we, as pilgrims and their guests, did not join in their devotions. It is true, we could easily have done so, but knowing how to excuse ourselves, we did not like to push our dissimulation any further. We had only to whisper into the ear of one of them that we were unclean. From that expression they inferred that we had the gonorrhœa, which excuse became a public secret ; and we thus got out of the difficulty. From Mooltan to Lahore we went on horseback. The journey from Bagdad to Lahore occupied four months ; *i. e.*, two by water, and two by land. On my arrival at Lahore, I found that the king, Runjeet Sing, with his army and the four French officers, was absent, having gone towards Peshawur ; but at the commencement of the rainy season, in the middle of June, they had all returned to Lahore, and I was well received. The first patient I had to attend, after my arrival at Lahore, and before I got public employment, was Achilles, an adopted son of General Allard. This boy was afflicted with a fistula on the spine, of long duration, and which had been several times superficially healed by the native surgeons. He was so reduced, that one could truly say, he was but skin and bone : " Ossa atque pellis totus est," which of course rendered the case most difficult. I was convinced that my medical reputation depended upon this case. General Allard told me that the boy would die, if not attended to, that he could no longer bear to see him in that pitiful state, and urgently solicited my aid. He did not at that time imagine that his darling Achilles would outlive him ; but the destiny of man lies hidden. Allard died at Peshawur, and was buried at Lahore; and Achilles returned from France to Lahore, where he also died, and was buried in the cemetery, near to General Allard's own tomb, which was in his adjacent garden.

I ventured to perform an operation, and that by force, for the boy made an obstinate resistance, when I placed him on a sofa. General Allard holding his arms and General Ventura his feet, while I made a cut along the fistulous sore, which caused him to be senseless for the following thirty-six hours, and to suffer with severe fever. My assiduous attendance accelerated the radical cure of the fistula, his strength visibly increased, and after a few months he regained his original plumpness, and, six years afterwards, when General Allard and his family arrived at Bordeaux, where I then was, I was astonished at Achilles' healthy appearance. On his returning to Lahore a few years afterwards, in company with Benjamin Allard, who went to take possession of the estates of his deceased brother, and to whom he officiated as interpreter in the Indian language, he fell sick, and died under the treatment of the native physicians. I was much grieved at the unexpected intelligence of his death, and paid him the last honours, by attending his remains to the grave. To encourage the suppuration of the opened fistula, I employed a mild, stimulating remedy, namely, cantharides infused in honey, on lint, twice a day, applied to the wound, by which it was soon cured. At the recommendation of General Allard, shortly afterwards, Rajah Suchet Sing, the younger brother of the minister, requested me to accompany him into the mountains, to attend him there professionally, to which I readily agreed, as, in consequence of my recent illness, I was very weak, and the summer heat of Lahore was intolerable. Besides that, my friends, the generals, advised me to accept the offer on account of the great influence the young Rajah Saheb possessed as one of the first personages at the court, and as by curing him I should establish my reputation.

Although my post was at that time not fixed, and consequently I did not depend on, nor was I subject to any one I nevertheless imagined that my departure for the mountains had met with the consent of Runjeet Sing. But it was not so The young Rajah, who had a secret disease, had induced me privately to accompany him, whilst Runjeet Sing, in my four months' absence, inquired after me several times of General Avitabile, who had first introduced me to him. It was, probably, for that reason that he detained me for nine months without giving me my dismissal, or appointing me to any office. General Allard said to me one day, jesting, "It is very difficult to get an appointment here, but still more so to get one's dismissal, when once in office." He himself, feeling an excessive longing to revisit his dear native land, after an absence of so many years, petitioned for a short leave of absence, which the sly Runjeet Sing repeatedly promised, but a long time elapsed before he obtained it.

On the third day after our starting for the mountains, we arrived at Suchetghur, at the foot of the hills, not far from Samba. We made our journey partly on horses, and partly on elephants. At that place, the rajah had his stables and cannon-foundry, and several new-cast cannons and mortars were tried in his presence. One of the former burst, and a gulendas (Indian artilleryman) was stunned. The rajah requested me to examine the man, who complained of a violent pain on his right side, accompanied by severe shivering; but, to the great astonishment of all the spectators, there was not the least trace of any external violence, whereupon the rajah himself, considering the case insignificant, opposed my wish to bleed him, and sent him some of his own *mumiai*. But at ten o'clock at night, about five hours after the accident had taken place, a messenger was sent by the rajah requesting me to attend the man, and bleed him. I instantly complied, and found that he had been, according to the custom of the Hindoos, taken out of his charpai (bed) and laid on the floor, where he expired in agony before I could give him any assistance. I do not know whether his liver was injured or not, a *post-mortem* examination not being allowed to be made; but it certainly was an extraordinary case, such as has never occurred during my medical practice of thirty years. His death must have been owing to a shock from the piece of hot metal, which, in passing near him, had injured some important organ necessary to the support of life, as fright alone could not have caused such violent pains and so sudden a death.

From Suchetghur, we were conveyed in palanquins in two days, in the mountains, to Ramnuggur, where the rajah had, besides his castle, a fortress, in which his treasures were concealed. We passed the rainy season on the hills; and in the autumn we descended, in order to witness the Duseire-feast at Umritsir. Thence, we went, with Runjeet Sing to Nadoun, on the Beas river, where the Maharajah married the two daughters of the famous Rajah Sansar Chund, both orphans, and brought them to Lahore. We passed Jowalla-Meki, a sacred place in the eyes of the Hindoos, where there is a volcano. From thence, I travelled, with Rajah Suchet Sing, along the hills to Besouli, Jesrota, and Nurpore, where he was appointed receiver general of the revenues.

On my return to Lahore, I was informed, by General Allard, that a number of his dragoons had been bitten by a mad jackal in the night, while they were endeavouring to kill it. Several of the soldiers, who were seized with hydrophobia, had died, some of them in the barracks, and others on their way home. The general made me the offer of experimenting on some of the bitten soldiers, who had already applied for leave of absence, that they might die near their families. I consented to it, and eighteen men were placed under my care. I was happy to find, in consequence of my treatment, that not one of them was attacked by hydrophobia. Thereupon, General Allard recommended my mode of treating this malady to Dr. A. Murray, who was on a visit to Lahore with the political agent of Loodiana, Colonel Sir C. M. Wade. They both requested me to publish it for the benefit of suffering humanity, to which I agreed without any reserve; and it was read in a public assembly at Calcutta, July 2nd, 1831, and published. I take the liberty to introduce an extract :—

"Dr. Honigberger's object, in the treatment of hydrophobia, is to keep up a copious suppuration from the part bitten by the rabid animal, which he accomplishes, at first, by applying the actual cautery, and afterwards by using stimulants to the wound. He also administers a compound of mercury and extract of tobacco, in pills, until they produce a flow of urine ; and at the same time he recommends tincture of cantharides in an emulsion of bitter-almond to be repeatedly given, until a slight degree of dysuria is excited. Various other remedies and local applications are also spoken of as useful in hydrophobia. It does not appear that any other person has yet made trial of some of the remedies proposed by Dr. Honigberger."

This was my treatment twenty years ago, when I practised Allœopathy ; but, since that period, I have made many interesting trials and experiments.

A short time after the publication of the above-mentioned method, I had a case where I tried, as a preventive, the endermic application, *i. e.*, I applied on the somewhat enlarged bitten part some extract of nux vomica, upon which the patient passed an unquiet night, dreaming of dogs running after him. I thought it a bad omen, and regarded it as a symptom of the approach of hydrophobia ; and I did not rely on the local application only, but gave him also, internally, a pill of the same remedy (extractum nuc. vomic.) one grain, mixed with three grains of carbonate of soda ; to which he considered he owed his recovery, as it caused an evacuation.

I introduced to our distinguished guests, Col. Wade and Dr. Murray an Akalee or Nahung, whose nose, ears and hands had been cut off by order of Runjeet Sing (he had even deserved the gallows), and whose nose had been so well restored in the mountains that we were all surprised, and confessed it could not have been better done in Europe. As we know, from history, this operation was even in the remotest antiquity, practised by the Hindoos ; and they formed the nose out of the cuticle of the forehead, which proceeding is now, and always will be the same. In Europe, where cutting off of noses is only in use, in exceptional cases—as when ulceration or other circumstances make it requisite—this operation is usually performed with the cuticle of the arm, and judiciously too, as, according to our custom, the head mostly is uncovered, and a scar on one's forehead, with a new nose on the face, makes rather an ugly appearance; whilst, in the East, the scar remains hidden beneath the turban.

In time of peace, the Nahungs gave a great deal of trouble to Runjeet Sing. On one occasion, he was even forced to place two pieces of cannon outside the Delhi Gate of Lahore, in the vicinity of Seidgenj, where the robbers congregate, because this band dared to intercept the communication of that city. They shut themselves up in Meea-Meer, five miles distant from Lahore, thence they made their appearance as rebels, but they were defeated, and forced to depart, and from the town also, to Umritsir. The individual just alluded to as deserving the gallows, had cut off the arm of a sentinel, for having prevented him from entering the tent of the king by a private entrance. The Nahung had a servant with him, who underwent no punishment, because he did not behave in an aggressive manner; but the offender, by the order of Runjeet Singh, lost his ears, nose, and hands, by the same sabre with which he had so skilfully cut off the arm of the soldier on royal duty. After the sad execution, he ran to drown himself in a well, but was prevented by the people who were accidentally present. When the king was informed of the fact, the culprit was sent to me, and put under my care and medical attendance, with strict orders to watch him, to prevent his committing suicide, and to present him, when cured, to the king. According to his own statement, he was drunk with bhang (hemp) when he committed the crime, and his only intention for intruding on the king had been to ask a gapa (gift). These robbers do not like to enter military service; they prefer begging, and living by pillage.

Rajah Heera Sing, son to the minister Dhyan Sing, who was a favourite of Runjeet Sing's, was afflicted with diabetes, and we (I and the five native physicians) were consulted, at the palace garden of Hazooree Bagh, in the presence of Runjeet Sing, and on that occasion I made mention of milk-sugar. As neither the Maharajah nor his physicians had ever heard of any sugar prepared from the milk of cows, they were curious to see a specimen of it, and I was ordered to prepare some in the gulab-haneh (rose-water house), in the presence of the fakir, Noor-oo-Deen ; but they had scarcely patience to wait for its preparation. I produced some white and fine crystallized milk-sugar, which I presented in a box to Runjeet Sing, of which he gave a few pieces to a boy to taste, but he did not find it so sweet as cane-sugar, so no one spoke any more about it, and the milk scene was thus at its end. The gulab-haneh, where the rose-waters and the bedemusk (aqua flor. salicis Babylon), which they use as cooling beverages in the hot season, were distilled, was the very place where I at first practised, and it was there I gave lessons in pharmacy and chemistry to the fakirs Aziz-oo-Deen and Noor-oo-Deen. The spirit produced from Cabul grapes, for the use of Runjeet Sing, was distilled in that place in my presence, by his own people, because every thing eatable or drinkable, destined for the Sikhs and Hindoos, must be prepared with their own hands, no Christian or Musselman being permitted to touch it, lest they should pollute it. There were also the royal magazines, under the care of Noor-oo-Deen, where I prepared different opiates, and many amusing metallic oxydes (kooshtegee), to please the fakir and Runjeet Sing, for which they held me in high estimation. Among others, I prepared some morphine, with a large dose of which the Maharaja would surely have killed a famous opium-eater, if I had not been consulted in time, and administered to him some antidotes. I thought it strange that no one at Lahore was aware of the existence of coffee, and its usefulness. Even the learned fakirs, Aziz-oo-Deen and Noor-oo-Deen (brothers), who were of Arab descent, knew coffee only from their books, under the denomination of *bun*, and the sample which I showed them in 1832, in the Durbar, was the first they had ever seen; but when the English arrived it became generally known. Neither had they any notion of our cantharides; for which they substitute meloe telini, a fly of greater efficacy, containing more cantharidine than cantharides. They are seldom employed by the native physicians for blistering, although they know the utility of them in cases of hydrophobia.

Besides what had been mentioned on the effects of blistering in the description of my own disease, the following may likewise serve as a proof how beneficial that process is when properly employed, and it may, in some cases, even save a patient's life.

General C——, had brought on a disease, by an external misapplication of mercury, while he was with the court at Umritsir. It was in the warm season, and on the fourth day after the application, he became so indisposed that my services were called into requisition. The native physicians had previously administered different remedies, but without success. On examination, I found that the stomach and intestines were affected, which disturbed the functions of digestion, and caused a violent purging, with a burning of the anus; I commenced by bleeding him, and applying leeches; after which, the diarrhœa having been suppressed, an intermittent fever, exhibiting itself at various periods, of from three to seven days, was the consequence. Observing no improvement in the health of my patient, I conceived that the heat of the climate exercised an injurious influence over him, and that no hopes of his recovery could be entertained unless he were removed. I therefore solicited permission for him to remove to a cooler locality, upon which we were sent to Deenanuggur, in the proximity of the mountains, to which place the Maharajah intended to retire with the court.

The disease having lasted three months, and the patient becoming weaker, he began to complain of a burning at the region of the heart; I tried to apply some leeches, but

I was obliged to cease, owing to his falling into a swoon. He daily grew worse and worse; and shortly after became delirious, with his eyes open, and his feet cold. The officers of his brigade, who were accidentally present, shed tears for their general, whom they expected to lose. I freely confess, that I had no hope of his recovery, seeing that his strength was daily declining. In this desperate state I applied three blisters, one on the nape of the neck, and the other two on the calves of his legs; at the same time I gave him my favorite opiate (opium, camphor, ipecacuanha and tartar emetic): and he thus was saved. In the same night an eruption appeared, consisting of many thousand pustules, principally on the neck, shoulders, and groins. From that moment the disease visibly diminished; his convalescence took a rapid course, and after a few weeks he was entirely recovered.

During the time of my patient's convalescence, rajah Suchet Sing came down from the hills to Deenanuggur, as was supposed, to meet the court. One day, the kind Rajah Saheb invited me to accompany him in a boat, on a duck-shooting excursion, on an extensive lake. As the rajah had not his own parasol with him, I gave him mine out of politeness; for as I was shooting, I did not want it. It was extremely hot, and I had nothing on me but a thin shirt, not even a waistcoat or jacket, so I was exposed to the burning rays of the sun for some hours, and the consequence was a severe coup-de-soleil. My friend C——, on witnessing my state, despaired of my life, his "Tissot" stating that a coup-de-soleil was extremely dangerous. But how great was his surprise, when he saw me recovering on the third day! Happily, the attack did not affect my head, but only one of my shoulders, and by applying leeches and poultices I recovered.

The king of England had at this time sent five immense horses as a present to Runjeet Sing. Alex. Burnes had brought them up the Indus, and they were much admired for their size and uncommon height. One of them was lost on the way, and another became the famous riding-horse of the Maharajah, who, being of a very low stature, appeared, when on the back of the animal, like an ape on an elephant. This horse fell sick, and although I had him immediately uuder my care, and spared no trouble; he became, like other dead animals, food for the dogs, carrion birds, and Pariahs, the lowest caste in India, who eat any animal, whatever may have been the cause of its death.

The horse had several ulcers on his legs, which having been healed by internal and external remedies, caused convulsions, and in that state he perished. I afterwards had other opportunities of curing similar ulcers with a simple remedy, according to my medium system, namely, by lamanaria saccharina (probably because it contains iodine), such ulcers being a kind of scrofula. This disease occurs very often in the Punjab, and the natives call it Zeherbadi (venomous swellings), as it ulcerates, and secretes a serous and corroding matter. By adhering to the same system, I also cured horses affected with glanders. Arsenic and dulcamara alternately administered, in small doses, in the morning and evening, proved very effective. The French veterinary surgeons administer for this disease hydrochloric acid, which, diluted with water, they pour into the mouth of the horse, or use it as a local embrocation: this I learnt from the celebrated naturalist, Victor Jacquemont, on his visiting Lahore, *en route* to Cashmere, &c., and he declared glanders to be incurable. At Vienna, as in England, I believe, they kill at once horses affected with that disease.

During the congress of Rupore, on the frontier of India, I attended, at Wuzeerabad, the governor of that province, General Avitabile, who, having sprained his ankle, had called in the native surgeons, barbers and bunglers, and they had so assiduously applied irritating poultices and embrocations, that the leg became inflamed, and was approaching to mortification. Under my treatment, the patient recovered, and the leg was restored to its former functions. Subsequently, he was afflicted with a contraction of the muscles of the face, which, on account of his long, crooked nose, appeared the more striking; this disease I ascribed to his immoderate indulgence in champagne, which affected his brain. Although I cured him at that time, two years ago he died suddenly of apoplexy, from continuing the same excess, in his own country. Having acquired immense riches, he returned to Europe, to enjoy in his native land (Naples) the fruits of his exertions, and there he died in the autumn of his life. Peace to his ashes! although many an unfortunate man was hung by his orders, at Wuzeerabad as well as at Peshawur, where he exercised his sway in a most arbitrary manner. The pleasure which he took in seeing people hung by dozens must be attributed to the affection of his brain. General Allard told me that the Maharajah once reprimanded him for having executed some musselmans; whom General Avitabile had ordered to be hung because they were of opinion, that, under the protection of a European governor they might be at liberty to eat beef! The opinion of Runjeet Sing was, that he ought to have imprisoned the criminals, and then allowed them to escape. It is well known, however, that General Avitabile was an active man; that he introduced many useful reforms into the country, and was of good service to the English army on their march to Cabul. Living in his house for three years, I had an opportunity of knowing him well; I therefore, conclude with the proverb, "De mortuis nil nisi bonum;" particularly so because I am indebted to him for the following important discovery:—During the time I was performing the before-mentioned cures at Wuzeerabad, I lost, on a hunting excursion, a hare in the copses, which we thought to find in a burrow. Wishing to get the hare, I sent to a village for some bels (pokers), in order to enlarge the hole. We succeeded in doing so; but great was our astonishment when, instead of the hare, we caught a musk-deer, which diffused so strong an odour, that I was seized with a headache, which lasted for three days. The man who dragged him out, was so frightened at finding an animal previously unknown to him, that he instantly threw it down, and our hounds bit it so violently that it was nearly killed. Having taken it home, I was advised by General Avitabile to cut off the musk-bag, which I did, and keep to this day; it being considered that unless that operation is performed previously to the death of the animal, the useful substance of the musk-deer will entirely disappear; the rest of the animal was regarded as useless, which I now regret, believing that it was the most valuable specimen I ever met with, as I have never heard of such animals being found in the plains of India. Those to whom I showed the musk-bag in Europe, suggested that the animal had found his way there from the Himalaya, and it might have been so; but the odour and appearance of the musk of Cashmere and Thibet is quite different. The exterior of the bag of this animal resembles that of the musk of China, it has smooth, soft, and short hair; but the interior is a yellowish brown mass, as hard as bees-wax, whereas the Chinese musk is of a reddish-brown colour, and in grains of a friable nature. Without having prepared the bag, I put it into an iron box, and found that in the rainy season the insects had destroyed the external hair, without having touched the internal parts. The musk has, like that of China, a strong, agreeable scent.

I thought that where one animal was found, more of the same race ought to exist, but I could not purchase any of a similar description. I now regret not having examined the hole where the precious animal was caught, as its companion might have been there, neither did I preserve the skin. Still I hope that the publication of this incident will induce English sportsmen in India to try to obtain the prize which escaped me, although the animal must be very rare, as neither the native physicians nor the druggists possess any knowledge of it. When in search of them, it ought to be considered that these interesting creatures are shy, prefer solitude, and live in copses, where their holes are made deep in the ground, beneath bushes, and thus they are saved from total extermination. Many naturalists are of opinion that the subject in question might perhaps have been another kind of animal, which possessed the same odour, just as different plants emit a similar scent. The exultation I felt on having found a real musk-deer, caused me to neglect making a proper examination of its characteristic marks, its prominent tusks—being satisfied with the scent. To the best of my recollection, the size was that of a hare, and it was of a slender cylindric frame.

Whilst I was residing at Wuzeerabad, a young Hindoo lady (katretee) came to call on General Avitabile with presents, as a token of her gratitude for his having preserved her from the fate of a Suttee, *i. e.*, being burnt alive with the body of her deceased husband; which proves that many of these victims of Brahminism feel an aversion to that horrid ceremony. The woman confessed, that on the day of the burning of her husband, and in her extreme grief, she was ready to sacrifice her life, hoping to enter paradise with her partner, but that now she felt more happy at having been preserved.

Runjeet Sing related to me that Dr. Allen (an American, and governor of Goojerat) used secretly to employ his time in his fortress in the practice of alchymy. I could not forbear laughing at the idea of his expecting to convert common metals into gold, as the conversion of quicksilver into silver was found to be quite impossible. Subsequently, my assertion was verified by the discovery he made, that the doctor's alchymy consisted in manufacturing false coin. Runjeet Sing reposed much confidence in me, and insisted on my accepting the command of an artillery department, or the office of governor of a province, like the Generals Ventura, Avitabile, and Dr. Allen; this, however, I refused, deeming that I had not sufficient abilities to execute such an office properly; but upon his giving me the choice, I accepted the management of a gunpowder manufactory, and also a gun-stock establishment. Notwithstanding my numerous occupations, which were very lucrative, I was affected with nostalgy, *i. e.*, I felt an irresistible longing to visit my native country, which I had not seen for many years, to such a degree, that my sole thoughts and endeavors were how to secure my return home. I was so occupied with this idea, that if they had offered me the Koh-i-noor (which is valued at half-a-million) to remain there for the remainder of my life, I should have refused it. General Allard's words : "It is difficult to get an appointment here, but, when obtained, it is still more difficult to quit it," were continually in my thoughts, and it cost me much trouble to obtain my dismissal, or rather my liberty.

Runjeet Sing was a man whose talents and prudence had acquired for him a great reputation, whose memory is honored, and whose name will long occupy a glorious place in the history of India. Although descended from a noble family, being the son of a sirdar, he could neither read nor write. He had lost one eye in his childhood, in consequence of the small-pox. His external appearance was not handsome, being remarkably short, delicate, and with indifferent features, which were, however, counterbalanced by his talents. He had an extraordinary memory. The prominent trait of his character was, that he rarely did what was required of him, and acted often contrary to what he said. In general, no one was informed of the place to which he intended to go, nor of the time appointed by the astrologers for his departure. The dark side of his character, was his extreme devotedness to sensuality, spirits, and opium, by which he shortened his life. I was an ocular witness of the spectacle, when he was married at Umritsir, to the Goolbegoom (rose-lady). She had been for the last few years a kenchinee (dancing girl) in the service of Runjeet Sing, and she knew so well how to ingratiate herself with her patron, that he did not hesitate publicly to celebrate his nuptials, and declare his marriage a legal one; for he cared not for public opinion, deeming that a sovereign ought to have the highest authority, and an independent will. She forsook the Mahomedan religion, continued to drink spirits, and she ate pork, just like Runjeet himself, and afterwards lived a retired life. She ruled the country, but only for a short time, and she actually caused (in concert with himself) her own husband Runjeet to be imprisoned, taking, however, advantage of that opportunity to extort money from the minister, as he was ready to ransom his lord and master at any price. The whole affair was, in fact, a plot, concocted between her and Runjeet Sing. A royal princess had died, whose fortune, according to the custom of that country, ought to have been taken possession of by Goolbegoom, as the regent princess. The inheritance, which consisted chiefly of jewels, was not sufficient to cover the deficiency of the maharaja's treasury; and the minister to whom he applied for assistance could not afford, or would not provide the sum required. In that difficulty, Runjeet Sing played the thief, and stole (as previously arranged) the said jewels; at which the Ranee Goolbegoom manifested such indignation, that she cast him into prison, firmly convinced that the miserly minister would no longer hesitate to procure the money required for the release of the sovereign, who was then undergoing such ignominy. Similar oriental tricks were not uncommon with Runjeet Sing, but this is not the place to enumerate them.

My return to my native country was *viâ* Mooltan and Dhera-Ghasi-Khan, where General Ventura was then governor. As I had provided myself with vaccine matter to use for my journey, the general wished me to vaccinate his darling child. Madame Ventura was opposed to my commencing with her little daughter Victorine, so her husband ordered some poor children to be brought from the bazaar at Dhera, whom I vaccinated, and to each of them he gave a rupee, as a remuneration. On the eighth day, on which the children ought to have come to me, that I might take the vaccine matter for further use, no one appeared, and I was told that their alarmed parents had removed them from the town. The parents had heard a rumour that on the eighth day, on their re-appearance, the Feringhee (European) doctor would cut the *moomiai* from their arm, which operation was supposed to endanger life; but on General Ventura's threatening the kotoal (police officer) with imprisonment, one of the boys was brought to me on the following morning, from whom I got vaccine matter enough to enable me to vaccinate several other children, among whom was Miss Victorine, at the harem of the general. The people having thus been convinced of their foolish error, came in numbers to my abode; the population of all the neighbouring villages, young and old, wished also to be operated on. Here again I had the opportunity of making some medical and surgical experiments, obliged as I was, to wait four months for the caravan of the Loanis, who were purchasing indigo in that neighbourhood, to carry it to Bokhara. My intention was to accompany that caravan, and to continue my journey from Bokhara to my native country, by crossing Russia. I learned afterwards, that after my departure from Dhera, Runjeet Sing began to be indisposed, and he sent messengers after me, to induce me to return, but they did not overtake me.

From Dhera-Ghasi-Khan, I went with the caravan to Dherabend, situated on the upper part of Dhera-Ismail-Khan, at the foot of the mountain, where the women, children, horses and sheep of the Loanis were residing beneath their tents. Wishing to secure a supply of vaccine matter, on my journey to Cabul and Bokhara, I endeavoured, immediately on my arrival at Dherabend, to operate with it; but it was a difficult task, as the heat was excessive and increasing. The Loanis, however, agreed to undergo the operation as soon as they had reached the cooler regions of the mountains. But during this interval the vaccine lost its virtue, which I regretted, especially at Cabul, as the small-pox was raging there in a most terrific manner; so that, during my four months' stay at the house of the Nawaub Djubber-Khan, two of his daughters died. On my request, the Nawaub ordered inquiries to be made in the whole circuit of Cabul, to discover cows affected with cow-pox; but in vain. At Cabul, this operation was quite unknown. At that time, I had forgotten having read somewhere that vaccine matter might be procured by inoculating the cows with the venomous matter taken from the small-pox, and that the venom is thus turned into a remedy.

The short description of my journey from Lahore, *via* Dhera-Ghasi-Khan and Guznee, to Cabul, was published by Colonel Sir C. M. Wade, in 1834, in the report of the Asiatic Society at Calcutta, with a map attached to it. The collection of plants which I made on this journey, I handed over to the late Baron Jaquin, Professor of Botany at Vienna, who placed them under the care of the late Doctor Endlicher and Professor Fenzel, to arrange them; a part has been already published, under the title of *Sertum Cabulicum*, and the remaining larger portion is near its completion, by Professor Fenzel. As for my collection of antiques, they are not unknown to the archæological world. They were published in the year 1835, by the Asiatic Society at Paris, to which I had communicated all the results I had obtained by means of opening the cupolas (tombs) of Cabul and Jellalabad, as also the coins and cameos which I bought when traversing Bokhara. On account of this communication, I was admitted an honorary member of the Asiatic Society at Paris; but my collection thereby lost its pecuniary value in London, so that I was obliged to forward to Paris two gold pieces (mokadphisis) to a certain M. Rollin for 3,000 francs, that sum exceeding any offer made to me in London. Among other valuable curiosities, there was a Bactrian papyrus-scroll, which had not then been opened, and the reader may find it lithographed and published by the Asiatic Society at Paris in 1835. I believe that to be the only Bactrian manuscript which has ever been found. Having packed this collection in a case, I sent it from London, addressed to the banker Geymuller, at Vienna, who afterwards became bankrupt, and the box containing those valuable curiosities remained full fifteen years at the custom-house at Vienna, unknown to me, notwithstanding many inquiries. To my astonishment and regret, I learned, on my arrival at Vienna (July 20, 1850), that the box, after an interval of fifteen years, had been sold by auction, a forthight previous to my arrival (July 5), for about three pounds, as belonging to the creditors of Geymuller, with a pretext that the real proprietor no longer existed. I could not discover into whose hands these precious antiques passed; and thus, in all probability, the invaluable contents of the Bactrian scroll will be lost for ever to the scientific world! Besides the antiques which I sold in earlier years to different private persons at Cairo and Alexandria, the various cabinets in St. Petersburgh, Vienna, Paris and London, possess a number of those which I collected.

At Cabul I opened a great many cupolas (tombs), under the protection of the Nawaub Djubber-Khan, and by so doing aroused the suspicion of Dost Mahomed, who thought that I was carrying immense riches out of the country. Although I was so prudent as to deliver all the articles I extracted to Dr. Gerard, who was then at Cabul, on his return from Bokhara to India, requesting him to hand them over to General Allard, at Lahore, that he might convey them to Bordeaux, yet Dost Mahomed gave orders to the Governor of Bamian to have me plundered at the frontiers; and thus I was robbed of all at the fortress of Akrabad; but I again received my property by the interference of the Nawaub Djubber-Khan and General Avitabile, the latter being then Governor of Peshawur. Fearing the cruelty of Mir Muradbeg, at Koondoos, I delivered at Cabul all my luggage to the caravan ready to set out for Balkh; and dressed in the costume of the Affghan people, I proceeded incognito, accompanied by ten men, some of them my own servants, and some belonging to the Nawaub. My guide was the old grey-beard, Kheiat, the same who conducted Alexander Burnes and Dr. Gerard to Bokhara.

We left Cabul in November; it was excessively cold, and we lost, during a heavy fall of snow and a strong wind, on the highest summits of Mount Caucasus, two of our people, but we happily met with them again at Bamian. The ill-repute to which my opening the tombs had given origin, preceded me. The Affghans and Hozaras hunted after us, when they ascertained who I was. Arrived at Bamian, we got a room in the fortress, by presenting the letters of recommendation which Dost Mahomed and the Nawaub had given us; but they frightened us, by saying that there were robbers in the environs, and on our road. Yet they promised to give us an escort, on account of which we were detained until the next day, as the equipment of our escort required some delay. Meanwhile, orders were given in the fortress of Akrabad to surprise aud rob us in the mountains. It was fortunate for us that a part of the garrison of the fortress was absent, and those soldiers who were present had not their muskets in order, consequently, they were unable to contend with us. Neither would it have been an easy matter for them to defeat us, provided as we were with good arms, and determined to oppose any attack. The soldiers themselves were aware of this cricumstance, consequently, they thought it more advisable to allure us into the fortress, and plunder us during the night, and I there experienced the truth of the saying, "Man must not despair in misfortune, neither be proud when in prosperity." I patiently allowed my hands to be secured, whilst I kept a small double-barrelled pistol loaded, in one of my high boots. At a favorable moment, my guide, Kafileh Bashi Kheiat, tried to liberate me, for which he received a sabre-stroke on his thick fur, happily, however, without being wounded. The robbers thought we had a great quantity of gold and silver concealed, and demanded 1,000 rupees for my ransom; but a man of the Nawaub's, to whose care I was committed, effected my release for four pounds of rice, which was weighed in their presence. The fact was, that this set of robbers were urged on by their hunger as well as by their want of money. After having given them all I had in my possession, their chief was reconciled. Laying one hand on the Koran, he produced with the other the order that had been issued for having me plundered, which was from the Governor of Bamian; all the things which were taken from me were enumerated. On my arrival on the other side of the mountain, I immediately dispatched a man with letters to the Nawaub, in which I described the ill-treatment I had sustained. I was afterwards informed that the Nawaub had reprimanded his brother Dost, and that the Governor of Bamian was removed from his post, all my things being returned to General Avitabile, from whom I received them. Had I, in my first excitement, opposed them, and fired at them, I should have been murdered.

At Holm I was recognised in the court-yard of the receiver of the customs, notwithstanding my Affghan costume, and though still on horseback, I was requested to alight there and take up my quarters. There is no doubt that I was betrayed by my own attendants, especially by Kheiat, who feared he would be punished when the caravan, which was coming behind us, should arrive, and give information of his having been my guide, and his passing me secretly through that country. The receiver of the customs instantly dispatched a man to Koondoos, where his superior officer, Utmaram, a Hindoo, minister to Emeer-Murad-Beg, resided. When informed of this circumstance, I sent off one of my attendants with the letter of recommendation which the Nawaub Djubber-Khan had addressed to Utmaram, in which he recommended him to take care of my person, or else he would destroy his property at Peshawur. This letter made such an impression on the minister, that the receiver of the customs received an order to forward me instantly and secretly, by an escort, to the frontier; fearing that if the Emeer-Murad-Beg should learn that I was there, he might insist upon my coming to Koondoos, and keep me there a prisoner. Thus I arrived safely at Balkh, where I waited for the caravan with my luggage; and the winter being very severe, I ordered a pair of kadjevahs. These are large baskets, which are placed on the camels, the interior of which being lined with woollen rugs, they prove to the traveller, who is accustomed to cower down, or sit with outstretched legs, a very comfortable contrivance. During two days, while we stopped on our way on the left bank of the Amoo (Oxus river), I did not stir from this warm abode; for the kadjevahs are ample enough to allow one to keep in them a charcoal fire, as also to perform the required necessities; and the weather was rather disagreeable; rain, wind and snow varying alternately. Thirty pairs of similar kadjevas, ranged in a square, formed a large yard. Several of them were filled with slaves (Parsians and Hozarahs). In my neighbourhood there was one in which there were four little girls; but as they were carefully watched, it was difficult to get a sight of them; they were going to Bokhara, to be sold there.

The Nawaub had made me a present of two ponies, called chargoosh (*i.e.*, four-eared, because of their ears having been slit); and they were of great use to me in the Desert from Cabul to Russia. They instinctively dig up the roots below the snow for food.

On my arrival at Bokhara, I delivered the letter of recommendation which I had from the Nawaub, addressed to the minister Hoshbegi. His first inquiry was, whether I knew Jussuff Wolff and Alexander Burnes? "Wolff," continued he, "was a very good-hearted man; but as for Burnes, he was a deceiver, because he told me, up to the last moment, that his intention was to go to England, *via* Russia, whereas he returned to Hindostan, *via* Khiva." He was convinced that Burnes was a spy, and asked me if I would act as he had done. I was told that there were 600 Russian slaves at Bokhara, most of them fishermen from the Caspian sea, or prisoners from the frontier. During my four months' stay at Bokhara, a Russian spy, Monsieur D—, was also there, whom the Governor of Orenburg had sent with presents to the Government, and who, although a Frenchman, imitated the musselmans so well, as not to be recognised as an European, for he knew both the Arabic and Persian languages; but the Nogais (Tartarian musselmans, under Russian protection) informed against him, and urged his being decapitated, lest he should inform against them for having transgressed the ukase, according to which, no Russian subject was allowed to go to Bokhara. They availed themselves of the opportunity, and accused him of the crime of being a heretic, who had visited all the sacred places of devout musselmans; they asserted also that he was in possession of a diploma obtained from the Ulemas (learned, literary men) in Bokhara, for converting the musselmans living in Russia. Hoshbegi examined the diploma in my presence, and stated that it contained nothing more than the assertion that D—had undergone a severe examination in the Arabic language, to the satisfaction of his examiners: thus he was acquitted ; but his accusers caused him to be brought before the Emir, when he and his diploma were again examined, with, however, the same result.

A short time before my departure, Hoshbegi requested me, by the bread and salt whith I had eaten in his house, to write to him from Russia, informing him whether this *eldjee* (ambassador) was a Christian or a musselman. I was of opinion that it could be easily ascertained, even at Bokhara, by examining his body ; besides that, his light hair indicate, that he was not an Arab. The minister probably did not like to urge the matter any further, because Monsieur D. had brought him some valuable presents. When I entered Bokhara, I was forbidden to write ; and I did not transgress that prohibition. It is probable that the Englishmen who came shortly after my departure to Bokhara (Colonel Stoddart and Captain Conolly) acted otherwise, which led to the discovery of their being spies, on account of which they were beheaded. Dr. Wolff, whose acquaintance I made at Lahore, and whom I saw last year in England (at the Isle Brewery, near Taunton), told me that these two Englishmen had been taken as spies and convicted, and that it was Ubd-ool-Sumet Khan, a Persian rogue, who informed against them, and afterwards caused Hoshbegi to be beheaded ; and who, eventually, was himself decapitated.

In consideration of my attendance on the various patients, I obtained, by order of the minister, permission to pass on horseback through all the bazzars of the holy city, accompanied by a servant of his. Nevertheless, I observed many fanatic students plotting against me, on whom I had my revenge, although not intentionally. I am sorry to say that a student of the high college died in consequence of an operation performed by me. My enemies, however, could do me no harm, as I had effected several important cures, among which was that of the Emir himself, whom I recovered from a gastric-bilious fever. The unfortunate operation was the extraction of a stone from the bladder; and the proverb is true, which says—"Non est in medico semper relevetur ut aeger, interdum docta plus valet arte malum." I had a presentiment on that occasion that I should not succeed in the operation; the patient was already so weakened and enervated, that I felt no wish to operate on him, and yielded only to the request of the minister, who told me that the student was about to kill himself in despair, in case I persisted in my refusal. To secure myself from reproach, should the operation happen to fail, I caused a document to be drawn up, with the signatures of the patient and his brother, declaring me not be responsible for the result of the operation, as I undertook it only because they insisted on my doing so. This document was legalised by the seals of the Emir minister, and judge. I performed the operation in the presence of several witnesses, whom I invited for the purpose, among whom there were several hakims. The extraction of the stone was performed in one of the apartments of the high college. Fortunately I used the apparatus altus, or I should certainly not have been able to extract it. The patient behaved very quietly during the operation, which was more than I had expected, and said nothing but "Ya Allah! Ya Allah!" (O God! O God!) To my grief, and to the surprise of all present, the stone was found to be immoveable, having grown into the substance of the bladder, in such a manner that I have never seen or heard of a similar case. The reader may imagine the difficulty, when, while such operations usually occupy only two or three minutes, I was fully five and twenty minutes engaged in loosening with the fingers of both hands the stone, which had upwards of twenty points, every one of which resembled a thick apple-stalk, half-an-inch long. The size of the calculus, however, did not surpass that of a hen's egg, and it was as white as crystallized sugar; an engraving of it may be found in the second volume.

I instantly sent the stone to the minister Hoshbegi, at the fortress of Registan, with the melancholy assurance, that to heal the wound was impossible. In the meanwhile, I availed myself of the opportunity to request from the minister some genuine Persian mumiai, this remedy being considered in the Arabic Materia Medica a specific against wounds and fractured bones. I administered one grain to the patient daily. After a few days had elapsed, he began to have an appetite. The minister, who took great interest in the case, sent twice a-day to inquire about the state of the student; and on hearing of this false sign of recovery, he said that my fears about the restoration of my patient were certainly groundless. "Would to God," replied I, "that my prognostic may turn out false, and that I may be obliged to owe the restoration of the patient to your mumiai;" but up to this moment all the operations that I had performed, when the stone was but slightly attached to the bladder, had always failed; and in such cases, mortification ensues, generally on the fourth day after the operation, which puts an end to the sufferings of the patient. He took his leave, uttering the consoling words, "Trust and rely on God," which I indeed did; for in sixteen days after, the unfortunate student died of weakness and exhaustion, the bladder being perforated like a sieve, and thus defying surgical and medical art. Feeling the approach of death, he thanked both me and his brother for our attendance, declaring that his early death (he was about twenty years of age) was not the consequence of the inefficiency of the medical art, but the fulfilment of the inscrutable will and decree of God, the Ruler of all beings!

Hoshbegi was in one and the same person, Wuzeer, Receiver of the Customs, Druggist and Hakim to the Emir. Like all the literary men in the East, he not only possessed medical knowledge, but he was likewise the confidential friend of his princely highness. He was also charged with the preparation of the victuals for the Emir, who was somewhat over twenty years of age. All dishes, before they are placed on the table of the prince, must be tasted by Hoshbegi, in the kitchen; he puts them afterwards in a locked basket, of which he and the Emir only have the keys.

The Emir having taken the above-mentioned bilious fever, I was introduced to him by Hoshbegi. I administered the usual emetic, which had a good effect, and Hoshbegi requested the recipe of it. He asked me also for some tartar-emetic, quinine (with which last he was acquainted through Dr. Gerard), and phosphorus, the latter for his recreation.

Among the many patients I had to attend during my stay at Bokhara, was one affected with asthma, whom I was ordered by the Emir to cure, as he was a relation of his own, and the recovery of whom produced some sensation. This man was troubled upwards of twenty years with a spasmodic and periodic asthma; he was already very weak and exhausted, yet I succeeded in curing him.

Hoshbegi was very much pleased with my information, and was anxious for instruction, so we passed many hours in conversation. A short time after the death of the aforesaid student, he asked me how the stone is produced in man; this I explained to him clearly. At this time, the Emirakhoor (chief groom) gave me two stones from a horse, each the size of a goose egg, which had been ejected, along with the excrement, in the interval of a year, and which probably had been formed in the stomach or intestines. I remember relating an anecdote to him on that occasion, which I venture to introduce here, it having very much pleased Hoshbegi. A mother on the Lebanon, whose boy I operated on, told me she well knew the cause of the formation of the stone in the body of her son George. I begged her to tell me her opinion, and she went on saying: "My husband, who is a butcher, is addicted to drink; he departed for the fair twelve years ago, when I was nursing George. His intention was to buy some oxen, and he took a large sum of money with him, of which he was robbed while in a state of intoxication. When I heard this, continued the woman, it made a very serious impression on me, and I suppose that my baby was also affected with my grief, as I observed on that very day he was unable to pass his urine, in spite of all his exertions, until he was relieved by suction. From that time he enjoyed good health for several months, yet this stoppage came on periodically, that is to say, as often as the stone obstructed the urethra, on which occasion he used to rub the part, stamp with his feet, and cry for help." After this relation she begged my pardon, adding, "one ought to conceal nothing from the doctor. Yet," continued she, "I have still one circumstance to communicate to you; previously to the operation, my child had the bad habit of wetting the bed; but he has never done so since."

In the present state of medical knowledge, it is impossible to assert whether the cause of the production of stony concretions be connected with the sensations of the nurse, or whether other circumstances co-operate, as we find snch concretions in different parts of the body, not only in the urethra, urine-bladder, kidneys, and the gall-organs, but also in the stomach and intestines of horses, oxen, goats, &c., as just mentioned. But there is no doubt that they are substances of the animal body. We have in ourselves different mineral substances, and a sickly habit causes them to accumulate. I once found five tolerably large stones pressed in the neck of a bladder to such a degree, that I cannot conceive how the man was able to void one drop of urine. Several cases occurred to me, in which, a few years after the stone had been extracted, new ones accumulated, because the origin of the disease was not eradicated; and I recommend every operator to combine an internal with an external treatment, the extraction or the crushing of the stone being nothing but a palliative.

At Bokhara, I found that the guinea-worm (Dracunculus) occurred very frequently. At Cabul, I saw a strange case of this kind, in which a merchant had drunk the water from which it orginates a year previously at Bombay. The worm was at the hollow of the knee. Upon its appearing and being pulled, it broke, and the knee was very much inflamed and swollen. Feeling an accumulation of matter, I made an incision, upon which it began to flow. I kept the wound open for several days, and ordered the swollen parts to be embrocated with wax-oil, and in a few days it was entirely healed. In a severe swelling of the testicles, which was the consequence of an external injury, the same remedy proved efficacious.

Oil distilled from wax (cerelæum) is employed by the native physicians of the East in various diseases, especially in paralysis, contractions, swellings, wounds, itching, impotence, colds and cholera-morbus. The embrocations are generally performed in the rays of the sun. In cholera-morbus, they drink hot broth afterwards; hot bricks are enveloped in rugs and applied to the soles of the feet, they are then covered with woollen-sheets over the head, to produce perspiration. In similar cases, the Bokharians administer a Turcoman-sudorific remedy, with which a native physician assured me he had cured many cholera patients. The medicament is as cheap as it is simple, and should be used in case no other can be obtained at the moment. They procure a quantity of wheaten bran, sift it seven times, and as many times wash it superficially, then rub it in water with the fingers, and strain it; the strained water is simmered until reduced to one-half, to which they add some garlic and almond oil, and it is then drunk lukewarm. The garlic serves, as the physician told me, to drive away the evil spirits. The physicians of Europe may learn by this what remedies ought to be employed when patients are haunted by evil spirits, a thing which occurs occasionally in the case of ladies. The same doctor also informed me by what means they got rid of the cholera at Bokhara. A procession was arranged, during which they buried in the middle of the city a new horse-hide, which is easily procured there; as the inhabitants of Bokhara eat more horse-flesh than any other kind of meat, and which is probably the cause of this odd idea. The Affghans have also a peculiar method of curing nervous fevers. They envelop the patient in the skin of a newly-killed animal (goat or sheep), in which he falls into a perspiration, and in this state he is left for a whole night. A decoction of bran is also said to be a good sudorific, but considered as a mild one, and is not generally in use.

To cure the guinea-worm, the natives of the East make use of many curious remedies, which will be found in the second volume.

At Bokhara, I met two unfortunate Armenians from Astrakhan, who requested me to use my influence in their behalf. Three years previously, when Count Suchtelen was Governor of Orenburg, they had laid claim to a considerable sum due to them as their legal portion of an inheritance at Bokhara; to which place they received letters of recommendation from the governor, and were sent thither to urge their claims, with directions, should they not succeed, to return to Orenburg, and the Russian government would assist them. On their arrival there, the settlement of their affairs presented some difficulty, as the government had confiscated the legacy, under various pretexts. The two heirs—who, in their endeavours to obtain their property, seemed not to have lost all hope, in spite of the evasive promises they had for many years received—thought it requisite to use their utmost energies to get their rights at last; for which purpose they solicited my assistance, representing to me their awkward situation, and saying that the Russian ambassador, who had recently arrived, refused to interfere, but by my influence they hoped to obtain a happy result. I could not reject their application, and by so much the more, as I was informed that the Russian government was desirous to negotiate for the liberty of its subjects then in slavery at Bokhara. These two Armenians were indeed in a state worse than slavery, because they were not accidentally flung on this territory, but were sent hither to obtain their rights. I resolved therefore to interfere for them. I felt myself, in fact, compelled to do so ; for had I refused my assistance, the poor men would have been detained, in consequence of the heavy debts they had contracted during their three years' stay at Bokhara. I accordingly addressed myself in this affair to Hoshbegi, begging him to take pity on these men, and to interfere in their behalf. He received myself and my petition very kindly, but appeared little disposed to do anything for the younger of the supplicants, as he had uttered some threatening words when asking for justice ; and he added, "they may plead their cause before the tribunal." But the judges refused to listen to their petition, alleging—first, that they had not appeared to make their claims immediately after the death of the testator; secondly, that those who appeared as heirs, being Russian subjects, could not be considered as legal claimants, but were reckoned among Christian sects, and treated as heretics; and, thirdly, that the whole legacy being the result of a trade not tolerated in the Koran, *i. e.*, wine, it ought to have been confiscated, as it really was. I solicited Hoshbegi to permit me to pay the debts of these poor men, and to take them with me to their home in Russia. This I obtained without any difficulty, so I liquidated their debts, and took them with me, accompanying the caravan with which the Russian ambassador also set out for that country. The most costly thing I carried with me from Bokhara, was a very beautiful horse, of a breed called *argomak*. This horse, the beauty of which was admired by every connoisseur, was provided with all its appurtenances; such as a silver bridle, a Bokharian saddle, a richly-adorned caparison, &c. This noble animal was a stallion four years old. I destined it as a present for his Majesty the late Emperor of Austria, Francis I, with a view to its serving as a riding-horse and a sire. I ventured to do this as an Austrian subject, and after an absence of twenty years, to manifest my loyalty and faithfulness to my monarch. My wish to perform this act of duty in the proper costume, was the cause of my appearing habited as a native of Bokhara, in the years 1834, 1835, and 1836, when travelling through Europe.

The journey from Bokhara to Russia, which I performed in thirty-five stations, was one of the most pleasant I ever had in the whole course of my travels, as no impediments from the elements, or other disastrous occurrences, happened during the route; yet, to make good the proverb of Solomon "There exists nothing perfect in this sublunary world," we had a little episode, which I will here relate. Passing the river, Sir—known in antiquity under the name of Jaxartes—we arrived at a custom station, where they demanded an enormous toll, which we had not any right whatever to pay. An awful quarrel arose, and we were about preparing for a fight, when our antagonists, perceiving our arms, began to feel a little more respect for us; they still, however, continued to make a noise and to vociferate, and made fire-signals for their brethren in the desert to hasten to their assistance. But the affair was soon settled, and we went on our way without any further molestation. With regard to mercantile interests, I must here add, that among the products and manufactures, native and foreign, of Bokhara, are lamb-skins, dyed linen, horses, indigo, Cashmere shawls, &c. Respecting indigo, I may observe that it was most impure stuff, for I observed that one-half of it was nothing but particles of clay, in the same shape as it is brought by the Loanis from Dhera-Ghasi-Khan, Moultan and Bhawulpore. How much might be saved in the carriage, and in duty at the custom-houses, if the indigo were purified previous to exportation! We were almost induced to take with us a great quantity of sarsaparilla from the desert, but I soon recognised it to be a mere substitute for the real article. Among other objects which attracted my attention in the desert, connected with scientific knowledge, was the kumiss (fermented mare's-milk), a favourite beverage with the Kirgis, and also with the inhabitants of the Russian

Page 74

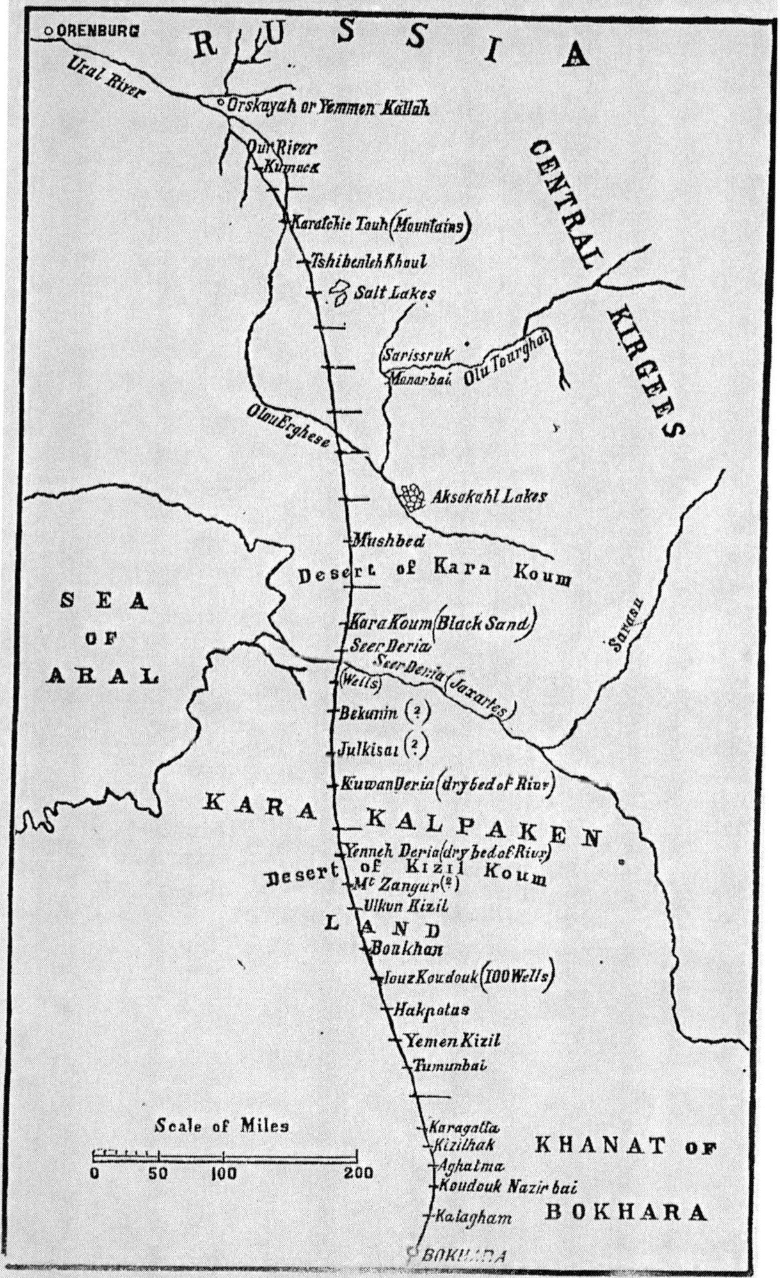

ORENBURG
RUSSIA
Ural River
Orskayah or Yemmen Kallah
Our River
Kumack
Karatchie Touh (Mountains)
Tshibenleh Khoul
Salt Lakes
CENTRAL KIRGEES
Sarissruk
Manarbai
Olu Tourghai
Olou Erghese
Aksakahl Lakes
Mushbed
Desert of Kara Koum
SEA OF ARAL
Kara Koum (Black Sand)
Seer Deria
Seer Deria (Jaxartes)
Sarasu
(Wells)
Bekunin (?)
Julkisai (?)
Kuwan Deria (dry bed of River)
KARA KALPAKEN
Yenneh Deria (dry bed of River)
Desert of Kizil Koum
Mt Zangur (?)
Ulkun Kizil
LAND
Boukhan
Iouz Koudouk (100 Wells)
Hakpotas
Yemen Kizil
Tumunbai
Scale of Miles
0
50
100
200
Karagatta
Kizilhak
Aghatma
Koudouk Nazir bai
Kalagham
KHANAT OF BOKHARA
BOKHARA

boundaries. I could give a great many proofs that the kumiss is a very wholesome and nutritious beverage. It may suffice to mention here, that the governor of Orenburg returned at that time from the Ural Mountains, where he had used the kumiss as a cure with great benefit. I may observe also, that it is introduced at the tables of the nobility at Orenburg and several other places. It was especially drunk by weak persons and children, as a wholesome potion. Kumiss is a palatable and intoxicating drink, it being produced by fermentation, and consequently spirituous. They prepare it by pouring the mare's-milk into seasoned goat-skins, which are continually tossed about until it begins to ferment. According to the opinion of the Kirgises the kumiss is better when the milk is procured from mares of different colours. The fresher it is, the better for the health. To give the reader a slight synopsis of my journey from Bokhara to Russia, a little map, on which the thirty-five stations are traced, is annexed.

On my arrival at Orenburg, I was greatly delighted to meet with several German generals, who were in the Russian service, and also German physicians. The deep impression which this meeting made upon me, can only be conceived by those who, like me, had for several years been deprived of all intercourse with their countrymen. But that enthusiasm was increased still more, when I was told that a new mode of curing diseases had been discovered, diametrically opposite to that which had hitherto been followed.

Who will blame me for having this irresistible and ardent desire to see Europe once more ? Providence had appeared to yield me an opportunity of extending the horizon of my knowledge, for the benefit of mankind ; and the same internal voice which twenty years before had induced me to abandon my friends, my relatives and my dear native country, admonished me also to renounce the favor of a powerful ruler, the prospects of becoming powerful myself, and the influence by means of which I could enjoy the most splendid ease, in order to be instrumental in introducing a hitherto unknown healing system.

From Orenburg I continued my journey by post over Kazan to Nishni-Nowgorod, and I arrived, without any material accidents, at the latter city. It was just the time of the fair, to which people from the nearest and remotest countries were flocking, to purchase and sell their merchandise. Provided as I was with cash, I lent a willing ear to some friends, who, from their local knowledge, advised me not to take ready money with me, but to buy sable skins. They gave me this advice, as sables would not increase the bulk of my luggage like other merchandise, and added that the skins could be disposed of with considerable profit. For that purpose, I called on one of the principal houses which dealt in sable skins, where I had the opportunity of making the personal acquaintance of the governor of the place, whom I met by accident. I made a bargain in his presence, the merchant engaging to be content with a profit of ten per cent. This induced me to purchase to a considerable amount, which I immediately paid, after having received the goods. During these transactions, the governor asked my interpreter who I was, whence I came, and whither I was going. Having got satisfactory information, and having learned at the same time that I was in possession of a beautiful horse of the finest breed, he requested me to show it to him when it arrived. When I left the merchant, my interpreter told me that the sable-dealer wished that none should be acquainted with our arrangements, and that he would send me, the following morning, a man who knew well how the skins ought to be packed. This circumstance created in my mind a suspicion of his dishonesty. To ascertain the fact, I went early on the following morning to a merchant whom I knew, and communicated to him my impression. After having examined the skins, he declared there was not a doubt about my having been cheated by the dealer, and he himself offered to supply me with the same quality of article for half the price which I had paid. He advised me to go instantly to the merchant, and propose to him either to add a portion more of sables, or that I would make him a present of the ten per cent., and he should take back his goods, and return me my money. But he was not willing to yield to either one or the other, so I could only follow the advice of my friends, and inform the police of the fraud, in order to get back my money. Whilst at the police-office, I was, to my surprise, arrested by an order of the governor, and taken before him. The first inquiry he made was about my passport; I produced it, and after a strict examination of its contents, he began to question me, why I had let seven days pass without having presented it to the legal authorities? I simply replied, that living in a public hotel, where no one asked me for it, I thought such a course unnecessary. This reply seemed unsatisfactory to the governor. He dwelt upon the fact, that as I knew fourteen different languages, I ought to be acquainted with the Russian, for I was then conversing with him in French; he also said that as I had asserted I was an European Christian, clad in oriental costume, I must enter the category of spies, especially as I had been audacious enough to attempt to injure one of the most respectable mercantile-houses, by casting a blemish on its character, and for which he would himself be security. I was led back again to the police-office as a prisoner, where I was detained from nine o'clock in the morning till three in the afternoon, without their offering me so much as a seat. Meanwhile a police officer was dispatched to the hotel, where my room was opened, and everything rummaged, but they could find nothing suspicious. Whilst they were thus engaged in the examination of my effects, my horse arrived, and was put in the stable. When the police officer saw my horse, he came to me and pressed me to sell it to him, but I declared that having destined it as a present to my legitimate sovereign, I would not sell it for any price. At three o'clock, I was informed that the passport which they gave me at Orenburg, and which ought to have been sufficient to convey me to my native country, must remain at the police-office, and instead of that, I was to receive an official certificate, with which I was ordered to depart for Moscow within twenty-four hours. After having left the police-office, I waited on some of my German friends, who pressed me to leave Nishni-Nowgorod as soon as possible, as a rumour was current that the emperor had arrived at Moscow, and that post-horses had already been ordered to bring him to Nowgorod; so that the greatest danger menaced me, namely, being shut up in a dungeon, to prevent my making complaints to the monarch. These friends accompanied me to my hotel; but how great was our astonishment on seeing the door of my room open, and a part of my effects stolen! But that astonishment reached its height when, on going into the stable to speak to the groom, we found him absent, and the horse bleeding, and on a closer examination, saw that the tendons of his legs had been cut across. It was quite natural that the suspicion of the theft and mutilation of the horse could only fall on the absent groom, and as his immediate capture was impossible, I was obliged to arrest the Bokharian merchant who was security for him. I addressed myself to the police-officer, who was instructed by my friends, and who came in person to make an inspection at the hotel. After the imprisonment of the Bokharian, the groom, who had escaped, came of himself to take the place of the captive. It being impossible now to take the horse with me, I sold him for a mere trifle to one of my friends, an Englishman, Mr. Strubing, who bought him for a sire, and who was so kind as to take upon himself to manage my affairs, for which I gave him full power, and a document was drawn on stamped paper, in the presence of the official authorities. Soon after my arrival at Moscow, I received a letter from Mr. Strubing, informing me that my groom had been released immediately after my departure, without any further process. The merchant, M. Lomoff, with whom I transacted the business of the sable skins at Nowgorod, having been a citizen resident at Moscow, I thought it but right to lay the case before his Excellency Prince Galitzin, Governor of Moscow. But great was my astonishment at my unfriendly reception by the Prince, who said he had not the best opinion of my character, on account of the bad reports which had reached him. I met with the same fate at Count Benkendorf's, on whom I called when he was there with the suite of the Emperor. It is impossible to conceive the difficulties I had to struggle with in getting a passport for the continuation of my journey to St. Petersburgh, as they had retained mine at Nowgorod.

As I was naturally extremely desirous to restore my injured reputation, I required that a commercial jury should be summoned to decide between me and Lomoff. Several months passed away fruitlessly, but at last that jury, consisting of two Russians, two Germans, and two Greek merchants dealing in furs, decided the matter in my favor. Lomoff would have been obliged to return the money had he not in the interval become bankrupt, but one of his relatives received the skins and paid me a part of the amount. During the settlement of the above transaction, I made an excursion to St. Petersburgh, of which city I had heard so much, and what I saw there exceeded my expectations. I will not mention the delightful situation of this city, nor speak of its magnificent palaces, churches, and public buildings; neither will I depict the imposing aspect of the majestic-flowing waters of the Neva; nor describe the various other external objects which have already been painted by others. I will only mention one particular circumstance, which rendered my stay in the metropolis, although for a very short time, most agreeable. It was the kind reception I met with among all classes of the inhabitants, from the highest to the lowest; especially among the former. I still retain in my memory one angel-like image, which appeared to me in the person of the Grand Duchess Helena. This intellectual and illustrious lady invited me to call on her, when she heard of my arrival, because she had been informed that I had seen at Lahore Victor Jaquemont, whose correspondence she was then reading. Her Imperial Highness conversed with me about different matters for two hours. She inquired principally about Cabul, Bokhara, and India, their political, physical and moral condition, and even the minutest particulars concerning those countries. Neither can I omit here to mention one circumstance, trifling as it is, for which I feel myself grateful even now. When I was on the following day on my way to see the Mint, as my oriental costume made me known everywhere, when I met the carriage of the Grand Duchess, that noble lady saluted me very kindly the instant she perceived me.

Being a native of Kronstadt in Transylvania, I thought it but right while in the vicinity of the Russian town of the same name, to visit it, a desire which must be excused, as that place enjoys a reputation for its nautical importance; but it happens very often during life that difficulties oppose our plans, and thus it was this time with me. I was to have gone there by steamer early in the morning, but a thick fog hovering in the atmosphere, rendering it impossible to start at the appointed hour, the crew waited for clearer weather. As it did not change, we departed at nine o'clock, but not far from the harbour we ran on a sand bank, and were not able to move any further. Happily there appeared an empty steamer coming up the river from Kronstadt, as if sent by Providence to our rescue. We went on board, and proceeded, after a short delay, to the place of our destination. On the steamer there was a respectably dressed young man, who spoke German, and whose behaviour demonstrated him to be of good breeding. After a conversation, in which he learned that my intention was to stay only that day and one night at Kronstadt, he proposed to me, in a very engaging manner, to take up my quarters in his house, an offer which I heartily accepted. On our arrival at Kronstadt, I accompanied him home; but the first sight of his rooms produced in me a very repugnant sensation; for everything in his abode indicated disorder and uncleanliness. My displeasure increased still more, when, after a short stay in his hospitable abode, he declared to me that he was ruined, having just lost in three days all his fortune by card-playing at Petersburgh. We had not finished our conversation, which took place close to the window that looked into the yard, when on a sudden the gate opened, and a troop of chimney-sweepers rushed in, whom my host informed me were his own servants. I looked for an excuse to leave as soon as possible the house of the chimney-sweeper; and afterwards I was informed that this profession is a very lucrative one in Russia, and that those who follow it are generally rich and respectable men.

Of what further occurred to me after my return to St. Petersburgh, I have nothing to relate, for I left the capital immediately after my arrival there, and set off for Moscow. The arrangement of my affairs having now been completed, I felt no stronger desire than that of again seeing my native country. It was in the winter season, and the ground was covered with snow, when about the middle of November, I left the old and venerable capital of Russia. I had my own carriage, and passed through the governments of Tulai, Orel, Kiew, Volhynia and Bukowina, and also through Czernowitz, Dorna, and Bistritz, to Kronstadt, my dear and beloved native town, where I arrived on Christmas-eve, in the year 1834, by the same road on which I had twenty years before left my home, full of lofty ideas, and impelled by my desire to see the Eastern world.

The season during my journey was inconvenient for me, as it would have been for any one in my situation. Although I had no longer to struggle against wild beasts and Arab robbers, yet the severe cold was almost insupportable, and still more so were the vexations and extortions I had everywhere to endure from greedy Polish Jews, and cunning treacherous servants. But even at the moment, when I had already left the Austrian frontier behind me, and fancied I saw my native land, I was near losing my life. It was in the middle of December when I ascended one of those snow-covered Carpathian summits, a short time before sunset. I had alighted from my carriage on account of the steepness of the road, when the vehicle suddenly overturned, and was precipitated down a tremendous precipice, together with the three horses and the coachman, and there they remained all the night long.

As for myself, I took refuge in a chardak (cabin where the boundary guards reside), and spent the night there. In the morning, my equipage was brought up by the efforts of the soldiers, with the aid of a great number of oxen, fetched from the neighbouring village. Who could have imagined that the coachman and the horses would have been alive after such a terrible fall? And yet the former was only hurt, and the latter lamed; but the coach was broken, and required repairs.

I cannot conclude this first part of my adventures without giving some account of the deep impression I experienced on treading again the soil of my native country, after an absence of so many years, in which I had had to struggle against so many difficulties. But the feelings of my heart reached their highest pitch, on entering those rooms in which I had passed my earliest happy age, and not missing either of my dear and beloved parents. My voice faltered, and tears began to flow down my cheeks, when I saw once more, after an absence of twenty years, my father, mother, brothers and sisters, pressed them to my throbbing heart, received their welcome, and felt their kisses. As they were informed of the day of my arrival, they had postponed the christening of my brother's daughter, and fixed it for the moment of my return, in order to heighten the solemnity of that ceremony, and to have me for her godfather. For that purpose, we went that very afternoon to the principal church, in which I had myself been christened, where a multitude of the citizens were already assembled to witness the holy act, the news of my arrival having spread through the town with the rapidity of lightning; some were attracted by curiosity. eager to see me in my extraordinary and splendid oriental costume. I also fancy that many of them were desirous of knowing whether I had lost the fluency with which I formerly spoke the languages of our country (Saxon, German, Hungarian, and Walachian). When they heard me speak them with the same facility as formerly, the interest they took in my person was still further increased. My parents and friends admired my oriental costume so much, that they requested me not to change it; and I yielded to their request, and afterwards visited many of the capitals of Europe in that dress.

I passed the remainder of the season at Kronstadt in the most agreeable manner; after which, I proceeded on my journey towards Vienna, passing through Hungary. Thence, I went to Trieste and Venice, Milan, Genoa, Nice and Marseilles; from this last, I made a short excursion to St. Tropez, to see General Allard's family, from whom I learned that the general had left India and was expected at Bordeaux. I proceeded to that city, and, after a three weeks' stay, I was so fortunate as to meet with the general, who brought me the box containing the antiques which I had forwarded to him from Cabul. I afterwards visited Paris, and came to England, by Calais and Dover. My companion on this journey was my brother, to whose daughter I had stood godfather. His accompanying me was owing to a strange and unfortunate accident which had befallen him.

On the very day on which I wrote to him from Orenburg, announcing my approach towards home, he had lost nearly all his fortune by a destructive fire, through which he was almost reduced to despair. In order to restore him to his former activity, I proposed that he should accompany me on my tour through Europe, which he willingly did.

At Paris, my steps were first directed towards the domicile of the father of Homœopathy, the celebrated Doctor Hahnemann. In Russia, I had been already told of the prodigious effects of his new healing system, and I earnestly desired to learn it at the source itself. The magnanimous old man and his lovely young wife received me in the most friendly manner, and I must not omit to mention, that the open and good-natured Homœopathist made many interesting revelations to me respecting his new method of curing. It was particularly important to me that Hahnemann recommended to me his apothecary at Kothen, Doctor Lehman.

The voyage from London to Hamburg, which I performed in a steamer, lasted a day longer than ordinary, and was one of the most dreadful and annoying I have ever experienced. We were overtaken by a tempest, by which the vessel was tossed about in such a manner that all the passengers suffered from sea-sickness. If I say that our feelings were those of a person whose bowels are being cut through with sharp knives, the comparison would remain far behind the real fact. At Berlin, I met with an old friend, Doctor Ehrenberg, the naturalist, whom I accompanied many years ago to the ruins of Balbeck; he was in good health, and we conversed about that journey; but Doctor Hemprich, his then travelling companion, had already left this world. According to Hahnemann's advice, I introduced myself, at Kothen, to Doctor Lehman, from whom I bought a considerable quantity of homœopathic medicines. From Kothen I went to Leipsic, Dresden and Toplitz, at which place was that celebrated congress of the Emperors of Austria and Russia, the King of Prussia, and the most celebrated diplomatists, as also a great number of the *élite* of the nobility. It may easily be imagined, that on such an occasion there was no lack of festivals and amusements, in which I took some share, as I met with a very kind reception, owing, perhaps, to my oriental costume.

From Toplitz I returned to Kronstadt, my native country, in order to pass the carnival there among my relations. In the spring of the year 1836, I went to Vienna, on particular business, and I stayed there till the autumn. In the summer of the same year, the long-dreaded guest, cholera, was raging in that capital. I myself felt the first symptoms of that dreadful and destroying epidemic. I had spasms and a diarrhœa; I therefore lost no time in applying my remedies, taking, every half-hour, a homœopathic dose of ipecacuanha. This remedy proved quite efficacious, and I was fortunate enough to be entirely recovered in the space of six hours.

As there are many substitutes for ipecacuanha, I think

it not superfluous to mention on this occasion, that it is only the genuine drug that can produce the desired effect. That by which I was restored, was from Doctor Lehman. The good result which I experienced in myself and others, from adopting the homœopathic system, induced me to extend the practice to a larger circle of patients. For that purpose I chose the capital of the Ottoman empire, which I thought particularly suitable, as it was at no great distance from my native country, and because I was acquainted with the oriental languages, habits and manners. Besides that, my pecuniary circumstances were rather embarrassed, as the reader may be aware, owing to the losses I had sustained in different countries, partcularly in Bokhara (by the Armenians) and in Russia (by my sable transactions). To carry out my plan, I petitioned for a passport to Constantinople, which I obtained without any difficulty.

I departed from Vienna, passed through Kronstadt and Bukarest for Gallaz, where I embarked, not as previously at Varna in an open vessel, but in a steamer bound to Constantinople. Contrary to my expectation, the plague was raging there at that time, and the Europeans kept themselves shut up in their houses, far from any contact with the world. Under such circumstances, I had no alternative but to wait for another opportunity. To do this with more comfort, I hired a small house on the shores of the Bosphorus, in a village situated in the most pleasant part of that country, from which I enjoyed a beautiful prospect. On the very evening of my taking possession of the cottage, I was called to attend a Greek lady living in my neighbourhood, who required my medical assistance. I was told that she had a fever. I found her in bed, complaining of being uneasy and costive, accompanied with a headache, so I ordered her an emollient clyster, which I myself was obliged to administer, as nobody could undertake to do it. But, to my alarm, I was informed on the following morning that she had died during the night of the plague, her husband having preceded her but a few days from the same complaint. The house of the deceased was immediately shut up. At that time the quarantine establishments at Constantinople were still in their original state of organisation, my small house therefore remained free, and luckily it was not infected with the plague. The circumstance of my not being myself affected by it—neither had I conveyed it to my household—induced me to believe that I had not any disposition to be attacked by that pestilential disease. I was also of opinion that the plague was not contagious. In order to have some experience in this matter, I tendered my services at once to the plague-hospital at Pera, where the poor patients were left to their fate, as no medical assistance or any other aid was to be had. Without any authority or permission, I attended them at my own expense. I proceeded, to the satisfaction of all the attendants and patients, to treat the infected according to the homœopathic principle, and my endeavours were mostly crowned with success. All this, effected by the most simple treatment, did not fail to procure me, in a very short time, a great reputation; so that, after the extinction of the plague, and the abolition of all quarantine, I was in great request among the most respectable private families. But, before I proceed to prove the efficacy of the minute doses of homœopathic medicines, I must first speak of a special remedy, which proved very efficacious, employed as a prophylactic or curative; and, I dare to say, with respect to the plague, it might be considered as a specific.

During my stay at Constantinople I frequently had an opportunity of making the observation that many individuals, especially Armenians, wore a string, to which was attached a bean, called Strychnos Faba St. Ignatii, as a preventive against the plague. Having been informed that this bean was acknowledged to be an effective one, I administered it in minute doses, as a medicine, and that with the best success. The particulars will be mentioned in the course of this work.

Among the above-mentioned private houses in which

they relied on my medical skill, was that of M. Shabert. The head of this respectable family had been formerly invested with the office of English interpreter.

It is the duty of a physician to have patience when he has occasion to attend old ladies; and thus I must crave the reader's indulgence while I relate what Mrs. Shabert communicated to me. She began thus:—" A young Greek stabbed my son with a stiletto; and, at the moment when he was about to cry out for assistance, the Greek was so malicious as to thrust the weapon into his mouth and cut a blood-vessel, from which a violent bleeding ensued, and it could only be stopped by immediate surgical assistance. He was taken to the consulate, in front of which it happened, and where he was employed. By the application of red-hot iron, the blood was stanched; but two or three days subsequently, the bleeding began afresh, and the patient felt exhausted; when the bleeding was renewed for the third time, he became much worse. On the ensuing night, he was restless, and in a state of great perturbation from his dreams. It appeared to him as if his adversary was running towards him, with the stiletto in his grasp. The attendant physicians, thinking this symptom to be the forerunner of another flow of blood, declared the patient's state to be very critical, being persuaded that, upon another bleeding, death was inevitable." In this awful position, the family proposed to the physicians to allow them a trial of homœopathy. They readily consented, in the hope of meeting with a good opportunity of rendering homœopathy ridiculous, and showing the public the inutility of that system. Mrs. Shabert having finished, her husband requested me to accompany him to the consulate, where his son was then lying, in order that I might cure him. I found the youth very much reduced, but tranquil in mind. His surgeon, a Frenchman, who was present, or rarher was waiting for me, told me he had, by a repetition, stanched the blood with a red-hot iron and other styptics, but that another bleeding was to be feared as soon as the scab should come from the wound, and as the parents of the patient were anxious to try homœopathy, he consented, and I administered, in his presence, three lilliputian pills of Aranea diadema (X°°°), and then took my leave. When I called on my patient in the morning, he told me that he had passed a quiet night, that his former physician had already been there, and on hearing that no bleeding had taken place, he had prescribed for him some pills; but he again and again repeated, that he felt no inclination to take them, as he preferred my medicine, which had proved so beneficial. Whilst I was preparing the medicament, the doctor, who was an Italian, came in, and was about to fasten a quarrel on me; but old M. Shabert took him by the arm and led him into another room, from which he disappeared, and I saw him no more. I repeated the medicine for eight days, at the end of which time he was completely recovered. I must observe here, that the Aranea diadema was prepared by Doctor Lehmann, at Kothen, whose medicines, as I have already mentioned, were recommended to me by Hahnemann.

What did the surgeon do in the meanwhile? To show that the recovery of the young man was the effect of his treatment, he ordered a dog to be brought from the bazaar, and cut through its crural artery, and then applied his styptic (creosote); but seeing that the wound did not heal, he allowed the dog to escape, and a short time afterwards the animal was found dead in the street.

Another case occurred in the above-mentioned family, with a female, which may serve as an example how small homœopathic doses not only produce effects, but sometimes cause great and beneficial excitement.

A sister of the young Shabert was troubled for many years with a megrim. This evil was accompanied with a nervous pain in the face, which made itself sensible at intervals of three or four days, in the early part of the day, like a disguised fever. In the moment of one of these paroxysms, I administered to her a dose of pulsatilla; but afterwards she became so much worse, that her husband, Signor Salzani, came to me at ten o'clock at night, in great alarm, to tell me that his wife had become almost mad, and that they had to use great efforts to prevent her from throwing herself out of the window. But this was her last paroxysm, at least she had no more during my stay at Constantinople. The dose of pulsatilla which I administered to her, was one drop of the third dilution on a lump of sugar; the tincture I had brought with me from Vienna.

At that period, the prince Abdool Mesjeet (now Sultan) fell dangerously sick, and I was told that his royal father had dismissed all the physicians, English, French, Greek and Turk, on account of their unsuccessful treatment, and that my reputation and fortune would be established if I succeeded in curing him. I replied that my rule was—"Noli accedere, nisi vocatus," adding, that only on the request of the Sultan would I undertake to attend the royal prince; his majesty, however, was fortunate enough to find a physician who performed the cure in a few days. The Sultan ordered those doctors who had attended his son formerly, to make their appearance again in the seraglio, and qresented him to them, asking whether they thought he was perfectly recovered. They expressed their astonishment at this unexpected and sudden recovery, and wished much to see that miraculous doctor, who had performed such a cure, in so short a time. The Sultan opened the door of a side room, out of which there issued an Armenian lady, in Turkish costume, whom he presented to them, smiling, as the miraculous doctor to whom his son owed his recovery, to the shame of the assembled doctors. To bestow on her greater honor, he ordered it to be publicly declared in all the Christian churches, that Mariam Khatoon (Lady Mary) had saved the life of the royal prince and was the only person who could cure the *gelinjik*, that being the Turkish term, derived from *gelin*, bride, and means the bride's disease. In Greek it is called nymphizze; it is a kind of cachexia, or hydrops alba. The royal Prince caught it in consequence of the measles, and they were in fear for his life, as his younger brother had died of the measles, having been improperly treated and bled during the disease.

As to the treatment which the Armenian lady employed, the following fact, which I insert, was generally rumored :—she placed the Prince in a heated oven (tandoor), which caused a profuse perspiration ; after that, she fumigated him with the burning flesh of a weazel, also called *nymphizze*, and his body was rubbed with oil. Besides this external treatment, she administered to him some medicines, of which the following three substances were the chief ingredients—ambergris, cochineal insects, and earth-worms. She ordered the Prince to observe a very strict regimen, not permitting him meat, or even broth, only light digestible fish (gelinjik balūgi), because of its name being like that of the disease. This disease occurring frequently in the capital, and weasel flesh being a costly thing, the druggists there sell it dried. There are many Christian women, Greeks and Armenians, at Constantinople, practising the cure of that malady, the principal remedy for which, I am told, is *Album* Græcum (white dung of dogs). It is a question whether phosphate of lime might not take the place of that disgusting remedy, as it consists of nearly the same substances. That disease is said to occur in consequence of wrongly-treated acute eruptions, especially the measles, or in consequence of sudden fright or excessive fatigue : it gradually increases in virulence. It is to be recognised by a pulsation behind the ears and other parts ; the pulse on the wrist is felt more up the arm than usual ; the eyes and feet are swollen ; the lips are pale ; asthma is felt in walking, with weakness in the knees ; finally, a slow consuming fever follows, which is succeeded by death.

I remained only two years at Constantinople, from the autumn of 1836 to that of 1838. During that time, my homœopathic practice was extensive, as there were only myself and the private physician to the Russian ambassador who practised the new system ; and it was so lucrative that I had no idea of leaving that place so soon, still less of returning to Lahore, until I learned from the Austrian internuncio, Baron Sturmer, who was in quarantine at Malta, and who had met with General Ventura, that the maharajah had ordered the general to make inquiries for me in Europe, and to persuade me to go back to Lahore. Accordingly, the general invited me to accompany him thither, after the expiration of his leave of absence in the autumn. I yielded to this invitation, and went in company with the general from Alexandria to Bombay, whence he proceeded alone, with the utmost speed, to Lahore, as Runjeet Sing was dangerously ill, and as at that time the English were preparing to place the Shah Soojah on the throne of Cabul.

General Ventura was accompanied by a shawl merchant, named Monsieur Le Boeuf, and a captain of cavalry, M. Mouton, with his lady. These three persons the general requested me to accompany to Lahore, as they were unable to speak Hindostanee.

At Bombay we went on board a native vessel, and sailed to Gogo, and thence we continued our way, partly in carriages, partly on camels. Among our fellow travellers there were some native shawl merchants from Umritsir. We took the shortest road, through Palee, Ajmir, Hansi, and Loodiana. We were hardly two days' journey from Gogo, when we were overtaken by two English captains, who had been ordered to examine our papers; for they looked upon us as if we were Russian spies. At Palee the plague was raging, as it had then been for the last three years. Previous to our arrival there, we passed a very pleasant evening with the family of an English captain. On this occasion I made the acquaintance of an English physician, Dr. Keir, who informed me that the English physicians in India do not agree in their views respecting the plague at Palee: for some of them consider the disease to be a pestilential fever peculiar to India, while others declare it to be the same plague that was so common in the East, and especially in Turkey and Egypt. He told me he would be very glad if I would write to him my opinion about it, should I on my journey observe the disease, as he considered it might be of great importance both to himself and to science, because I had had so much opportunity for studying the nature of the plague at Constantinople, adding that he intended to publish my report.

About noon we arrived at the infected Palee, where we ordered our tents to be pitched near to the large marsh, opposite to which the town lies. The first sight which presented itself to our eyes was the funeral trains of several of the inhabitants. After dinner, at two o'clock, I repaired to the governor, who was a Hindoo, and told him I was a traveller and a physician, and that I wished to see a few infected persons, and administer to them my medicines gratis, if he would kindly send some one to accompany me. He received me very affably, and yielded to my request. The man who accompanied me had not the trouble to escort me far, as in the very next house there were several patients, some of whom had only a short time to live. At these visits I neglected no circumspection and precaution. I never entered a house, but caused the patients to be brought before the door, where I examined them, writing down their names and their statements, and administering to them the remedies, and I departed without having touched any of them. The aspect of the town itself offered a sad spectacle : only now and then I met with a human being : the bazaars and shops were closed ; they told me that the greater part of the inhabitants had either died, or left the town ; and numbers of houses were quite deserted. The infected died in general on the third or fourth day ; and scarcely one among twenty recovered. I saw carbuncles, buboes, bleeding at the nose—in one word all that I had seen in the hospital at Constantinople. I no longer, therefore, doubted that the disease was a most virulent plague. It is true, that it was not the plague of Turkey, Arabia or Egypt, but one peculiar to India ; Palee being a province of that part of Asia. At four o'clock the same afternoon I returned to our tent, and retired to rest at the ordinary time, in the enjoyment of the best of health ; and I should have slept longer than usual, if Madame Mouton had not come to awake me, and announce that the camels were ready for our departure. The moment I began to rise, I felt a pain in my groin ; and a presentiment of having been infected with the plague, caused a rush of blood towards my heart, so that I had the feeling of one who had been stabbed with a dagger. The pain in the groin, the fever and my anxiety increased rapidly ; and it was with difficulty that I moved a few steps, in order to examine the painful part, upon which I discovered some buboes, the size of peas. I felt a burning pain, so I placed myself in the kajaweh (basket) on my camel, and we departed. The station we had to reach was five miles distant ; the reason why we made so short a journey was, that our only object was to quit the region of the plague, and even now I look upon it as fortunate that I was removed to a place where the healthy air probably aided the effect of the medicine which I had taken. As soon as we arrived at our station, I took some of the small pills of the above-mentioned Stryconos Faba St. Ignatii. Although Palee alone was infected by the plague, still the inhabitants of the village did not allow us to enter it ; they, however, brought us all we were in want of, and took the money from our hands without any scruple. During my scientific excursion to Palee, my fellow-travellers had shot some ducks on the marshes, and these were prepared for our lunch. I was invited to partake of the repast, but did not feel any inclination to eat, as I was burning with fever, and my pain was almost insupportable ; but not to cause suspicion, I took my place at the table, and the bits which I conveyed with one hand to my mouth, I transferred with the other to the napkin ; this I performed with the skill of an adept. After dinner, I repeated the dose of the same medicine, laid down, and covered myself all over, and in a short time I began to perspire to such a degree, that my mattress was wetted through. In consequence of this perspiration, I got rid of the fever and anxiety, and entertained the hope of being restored to health, although the pains in the groin still continued. The swelling of the glands remained for three weeks, as I did not employ any local remedy. After my complete recovery, I wrote to the English physician (on whose account I had visited the infected town of Palee) the result of my experience, and read the letter to my companions, who manifested their astonishment, and blamed me for having exposed them to the infection of such a dangerous epidemic. My answer was, that I only did my duty as a physician, and that those who were not pleased with such proceedings ought not to travel in the society of a physician.

I cannot tell how it was that I caught the plague, in spite of all my precautions, unless it was that when I was entering the town, there was a violent wind blowing, whirling the pestiferous dust up into the air; and this might have communicated the *virus* to my body externally, and even internally—externally, by absorption through the lachrymal glands of the eyes, the pituitous membrane of the nostrils, and the cavity of the ear ; internally, by the respiration of the lungs. The infection was not produced by immediate contact ; had that been the cause, I should certainly not have escaped it at Constantinople, if the predisposition to it lies in every one. At this time I must have had a predisposition for the contagion, for some days before I had felt an itching in the body, and a kind of plethora, owing to the irregular manner of living which is consequent on the inconveniences and difficulties of long journeys. It is certain that the plague does not require a long time to develop itself, as it made its appearance a few hours after my visiting the patients. In some cases an interval of two or three days may occur before the symptoms are visible. The malaria of Palee, I believe, is generated by the exhalation of the immense marsh, whither thousands of birds and reptiles resort, and which serves at the same time as a depository for all the substances ejected from the town. The government could easily prevent the obnoxious influence of this marsh, by converting it into fertile ground

Arrived at Lahore, I found my former patron, the maharajah, Runjeet Sing, seated on a chair, with swollen feet, and making himself understood by gestures and signs

Page 94

MAHARAJH RUNJEET SING

MAHARAJH KURRUCK SING

KONWAR NO-NEHAL SING

MAHARAJH SHERE SING

with his hands; his organs of speech being paralysed to such a degree, that he was not able to utter a single articulate sound, and other means of imparting his thoughts were not in his possession, as he never had learned to write.

From time to time I had occasion to relate many of the cures effected by the new method of homœopathy, by the aid of which I had cured myself in Vienna of the cholera, and lately in Hindoostan of the plague. Although they did not doubt the truth of my assertions, it was not without difficulty that they could prevail on themselves to trust me with the treatment of the maharajah, because the favourable season—it being spring—allowed the native physicians to rely on other trials which they had to make: meanwhile I succeeded in some homœopathic cures quite to my satisfaction. But the greatest sensation produced, was by a cure which I undertook at the request of the minister, raja Dhyan Sing. He committed to my medical care a native of Cashmere, Aboo Ibrahim, commander of his jesails (camel-artillery), in whose head, ten years previously, a bullet had been lodged, at an affair with the Affghans, and which no native surgeon had been able to extract, and in consequence he was paralysed on one side. I trepanned him, and extracted the bullet, which was stuck beneath the skull, and pressed the brain, without, however, affecting that organ. My patient having been a drunkard, and troubled with indigestion in consequence of his weakened stomach, I administered to him some physic, to accelerate his recovery; and I succeeded in restoring him to perfect health, in the short space of two months. When relieved from his hemiplegy, I presented him to the minister, and he introduced him to the maharaja.

Meanwhile, the excessive heat had come on. At this time the fakeer Azeez-oo-Deen came unexpectedly and called on me, as the native physicians were unable to improve the health of the maharajah. This man, who had formerly been physician in ordinary to the king, told me that the maharajah had never taken any remedy prescribed by a European physician, and that he used to give all the remedies which had been ordered him by the English doctors, Murray, Steel, and Macgregor, to his servants, to try the effect on them; but that he was now resolved to take my medicines, which I was to prepare in his presence. This I promised to do. It was then mid-day, the time when the durbar (assembly) leaves the palace, so, accompanied by the fakeer, I presented myself to the king. I found with him only the minister, Dhyan Sing. I had brought with me the tinctura dulcamara, and three empty corked little phials. First of all, I asked for a gudwai (water-carrier), and ordered him to bring the spirit that the maharajah was in the habit of drinking; this had been distilled, in my presence, from Cabul grapes, and it was rectified, because Runjeet Sing preferred strong spirits. I put the three empty phials into the hands of the gudwai, and ordered them to be rinsed with the same spirit, and afterwards each of them to be half filled with spirit, about one drachm in each phial. When this was done, I put just one drop of the essence of dulcamara (woody-nightshade) into one of those phials which the water-carrier held in his hand, and I ordered him to cork it and shake it. Then I desired the fakeer to mark it number "one," and I put a drop out of it into the second phial, causing it to be corked and shaken like the first, and marked number "two". In the same manner, the third dilution was made, and number "three" was marked on it. From this last, I ordered one single drop to be let fall on a lump of sugar, which, at my request, the maharajah put into his mouth, where it was retained until dissolved. I ordered the same dose to be administered to the patient every morning and evening.

During the preparation of the medicine, some persons who were standing by could not forbear smiling; and the fakeer himself was of opinion that such a minute dose could not be hurtful, should it even be supposed to be poison. But what was the result? On the first day there was no sensible amelioration in the health of the maharajah;

on the second day he felt somewhat better; and on the third he was in such a merry humor that, at five o'clock in the afternoon, he ordered the minister, Dhyan Sing, to put a pair of gold bracelets on my arms, valued at five hundred rupees, in his own presence and in that of the durbar; this present was accompanied with two Cashmere shawls of the same value, and, whilst I sat on the floor, the minister laid them upon my shoulders, the maharajah telling me that my physic had produced in him the best effect. It was, of course, quite natural that this event should fill my heart with joy, as it inspired me with the hope that the king would soon recover, and thus lay the first stone of my reputation and future fortune. This scene took place in the royal garden, Shahbelore, two miles from the city, where I had resided for three days. On the fourth day, early in the morning, the minister allowed me to visit my patients in the city; but while there, I heard that several mounted messengers had been despatched from Shahbelore to request me to return to that place. I galloped back; and on the road I overtook some hakims (Mohamedan physicians) and astrologers, travelling the same way, on elephants, on horseback, or carried in palanquins, from which I presumed that the maharajah had met with some accident, which made me very anxious. Arrived at Shahbelore, I was told that the maharajah had an attack of fever. On examining him, however, I could not find the least symptom of fever, it being in fact only excitement. The gudwai, who was in charge of the medicine, was of opinion that the fever proceeded from too great a dose, which the maharajah had asked for on the previous evening, namely, two drops at once; but I thought that could not be the cause of the alteration, one drop more or less not being able to produce such an effect. The physicians of the city were invited to a consultation. That was all they desired; for they had been touched to the quick on hearing that the maharajah was recovering, and that he had made me presents of gold and robes of honour. They would have preferred seeing the king die, rather than acknowledge me, an European, as his saviour. That was the reason why all my endeavours and all my demonstrations turned out fruitless. The prudent minister was of opinion, that it did not lie in his power to decide ; the fakeer, Azeez-oo-Deen, exercising such magic influence on the maharajah, that only by addressing myself to him could I obtain any decision according to my desires. I reminded the fakeer of his own words, that such minute doses could not be hurtful, even if it should be poison. Besides, I observed, that it was not every fever, especially when appearing in so mild a form, that could be of bad consequence, as nature sometimes cures diseases by re-action in the frame ; and that, under such circumstances, it was advisable to lay aside all medicine, and await the result. But he objected to that, saying that the maharajah was too feeble to endure such a fever. "But," continued he, "let us hear what opinion the other physicians have." All my arguments availed nothing. The consultation, at which the fakeer presided, was composed of a dozen hakims from Peshawur and Lahore, Hindoo physicians, astrologers, &c., each of whom imagined that he possessed the deepest knowledge of medical art. Most of them carried large books, to cover their want of real learning. In fine, they agreed unanimously to administer to the patient a majoon (electuary), of which jowahirad (precious stones) constituted the principal ingredient. The fakeer himself prepared and administered it to the patient ; but in less than a fortnight the maharajah gave up his temporal life. He died at the fortress in my presence, upon which the minister ordered the gates to be shut, but I readily obtained his permission to absent myself. The fakeer, who exercised great influence in the household of the royal court, and who had begun his career at Lahore as a barber, with a few boxes of ointment, did not live long after his patron, Runjeet Sing. Azeez-oo-Deen—of Arabian origin, and descended from the Ansari Arabs of the desert—was the oracle of Runjeet Sing. He, the prime-minister Dhyan Sing, and Dewan-Deena-Nauth, minister of finance, constituted the triad of which the privy-council of the king was composed. The latter has been recently promoted to the rank of rajah by the English.

The small doses of opium (every afternoon one pill of 3 grs.) which Runjeet Sing took daily, and the strong spirits he used to drink at different hours of the day, transported him into a kind of excitement, which manifested itself in the highest degree in the evening, after the enjoyment of larger portions of spirits. Every one loved and feared him at the same time. He had an army of 100,000 men, inspiring awe and respect, half of whom were regular and the other half irregular troops, with whom he might have enforced his laws on all the Hindoos ; neverthelesss, he entertained the greatest friendship with his neighbours the English, and manifested his favour towards the French, the Italians, and other European nations, by making them governors in his provinces. His disease was brought on by a severe cold, and by indulging somewhat too much in strong spirits. The latter I am told was especially the case during the winter in which the Governor-General of India, Lord Auckland, came to Lahore to pay him a visit. In the transport of his joy, he drank more than ordinarily. Probably, if an emetic had been given at the commencement of the disease, it would have produced a good effect ; but as the native physicians did not know of any good and effective emetic, and are fearful, also, of the effects of vomiting, they prefer using purgatives, by which sometimes the disease grows worse, as the case above related sufficiently proves.

It made a very deep impression on my feelings to have been prevented from making myself useful to the maharajah, and restoring to health the man on whose life was depending the happiness, peace and prosperity of that country. Every one whose forethought enabled him to throw a glance on the future, must have seen with pain and sorrow that a violent crisis menaced that country, by which a nation scarcely risen from barbarity might sink back into its former condition.

The first sad and cruel scene that I witnessed after the death of Runjeet Sing, was the Suttee, or burning of his eleven wives, along with the body of the deceased. There were four ranees (legal wives), and seven female slaves, who, animated with the superstitious hope of entering paradise with their lord and husband, were ascending the funeral pile with death-despising intrepidity ; they cowered round the corpse, and were covered with reed mats, on which oil was poured in profusion. This done, fire was set to the funeral pile, so that the poor creatures became suffocated by the smoke and flames before they could utter a cry. In order not to give the reader a false notion of the customs and manners of the Hindoos, it is necessary to observe, that no woman is compelled to be burnt with her husband ; they do it by their own free will, and it is a characteristic trait, that only those women devote themselves to that dismal ceremony whose fate had decreed them not to be mothers. Perhaps they follow their husbands to the other world, in the hope of obtaining there what was denied them in this sublunary one. But it is not the custom for men to be burnt, either with their wives or with other men ; nevertheless, the minister, Rajah Dhyan Sing, insisted upon being burnt with his lord and his wives ; but the welfare of the country depending at that time solely on him, he was prevented from undergoing this terrific ceremony. Runjeet Sing, a short time before his death, engaged this minister to assist his son, Kurrck Sing, whom he made heir to the throne, although he must have been persuaded of his incapacity ; and if Kurrck Sing had followed the prudent advice of his father, and had not yielded to the insinuations of his tutor, Sirdar Chet Sing, every thing would have proceeded in a prosperous manner.

Before I proceed in my relation of the late eventful occurrences at Lahore, I must give some more details to such of my readers as may wish to know the particulars of that abominable ceremony of burning the living with the dead, which at present occurs but rarely in places under the English government, by whom it is strictly forbidden. I witnessed the above-mentioned self-sacrifice, of which the following are the details :—

SING SEPAHEE MOOSELMAN SEPAHEE GOREKHEE SEPAHEE

VI

Early in the morning subsequent to that on which the death of the maharajah happened, I went down the Tukht (coronation-square), accompanied by Col. Henry Steinbach (lately in the service of the maharajah, Gholab Sing, in Cashmere, now in Europe), and we directed our steps towards the large yard, which we had to cross, in order to get betimes to a convenient place close to the funeral pile. This was erected between the walls and the fortress, in a small garden, the conflux of the people having been so enormous in the fortress. In the large yard, we observed one of the four ranees (queens) coming out of the harem on foot and unveiled, for the first time in her life. She was slowly proceeding towards the place where the royal body was lying, and she was surrounded by about one hundred persons, who kept themselves at some distance, while accompanying her. Close to her side there was a man carrying a small box, containing the remainder of her jewels (as she had already distributed some), which she made presents of, handing them one by one to the people on her right and left. Two or three steps in front of her, there was a man moving in a backward direction, his face turned towards her, and holding a looking-glass, that she might convince herself that her features were unaltered, and no fear visible on them. At the distribution of the jewels, Col. Steinbach made the observation that, had we stretched out our hands to receive a present, it certainly would not have been denied; but we thought proper to leave it to the poorer people, because we occupied lucrative posts. It is curious, indeed, that this was the very ranee whom Runjeet Sing married in the first year of my residence in that country, ten years having passed since I witnessed the nuptials at Nadoun. She was, as I mentioned before, a daughter of Sunsarchund, and she had a younger sister, whom the maharajah at the same time took also for a wife, and conveyed them both to Lahore; the latter, I am told, had died of consumption during my absence. As for the former, although I was present at her wedding, I nevertheless had never seen her before, and it was only on her last fatal walk, which she took to her funeral pile, that I could behold her. The funeral train, accompanied by many thousands of spectators, was now proceeding; all were on foot, their abode in the fortress not being far distant from the place of the ceremony. The four ranees only were carried, in open palanquins, behind the deceased, after them followed the seven female slaves, barefooted; some of them appeared to be not more than fourteen or fifteen years of age. The ranees, too, were barefooted, their silk dresses were simple, and without any ornaments, and they appeared to be indifferent to the awful though voluntary fate which awaited them. Perhaps our hearts throbbed more at the view of this dismal train than those of the poor victims themselves. The body of Runjeet Sing was placed on a board, to which it was probably fastened, and was carried on a light and decorated bier constructed in the shape of a ship; the sails and flags of the vessel were made of rich golden and silk stuff (kimkab), and of Cashmere shawls. A number of people carried the bier from the interior of the fortress up to the funeral-pile, there the board with the body was taken out of it and deposited on the ground, where, on what was a small garden, now stands a summood, *i. e.*, a tomb of the royal family Runjeet Sing, Kurruck Sing and No-Nehal Sing, *i. e.*, the father, son, and grand-child, together with their wives and slaves. The costly ornaments of the richly decorated bier were given to the mob; the Brahmins performed their prayers from the Shaster, a book written in the Indian or Sanscrit language; the Gooroos, or priests of the Sikhs, did the same, from their holy scripture called Grunthsaheb,* and the Musselmen accompanied them with their "Ya, Allah! Ya Allah!" A slow, but not displeasing rumbling of the drums and the murmuring of the people, gave to the whole scene a melancholy aspect, and was peculiar to the country. The funeral pile which displayed itself before the eyes of the spectators, was constructed of dry woods, amongst which

* *Grunth* is the holy book of *Baba-Nanuk.*

there were pieces of aloe ; it was about six feet high and square. After the prayers of the Brahmins and Gooroos, which lasted nearly an hour, the minister and other sirdars ascended by a ladder the funeral-pile, upon which ignitible matters and substances, as cotton seeds, &c., were strewn, and the royal body was respectfully placed in the middle of the pile, together with the board. After this, the ranees ascended the fatal ladder, one by one, according to their rank, the slaves followed, and the minister showed himself very officious in affording them assistance. The ranees placed themselves at the head of the royal body, and the slaves close at its feet. There they cowered, remaining in silent expectation for the fatal moment, when a strong thick mat of reeds being brought, with which the whole were covered, oil was then poured over the mat, the minister and sirdars descended, and the pile was lighted at each corner. In a few moments, the deplorable victims of an abominable and fanatic ceremony had ceased to exist.

The consuming of this pile occupied two days ; on the third, some of the bones and ashes of each of the bodies were collected in the presence of the court only, and separately placed in urns. After which ceremony, a preparation was made for a journey, with exactly the same pomp and splendour as if the maharajah and his wives were still alive. Thus their remains were conveyed in five richly caparisoned palanquins by numerous attendants and guards, accompanied by handsome presents, such as shawls, costly decorated elephants, horses, &c., &c., to the banks of the Ganges, where the Brahmins received the whole. The bones and ashes they put into the river, the other valuables they distributed among themselves ; nothing returning but the men. The tents under which the ashes of Runjeet Sing and each of the ranees were placed, were composed of the most valuable Cashmere shawl materials, the props of which were of gold and silver. Some millions of rupees were expended in this outfit. Upon the procession leaving the fortress, it traversed the streets and bazaars, the ministers and some of the principal sirdars on foot, with numerous others mounted on their elephants and horses. Thousands of persons were assembled in the streets, bazaars, and on the tops of houses, by whom flowers were thrown upon the palanquins. The curtains of the palanquin which contained the remains of Runjeet Sing were open, while those of his wives were closed, in the same manner as when travelling during their lifetime. The minister walked close to the palanquin of his royal master, being occupied in keeping the flies from its contents, thus showing his respect to the last. On the arrival of the procession outside of the Delhi gate, a final and profuse royal salute was given by the thundering of cannon from the fort and ramparts of the city, upon which the minister and sirdars returned, leaving the remains and presents to be conducted by the guard. The mourning lasted thirteen days, the colour of the costume being white.

After the obsequies of Runjeet Sing, his legitimate son, Kurruck Sing, ascended the Guddee (throne), who, besides being a blockhead, was a worse opium eater than his father. Twice a-day he deprived himself of his senses, and passed his whole time in a state of stupefaction. It was quite natural that the government could not long remain in the hands of such an individual. His guardian, or tutor and factotum, Sirdar Chet Sing, being desirous to become an independent minister, was a rival of Dhyan Sing, and was contriving to remove him. He intended to assassinate him one morning in the durbar. For this purpose he had collected in the fortress, where he lived with Kurruck Sing, his two recently organised batallions of body-guards, and had ordered the sentinels at the three gates, devoted to Dhyan Sing, to be changed early in the morning fixed upon for the murder of the minister; but this plot was not concealed from Dhyan Sing, and he hastened to prevent the treacherous act, in which he succeeded by the assistance of the royal prince, No-Nehal Sing and a few of the sirdars; and with the aid of his two brothers and some relations, Kurruck Sing and Chet Sing were assailed in the fortress before the break of day, when Chet Sing and all his relations and partisans were destroyed. This was the beginning of the bloody scenes in the Punjab, which could only end by the interference of the English.

After the murder of Chet Sing, the royal prince, No-Nehal, Kurruck Sing's only son, took possession of the government, and ordered his father to retire to his private house in the city, where he soon became indisposed. A few months afterwards he followed his father, Runjeet Sing, to the funeral pile. The rumour was current that he was poisoned, and the poison employed was also specified, but I do not believe it. Only it is a fact, that the son showed great indifference in regard to the treatment of his father, or for his recovery; and, during his father's illness he never saw him but once or twice, and then but a short time before his death; on which occasion the father was treated by his only son in a manner quite revolting, even to the natives around, which accounts for his having committed him into the hands of inexperienced physicians and faqueers. I, the only appointed European physician, was never called for during the king's disease, which lasted nine months. It is probable that the patient requested my assistance, but the son prevented my attending. Had he known that the death-day of his father would also be his own, he certainly would have behaved in another manner.

On the same day in which the king, Kurruck Sing, and his only son died, a curious event happened. Early in the morning. I was called by Meean Oottum Sing, eldest son of the Maharajah Gholab Sing, and he committed the Chief of his mountain troops to my treatment, he being every ill, promising me a pair of Cashmere shawls in case I should be able, as I expected, to relieve him hy the evening. My new patient was unable to void his urine, and was troubled with gravel in the kidneys. He recovered the same day, whilst Oottum Sing himself, as we shall see, met with his death. When I hastened into the house of the patient, summoned as I was by Oottum Sing, with whom he lived, I found both in a small room, and, according to the custom of the Hindoos, the patient was lying on the floor, whilst Oottum Sing was sitting on the bed, offering me to sit near him.

We were speaking about the disease of the patient, when suddenly a messenger entered, with the news that the Maharajah Kurruck Sing had expired a few minutes previously. The ceremony of the funeral-pile took place the same afternoon. Three of his wives were burnt with him; and I was present at that horrid, yet remarkable spectacle. The ceremony took place close to the same spot where Runjeet Sing was burnt, and nearly with the same rites. The court afterwards went on foot to the river, to perform their ablutions, according to the custom of the country, whilst I returned to my above-mentioned patient. Scarcely had I arrived, when I was told that I had been called for, and invited by the minister to attend immediately at the fortress garden (hazooree-bagh). I did not lose one moment, but repaired to that place, and found the minister waiting for me, who, as soon as he descried me, came, and seizing my hand, told me it was all over with Meean Oottum Sing. My surprise was increased, upon hearing that a piece of the wall falling upon him and the royal prince, No-Nehal, had crushed them beneath its fragments. Oottum Sing was killed instantly, and the royal prince considerably hurt. The minister conducted me to a tent, where I saw the prince; but he (the minister) enjoined me, in the most energetic manner, not to speak about that event to any one. The prince was on his bed, his head most awfully crushed, and his state was such that no hope of his recovery existed. With that conviction I left the tent, and whispered to the minister, in so low a tone that no one else could hear it, "Medical art can do nothing to relieve the unfortunate prince;" upon which, the minister requested me to wait there while he re-entered the tent, and, after a short stay therein, he came out, addressing me loud enough to be heard by all the assembly, who listened attentively, asking "whether they might give some soup to the Koonwar Saheb (royal prince), he wishing to have some." Whereupon I answered, "Of course; he is in need only of parsley;"—a proverb applied to those dangerously ill, and not expected to live. The minister's intention in questioning me thus, was to conceal at that moment the approaching death of the prince, in order to have time to make the necessary preparations, so that the peace and tranquillity of the country might not be disturbed, in which he succeeded so that the death of the prince remained a seeret for three days. This interval he took advantage of to recall Sheer Sing, Runjeet Sing's adopted son, and to place him upon the throne. In the meanwhile, the partisans of the deceased prince invited the ranee, his mother, Chund Kour, to come as soon as possible. Both arrived on the third day, only that Sheer Sing was rather later than the ranee, who had taken her position in the interior part of the fortress : and he was therefore obliged to camp in the garden (hazooree-bagh) outside the fortress. When both were at their respective posts, the death of the royal prince was made public, and the burning ceremony was ordered, which took place close to that of his grandfather. Two beautiful young ladies became victims of the flames with him. One female of the age of twelve years Sheer Sing detained, owing to her not being yet ripe for the ceremony of the suttee.

It would have been proper at that time to have made inquiries whether the falling of the wall by which No-Nehal Sing and Oottum Sing had been crushed, was accidental, or a premeditated machination of wicked conspirators ; but none thought it worth their while to make the inquiry, and the event was regarded as a punishment of God—the royal prince having neglected his royal father, and if he had not caused his death, had at least accelerated it by his negligence.

The absence of investigation induced the English to believe the death of No-Nehal Sing to have been a premeditated plot of Dhyan Sing, who, according to their opinion, ambitious as he was, saw in the prince the only impediment and obstacle to the sinister purposes which he had in view. As for me, having lived for a long time in that country, an ocular witness of the events, and having had the opportunity of closely observing the conduct and motives of the minister, I cannot agree with this assertion. Firstly, he would certainly have spared the life of his nephew Oottum Sing, whom he loved, and would have appointed another companion to the prince, and also have kept himself somewhat farther from the place at which the accident happened. He could not foresee the moment of the downfall of the wall, nor calculate the distance where he might escape the ruin : as a proof of which, his arm was severely contused and injured, for which I myself attended him. Secondly, he would certainly have arranged that Sheer Sing should be at hand, in order to raise him immediately to the throne, by which he would have prevented the consultations which daily took place in the fortress for foureen days, nntil at last it was decided that the Ranee Chund Kour, mother of No-Nehal Sing, and heiress, should occupy the throne, which she did not know how to maintain. There is more reason to suppose that the partisans of Kurruck Sing and Chet Sing were the authors of this plot against the prince, as he had intended to ask them for an account of their perfidious behaviour during his father's long illness, they having cheated and robbed him in the most shameful manner, and it was generally known that immediately after the funeral rites of his father, he (the prince) intended to order seven of their houses to be closed, and inquiries to be made.

During the conferences of the sirdars in the fortress, which lasted for a fortnight, the Ranee Chund Kour attempted the life of Sheer Sing ; but Dhyan Sing was soon informed of it, and warned his *portégé*. Sheer Sing did not forget it, and when he afterwards took the reins of government into his hands, it happened that during his absence from Lahore, the slave-girls of Chund Kour crushed the head of their mistress with a brick, whilst she was enjoying her siesta. Dhyan Sing proceeded, in the absence of the king, against the assassins, and caused their noses, ears and hands to be cut off, which was effected publicly, before the kotoali (police-office), and expelled them from the city ; but as their tongues had remained unhurt, they alleged that they only fulfilled the wish of Sheer Sing, who promised them as a reward a jaghir (some land). On that account, they were transported to the opposite side of the river Ravee, and were never afterwards heard of.

The Sikh troops had been often reviewed before their monarch or the royal prince, and on such occasions some were promoted or rewarded. This was abolished under the government of Chund Kour. She was only visible to some of her confidants. Her ministers and counsellors directed the helm of the state vessel, which moved on indifferently, as each one neglected the public welfare, and provided only for his private interest. In the course of time there naturally arose a general dissatisfaction. The minister, Dhyan Sing, perceiving the consequences of it, pretended to go with his younger brother Soochet Sing into the mountains of his native country, on a hunting party, to restore his health ; but, in fact, it was only a pretext for calling in Sheer Sing, to whom all the troops flocked to range themselves under his standard.

The following event may serve as a sample of oriental policy. Dhyan Sing's eldest son, Heera Sing, and his own elder brother, Gholab Sing, belonged to the faction of the ranee. They shut themselves up with her in the fortress, which was bombarded incessantly for three days and nights. It was only when the besiegers prepared to take the place by storm, that the besieged surrendered, under the following stipulations : the ranee shall henceforth live in the fortress, a convenient jaghir shall be granted to her ; and to the garrison, consisting of two batallions of dogras (mountaineers), the troops of Gholab Sing, a free retreat shall be granted. Their retreat was fixed to take place in the darkness of the night, and they were permitted to take with them whatever they pleased. Gholab Sing was during five days in possession of the fortress where the treasury happened to be. The troops of the mountains were ordered to go the opposite side of the river Ravee, until the coronation of Sheer Sing should have taken place. By Dhyan Sing and Soochet Sing's mediation, Gholab Sing and Heera Sing were reconciled with Sheer Sing, living with him on the best terms,and enjoying as before the greatest influence at the court. Had the party in the fortress gained the day, the issue of that civil contention would also have finished in favour of the Rajah's family. After the settlement of this affair, two of the rajahs retired into the mountains with their troops, laden with their stolen treasures, the two others remained with Sheer Sing.

The new maharajah addicted himself to immoderate drinking, aud indulged especially in champagne. The good feeling between him and Dhyan Sing soon reached its end, and they began to hate each other in the most acrimonious manner. Sirdar Ajeet Sing and his uncle Lena Sing (descended from the family of the Scindawalla, and related to Runjeet Sing) belonged to the party of the ranee, who had fought against Sheer Sing and Dhyan Sing; but they knew how to insinuate themselves into the confidence of both to such a degree that, without the knowledge of either, they destroyed both the maharajah and his wuzeer. They conspired with Sheer Sing to murder Dhyan Sing, but at the same time they also intrigued with Dhyan Sing to murder Sheer Sing. Both king and minister were well acquainted with their preparations for war, and knew also that the Scindawallas had provided themselves wirh gunpowder, bullets and soldiers. Sheer Sing was even repeatedly cautioned by his friends to be on his guard, to which advice however he paid no attention, and in an immovable manner allowed them to concoct their schemes. Each one believed that the stroke was appointed for his adversary, and, finally, it fell upon both. True is the proverb: "He who digs a pit for another, falls in himself;" for Ajeet Sing as well as Lena Sing had laboured for their own ruin.

Sheer Sing used to review his troops every day. On such an occasion, being in the royal garden (Shahbelore) for the pnrpose of mustering the Scindawalla's troops, and sitting before the window of a small room, to look at the soldiers, Ajeet Sing approached him and exhibited a

RANEE CHUNDA

MAHARAJH DULLEEP SING

SIRDAR JEWAHIR SING

RAJAH LALL SING

loaded double-barrelled fowling piece, as a nazerana (present), and at the moment Sheer Sing was stretching out his hand to receive it, he was shot with that gun on the spot. Ajeet Sing's troops, arrayed before the window, gave a volley of musket shots through the window, to kill the men surrounding Sheer Sing, and penetrated into the room to cut off his head. I was by accident not farther than ten steps from the place where the horrid crime was committed, and five minutes before his atrocious murder I had spoken to him in the garden under a tree, where he ordered me to remain until his return. The subject of our interview was a gunpowder-mill with machinery, which Dhyan Sing had ordered me to make. Sheer Sing had inspected that establishment four days previously (on a Sunday), and was so satisfied, that with his own hands he put on my arms two pair of gold bracelets, and ordered 500 rupees to be given to me, as an additional sum to the 900 which I already received as my monthly appointment. This having been only an oral promise, I went daily to the durbar, in order to receive an authority in writing, and was with him on the fatal Thursday on which he was assassinated. Whilst this crime was being perpetrated by Ajeet Sing, Lena Sing, his uncle, murdered, in a garden in the neighbourhood, the royal prince, Pertaub Sing, a boy only twelve years of age. This innocent victim of party fury was cruelly cut into pieces with sabres, at the moment when he was occupied with his Brahmins in prayers and giving alms to the poor; for it was a Sancrat day, the first day of a Hindoo month, on which similar ceremonies generally took place. The guardian of the infant child, Baii Goormuck Sing, Misser Belee Ram (the first treasurer), and other accomplices, did not wait long before they received retribution. From Shahbelore, the murderers hurried towards the fortress. On their way they met Dhyan Sing, who was on his road to Shahbelore, and they informed him of what had been done, and took him back to the fortress to execute their project of placing Runjeet Sing's youngest son, Dulleep Sing, on the throne. When they arrived in the fortress, they shot Dhyan Sing, cut his body into pieces, shut themselves up in the fortress, and proclaimed, by drum-beating, Dulleep Sing as king, and Ajeet Sing his wuzeer. Rajah Heera Sing, Dhyan Sing's son, who was at liberty, having escaped being murdered, knew how to gain the favour of the troops by his eloquence and promises, and they declared themselves ready to follow him. Confident with this armed force, he entered the city at midnight, surrounded the fortress, and blockaded it. The thundering of the cannon lasted twelve hours, till mid-day, at which time the small garrison was almost exhausted. At that moment, Heera Sing gave the signal for storming. A Spanish colonel, named M. Hurbon, in the service of the Sikhs, was one of the first on the battlements of the dismantled walls. Those who laid down their arms remained unhurt, only the ringleaders, Ajeet Sing, Lena Sing, Baii Goormuck Sing, Misser Belee Ram, and a few others, were destroyed in the *melee*. Ajeet Sing's head was delivered to Heera Sing, as a trophy, but his body, and that of his uncle, Lena Sing, were hung up on the outside of the city gates. Who would have imagined that the victorious Heera Sing should so soon have met with a similar fate!

With the body of Dhyan Sing, thirteen wives and female slaves were burnt. Heera Sing, his son, had been educated by Runjeet Sing, was endowed with wit and genius, and had received a good education, being able to read and write well; and knowing also how to treat the troops; which latter accomplishment he learned from his father. The young king (eight years old) had therefore a young minister (twenty-five years of age), who might have occupied his post for a long time, had he not been too much under the control of his guardian, whom he regarded as a deity. This guardian was a fanatic Brahmin, from the mountains, of the name of Jellah Pundit, who frequently induced Heera Sing to take false measures, by influencing his mind with astrological dreams and false prophecies, to the injury of the country. In fact, he only did that which pleased him, and ordered only what agreed with his extravagant ideas; this caused considerable confusion, and in consequence there was general dissatisfaction ; so it was thought prudent to remove Jellah Pundit. The troops themselves, with the king's uncle at their head, insisted on his being delivered over to them, to which Heera Sing manifested no inclination; this caused the flight of the latter, with his guardian, which they performed on elephants, laden with their riches. But scarcely had they gone a few miles from the capital, and crossed the river Ravee, on their way to the mountains, when they were overtaken by their persecutors, whilst stopping at a village for a few minutes' repose. They were overwhelmed, in spite of the brave resistance of Heera Sing's retinue; the village became a prey to the flames; and he and his escort were killed to the last man. Among those who perished in that affair was Meean Son Sing (a son of the maharajah Gholab Sing), whose head, together with those of Heera Sing, Jellah Pundit, &c., &c., was brought as a trophy to the capital.

It cannot escape the attention of an observer who has followed the course of the political changes at that period, that in this party contention a great deal of bloodshed and mischief might have been averted from the country, if the Sikhs had been endowed with more penetration, and if, instead of defending the cause of Heera Sing's party, they had ranged themselves under the banner of Ajeet Sing, and supported his interest. If they had arrested Heera Sing, as the circumstances then imperatively required, they would not only have prevented every future struggle, but brought also into their possession all the immense treasures which were at Heera Sing's disposal. But the proverb says, "Quem Deus vult perdere, prius dementat."

I intend to give to my readers a true picture of what happened to me at the assassination of Sheer Sing, being an involuntary spectator at this ferocious scene; and how I escaped the perils which threatened my own person. At the moment I heard the firing of the guns, and perceived all the people in motion; taking their weapons, I felt persuaded that the locality was not an asylum for a tranquil man; so I looked for a passage to make my escape from the garden—the scene of horror—and betake myself to the spot where I had left my horse and servants. These were still waiting, at a place which was separated from me by a small low garden wall, and a narrow ditch. I hastened towards them, jumped over the wall and ditch, and arrived safely at the spot. It was by a fortunate chance that I took this direction for my escape; my people telling me afterwards, that at the great entrance to the garden the bullets hissed and flew about, and that they were in great anxiety for my life. Thus I was saved in a critical moment, by taking a firm resolution, without any hesitation.

Having said thus much about my own preservation, I will now proceed with my narrative.

At the time of Sheer Sing's reign, we mustered about twenty Europeans, for the most part French and English officers, in the service of the Lahore government. It was the common saying, that we should bye and bye form a colony; but Jellah Pundit dismissed them from the service, one after the other, alleging economical motives, but, in fact, from religious fanaticism; so that I and the Spaniard only remained. But at last I too was dismissed. Nevertheless, I remained in the city; and cautiously made preparations for my departure, and for that purpose had sold all my effects at a very low price. I did this partly by the advice of my friends, partly by my own inclination, persuaded as I was that such misgovernment could not be of long duration, and anticipating what the future must bring forth. I did not doubt for one moment that they would bring the heads of the minister and his bad adviser as trophies to Lahore; and my supposition was realised by the result. The fanatics, the Akalees (immortals), or rather the robber-pack, the Nahungs, exhibited for money the head of Jellah, at Lahore and Umritsir: "That is the rogue," they exclaimed, "who induced the young Heera Sing to murder his uncle, the brave Rajah Soochet Sing, for which he wanted an army of 20,000 men, although his antagonist was only assisted by forty valiant mountaineers." This murder happened in a small mosque, five miles from Lahore. Jellah, the idol of Heera Sing, intrigued as a decided fanatic against the high priest of the Sikhs, Gooroo Baba Beer Sing. Under the pretext that this holy man was on good terms with the rebels and fugitives, and collected them in his camp, in order to surrender the country to the English, he spurred the minister on to send a part of his troops to the residence of the priest, and to take the fugitives prisoners. At this expedition, accompanied by great bustle, the Gooroo was shot, together with a great number of horned cattle (holy beast, sacred among the Hindoos and Sikhs), and numerous poor people supported by the charity of the priest ; part of them were driven into the river Sutlej, near to Hurekee-ke-Puttun (a ferry on the Sutlej), where they perished. Among the slain there was also Cashmere Sing, son to Runjeet Sing, who nad been driven from the fortress of Seealkote, which was given to him and his brother, Peshora Sing, as an appanage from their father.

Jellah impaired the civil list of the king, Dulleep Sing, and his mother, ranee Chund, and that of his uncle Jewahir Sing, to such an extent that they could not live in a style due to their rank. This prompted the brother of the ranee, Jewahir Sing, to allure Dulleep Sing out of the fortress on an elephant, and to take refuge with the troops of General Avitabile, but the kidnapper was received by the general in command, Misser Jodaram, a Brahmin, and father-in-law to Jellah, with, instead of friendly salutation, a stroke in the face, and he imprisoned them both, for which he lost his nose when sirdar Jewahir Sing became wuzeer. In the city the rumour was current that Jewahir Sing intended to convey Dulleep Sing to Ferozepore, to deliver him to the English. Early in the morning Heera Sing went out on horseback, and brought both the fugitives back to the city. According to custom, a salute of hundreds of cannons were fired on the entrance of Dulleep Sing, who was given up again to his mother in the fortress. Jewahir Sing was dragged to prison. At that time Jellah Pundit entered into a tender connection with a widow of Sheer Sing, and promised her that he would murder Dulleep Sing, and place her son, as legitimate heir of the Guddee, on the throne. The affair could not be performed secretly, and it reached the ears of impartial persons, so the ranee Chund became informed of this conspiracy, and that was quite sufficient to suffocate it at its birth. Women's cunning surpasses all skill, especially if the question conerns their own interest. First of all, she contrived to secure the good will of the treasurer, Lall Sing. Who would have thought that a man, who owed his splendid position to Rajah Dhyan Sing, and who lived always in the society of Heera Sing, with whom he contracted brothership, and with whom Jellah Pundit exchanged turbans as a token of true amity, would have played the felon against these friends, in supporting the ranee with his advice and activity? First of all he occasioned the release of her brother, Jewahir Sing, and gave him the required sums, with which he allured the Nahungs, in order to bring him out of the city. He succeeded immediately in attaching the discontented regular troops to his party; and at the head of his partisans, he appeared the next morning, on the place used for millitary displays before the fortress, asking from Heera Sing the delivery of Jellah Pundit; Heera Sing obstinately refusing the request, and feeling himself at the same time too feeble to oppose openly the mutineers, resolved to fly, as before mentioned, with Meean Son Sing, Jellah Pundit and his partisans the mountaineers, &c., directing their steps towards the river Ravee. Thus the whole body of the Sikhs became alienated from his interest, and his most intimate friends, pursued him with the army, and when he was overtaken, they killed all who could not escape. Lall Sing and Jewahir Sing re-entered the fortress victoriously about noon, with their trophies, consisting of five heads, whilst the robber-pack, as rear-guard, eager for booty,

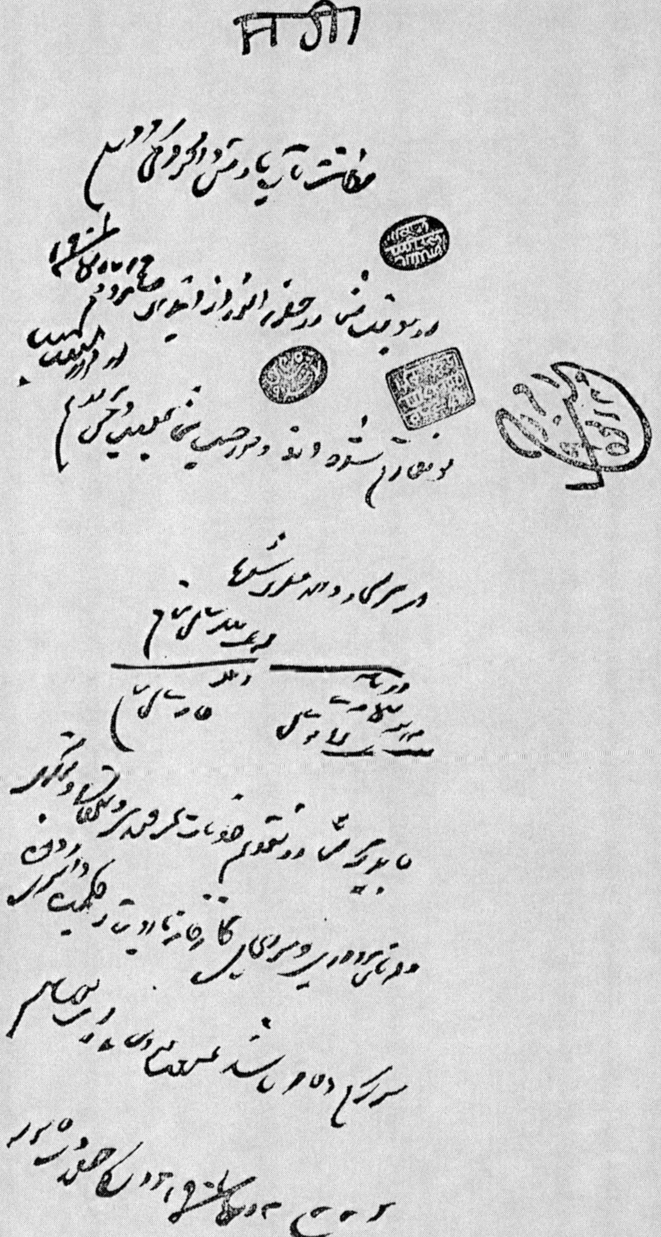

divided amongst themselves the riches, which the fugitives had taken with them. Every one hastened to present his nazerana (present), and to express his congratulation, and I did the same ; on which occasion the new wuzeer, Jewahir Sing, who replaced Heera Sing, recieved me, not only with a friendly smile, but I obtained again on the same day my former position as physican, and director of the powder-mill, &c.

Jewahir Sing, like his predecessors, did not long enjoy the possession of his dignity. He and the celebrated slave-girl, Mungela, formed one party of the opposition, whilst Lall Sing, and the ranee Chund, were the other antagonists of the government. On both parties depended the administration of the government, while, on account of the contrast in their views, they could not act in harmony. A pseudo son of Runjeet Sing, named Peshora Sing, brother to Cashmere Sing (who was killed with the high-priest), intended to excite a rebellion against the subsisting government, and took the fortress of Attock. Jewahir Sing, flattering him with promises, allured him out of the fortress, and gave orders that he should be secretly murdered. But the troops, among whom the victim had a great number of partisans and friends, got information of the treacherous assassination, and in revenge killed Jewahir Sing when riding on his elephant. Jewahir was aware what the troops meditated doing with him and endeavoured to avoid their invitation to enter their camp.

In the latter period of Jewahir Sing's administration, we lived under very critical circumstances; neither justice, order nor security of life were enjoyed by the community. The soldiers, having lost all discipline, acted as each thought proper ; for instance, if a soldier went into a bazaar to receive an old debt, he took it by force with tenfold interest. At the camp of Meean Meer, five miles from Lahore, there was a false report that I had concealed in my house some English spies, who were in communication with Jewahir Sing, to surrender the country to the English. Colonel Mouton was the only one who lived in my house, and who, a short time previously, had returned from France, in order to solicit a new engagement; and now and then the Spaniard, Hurbon, and St. Amand, a painter, called on me, these being the only Europeans at Lahore. On one occasion, some soldiers whom I attended, told me confidentially that the troops had resolved, if Jewahir should not come from the fortress into their camp on that afternoon, to assail the fortress and kill him there. Their intention, they added, was also hostile towards my dwelling, which they intended to plunder and burn, as they thought I was concealing English spies who were conspiring with Jewahir Sing to surrender the country to the English; they advised me therefore, to carry anything of value to a secure place. It was indeed, not before the last moment, when Jewahir heard, by the beating of the drums, that the troops were in full march to assail the fortress, that he resolved to leave his residence; which turned out happily for the city and myself, for had he not done so, Lahore would have been plundered and sacked. In leaving the fortress he was riding on an elephant, holding little Dulleep Sing before him on his lap. In his Howda (chair), there was a number of bags filled with gold and silver. He thought probably to ransom his life with it, but he was mistaken. The Ranee and Mungela, with many slave-girls, followed him on several elephants. When the train arrived at the camp, the soldiers first took Dulleep Sing from his lap, and sent him with his mother in a royal tent, erected on purpose for the court. Scarcely was that done, when they fired at Jewahir Sing, without any further ceremony, and the same fate awaited two of his attendants, named Baba-Ruttun-Sing and Chetta Payah. This catastrophe made such a deep impression on the Ranee and Mungela, that for many weeks they were quite inconsolable; they appeared before the public for several days with their hair loose, as if mad. Every morning they went from the fortress on foot, crossing the pret (place for exercising soldiers) in the garden where Jewahir Sing had been burnt with both his companions and five living women; there

MAHARAJH GOOLAB SING

RAJAH DHYAN SING

RAJAH SOOCHET SING

RAJAH HEERA SING

they gave free vent to their tears, to relieve their oppressed hearts.

In the year 1845 the cholera arrived at Lahore, having travelled through Turkistan and Cabul. At the same time Gholab Sing was brought from Jummoo, a town in the mountains, a prisoner to Lahore, and he might have congratulated himself on having escaped the persecution of Jewahir Sing; for it was well known that at different periods attempts had been made upon his life. The reason of Jewahir's hatred against him was that Gholab Sing had persuaded a great number of the Sikh troops to follow his banner, to whom he trusted himself. He was brought from Jummoo to Lahore, in consequence of his resistance to some government exactions. It is a remarkabie fact, that Gholab Sing, in spite of his fortress being blockaded by numerous troops, was bold enough to give an order to murder on the road the delegates of the Sikhs whom he himself had despatched with the subsidies requested by the government, as if he had regretted performing his duty.

During his struggles in the mountains, Runjoor Sing, well known to the English as the commander of the Sikh troops at the battle of Aliwal, had the command in the mountains of Jesrota. One of the most wealthy Brahmins of that country had been requested by some of his neighbours to take their moveable goods into his custody, for which purpose the Brahmin solicited of Runjoor Sing a guard, which he obtained. But when Runjoor Sing was apprised that valuables were stored in the house of the Brahmin, he plotted an intrigue for obtaining possession of them, and despatched a division of his men, disguised as robbers, to plunder the house. The Brahmins being convinced that this violence had been perpetrated under the protection of Runjoor Sing, flocked in numbers to Lahore, to make their complaints to Jewahir Sing; but seeing they could not receive any satisfaction from him, they all returned to their homes. The Brahmin at whose house the robbery was committed, was the only person who remained behind at Lahore, firmly determined not to leave the capital until he obtained satisfaction. After a long and vain expectation, he early one morning ascended a fig-tree, declaring that he would not leave that tree before he got reparation for the injustice which had been done him. When Jewahir Sing was informed of the fact, he despatched a soldier to compel the Brahmin to descend. The Brahmin, rather than comply, stabbed himself in the tree; upon which, Jewahir commanded the faqueer Noor-oo-Deen to order the jerahs (native surgeons) to cure the wound. On the same day I was by accident coming from the durbar, which that day was held in the fortress, and met the faqueer, when we went together in the Goolab Khana, at the Hazooree Bagh, where the faqueer had his business during the day. There we found one of the jerahs, who reported that the cure of the Brahmin was impossible, the bowels having protruded from his body, and could not be replaced. While I was inquiring what was the subject of their conversation, the faqueer related to me the particulars, and requested me to accompany the native surgeon to see the patient for a moment, adding, that he wished me to do my best to restore him to health. I went there, and found him in a small garden before the city gate (Tunksallee Derwazeh.) The other jerahs had already given him up as a lost man, and retired. On his abdomen I saw the protruding intestines, which, although unhurt, were of a bluish colour, by having been six hours exposed to the heat of the summer in that position. The patient, a lean man of about fifty years, was in the full possession of his senses. I sent for my instruments, and enlarged the narrow opening of the muscle and the peritoneum, so that I could replace the bowels, made a gastroraphy, and joined the wound. All this was done in a few minutes. During the operation, the patient said slowly "tenn, tenn, tenn," (saint, saint, saint); The assisting jerah gave me the title of ustad (master). After this, the patient was troubled by an annoying hiccup, which lasted for three days, and then he recovered. I presented him to the faqueer Noor-oo-Deen, and the minister. The latter did his best to appease him, and ordered some cows, utensils, clothes, and money to be delivered to him, and he retired satisfied. From this fact, every one will be convinced of the incapacity of the native surgeons, or jerahs, in the East.

After the death of Jewahir Sing, the ranee conferred on her lover, Lall Sing, the title of prime minister. She had been several times *enciente*, but had always procured abortion. The fact was a public secret. It is easy to imagine that neither civil nor military men respected or feared the ranee and her favourite. This was especially the case among the army, whose discipline was in the highest degree corrupted. Every batallion had two men called punches, or deputies, who dictated laws to the court, according to the resolutions taken by the assembly of the toops. This continued until the ranee and her lover became objects of contempt and disrespect, and were often abused publicly, and threatened by the troops. There was no doubt any longer that their days were numbered, and at that time they thought it necessary to put themselves under the protection of the English. How was that to be effected? It could only be done by making war against the English, by which, although her toops might be destroyed, and their opponents take possession of the country, they would be personally benefited. Another reason which may have induced the ranee to place herself under the protection of the English government, was possibly lest her fate might resemble that of her predecessors, should her adult son learn in what manner his father, and also his grandfather, had destroyed their own mothers (*vide* Major G. C. Smyth's " History of the Reigning Family of Lahore"). Thus she was between two fires, and thought her only safety was in English protection. The difficulty was, how to carry out their plot ; but they very soon found the means. At that time Teja Sing was governor of Peshawur, having succeeded General Avitabile, and was the only man who exercised a great influence over the troops since the time of Runjeet Sing. The ranee called on him for his advice. On his proposal, false documents were drawn up, which were read in the durbar, the contents of which were, that the

English had confiscated the incomes of the lands of the Sikhs on the other side of the river Sutlej, and had committed numerous outrages, and that they were preparing for war against the Sikhs ; therefore it was said to be necessary to have revenge, and attack them.

Lall Sing was proclaimed wuzeer, and Teja Sing Commander-in-chief of the troops. The Sikhs received their guree pershaut (consecrated bread) on the Summood (tomb of the royal family), where they administered an oath to each individually ; the Mahomedans on the Koran, and the Hindoos on the water of the Ganges.

The astrologers having named an auspicious day, they went, without any further diplomatic conferences, on their march. The English, although well acqnainted with all those disturbances aud confusions which happened in the neighbouring country, yet had not the least idea of being attacked by their allies, and were consequently not at all prepared for a war. On the other side of the river Sutlej, the four battles were fought—at Moodkee, Ferozeshahur, Aliwal, and Sobraon ; and the English, completely triumphing in the last battle, became masters of the country. Teja Sing, whom I attended at Lahore, made to me the candid confession, that, in circumstances like those to which the country was reduced, no other remedy was left for its salvation but to surrender it to the English. It is well known, that on the 22nd of December, 1845, Teja Sing arrived on the field of battle with a reserve of twenty-five to thirty thousand regular troops, after the English had fought a whole day and night, and consumed all their ammunition, on account of which they had been obliged to retreat. But the Sikhs with whom they had fought, believing themselves defeated, retired also, and the English returned and re-occupied their abandoned camp. That was the critical moment in which the reserve army, under the command of Teja Sing, arrived ; and he, being in correspondence with the English, did what he could to check the ardour of his troops by filling them with fear ; and he was the first who turned his back in order to

Page 123

RAJAH TEJA SING

RAJAH DEENA-NAUTH

FAQUEER NOOR-OO-DEEN

SIRDAR DOST MAHOMED

spare the English, he knowing their critical position. The army followed his example, and retreated also. That was the famous battle in which the confusion among the British troops reached its highest pitch—to such a degree, that they fired on each other. On this occasion, a Catholic priest, the only one in the whole army, lost his life, his long beard and turban causing the mistake. It is known, too, that the Prince Waldemar of Prussia was in the English ranks as a volunteer, and distinguished himself by his courage and calmness. Although he luckily escaped the peril, he was much afflicted by the sad accident of seeing his dear friend and travelling companion, Doctor Hofmeister, fall by his side, having been killed by a shot from the Sikh camp

On the 10th of February, 1846, the battle of Sobraon took place, which decided the fate of the country. Teja Sing, the traitor, took to his heels, and, on passing the Sutlej, he ordered the bridge to be broken down, leaving the greater part of his troops behind in a helpless state. The betrayed soldiers cried, with their hands folded and grass in their mouths, making themselves emblems of their holy animals, the cattle. It is said, that some of them exclaimed : "We suffer only the just reward for our sins ; we did not deserve any better fate, for there, beyond the river, is the land where we killed our gooroo with his cows." Major G. C. Smyth, in his history, says very truly concerning the attack on the gooroo :—"One of the first victims was the holy Bai, one of whose legs was nearly knocked off by a cannon ball. Utter Sing and Cashmere Sing, with some other sirdars, fell in the conflict which ensued ; and numbers of their people were drowned in the river in attemping to escape. The Sikhs lost all their reverence for their gooroo, the sight of the rich plunder which his camp afforded being a temptation too strong for their piety. Their only object now was to secure, every man for himself, as much of the booty as he could ; but for this they had to fight hard. When the struggle was over, the Baba was found breathing his last, in exclamations against those of his own caste and creed. He now produced many of the letters which he had received—the forgeries before-mentioned—to prove, as he supposed, the treachery and villainy of the Sikh chiefs and officers, who, as he believed to the last, had written these letters, instigating him to take the part of Utter Sing. 'When,' said he to the Sikhs around him, 'you and your chiefs and officers wrote these letters to me, with the most solemn promises, both to myself and Utter Sing, I relied on your good faith, and agreed to your proposals, in the hope of obtaining for Utter Sing and his family the means of a quiet livelihood; but you, calling yourselves Sikhs, are worse than Mahomedans. You have proved yourselves a vile, treacherous and unfaithful race, without pity or religion. Still, my dying prayer to heaven is, may even your wickedness be requited by good.' He then gave directions that his body should be thrown into the river, that his bones might not be left on such a land of iniquity," &c., &c.

Utter Sing was an uncle of Ajeet Sing, and brother of Lena Sing, who were the murderers of Sheer Sing, Dhyan Sing, and Pertaub Sing, &c., &c. They were all members of the Scindawalla family, and related to Runjeet Sing; for this reason, Utter Sing embraced the party of the Ranee Chund Kour, at the outbreak of the civil contentions. But the fortress of Lahore having been surrendered to Sheer Sing, Utter Sing took to flight, and solicited protection from the English. It was natural that Heera Sing and his counsellor, Jellah Pundit, should endeavour to catch him, at any price whatever; so they managed to bring him over to the Baba Beer Sing, in order to implicate the holy man in the affair. I related before, that Jellah Pundit, through religious fanaticism, hated the Baba for having given an asylum to the two unfortunate princes, Cashmere Sing and Peshora Sing, after having been driven, by Heera, from the fortress of Seealkote, which had been allotted to them as their property. Utter Sing permitted himself to be deluded by false promises, and repaired to the appointed place, where directions

Page 124

CHARAENA SOWAR

NAHUNG

were afterwards given to capture him alive. The plot miscarried, it is true. Utter Sing was overwhelmed by a superior force, but he shot at and killed the general who was about to capture him, which caused the ensuing battle.

The Sikh army having passed the Sutlej, the soldiers became aware that their leaders were playing the part of traitors, not doing anything they ought to have done. In the before-mentioned history of Smyth, we find the following passage :—

"They gave vent to their alarm and indignation in fierce reproaches on the treachery of their leaders ; but that was all they could do. 'We knew,' they said to their leaders, 'that you had leagued with the court to send us against the British, and to pen us up here like sheep, for them to come and slaughter us at their convenience ; but remember, that in thus acting, you play the part, not only of traitors to your country, but of ruthless butchers and murderers. You destroy a whole army, which, whatever its faults and crimes may have been, has always been ready to obey the orders of the state and its officers. We might even now punish you as you deserve ; but we will leave you to answer to your gooroo and your God ; while we, deserted and betrayed as we are, will do what we can to preserve the independence of our country," &c., &c.

During this war of the Sikhs against the English, the Rajah Gholab Sing remained neutral at Jummoo, in the mountains. It is true he promised his support to the Sikhs, but he hesitated in fulfilling them as long as possible. A short time previous to the last battle, at Sobraon, some hundreds of the Sikh delegated punches (deputies) succeeded in drawing out the "bear," as they used to call him, from Jummoo, his den. Under the pretext of getting the order from the ranee herself and the durbar, he went, accompanied by them, to Lahore. But this was only done in order to procrastinate. Arrived at Lahore, I called on him, because we were well acquainted with each other, and he asked me for my advice how he ought to act in that critical position. He complained of the embarrassment he was in; "because," said he, "the same Sikhs who murdered my brothers and sons, and who, under Jewahir's administration, attempted my own life, are now endeavouring to draw me into the field, in order to fight against the English." I advised him not to mingle with the affair. This agreed with his views, the Sikhs having already lost three battles; and it was more than probable that the fourth, which must decide the destiny of the country, would be their last. The treacheries of the chiefs having been well known to him, I made him aware how prudent it would be to demand the eighteen English prisoners at Philoor, and to send them to my house, which he did. Meanwhile, the news of the defeat at Sobraon reached us, and that the English had passed the Sutlej. They requested Gholab Sing to repair to Kussoor. He despatched the English prisoners (among whom there was Doctor Benet) on elephants into the English camp, having previously made them presents at the durbar; and three days after, Gholab Sing followed them.

He chose me to accompany him as a private counsellor; at the first station, Kanekatch, about fourteen miles from Lahore, we received news from the city which intimidated me. It was rumoured that the defeated Sikhs had collected the rest of their troops, and intended to kill their commander, the traitor Teja Sing; and having done so, that they then intended to divide into two parties, one to march towards Lahore, to plunder it, and take revenge on the ranee and her paramour; and the other to attack Gholab Sing and his retinue, for having first promised them his assistance, and instead of that, intending to go to Kussoor, to surrender the country to the English. Fearing to be attacked during the night, no one allowed himself any rest. Gholab Sing placed four cannons which he had with him, under the command of Captain Gardner, at some distance from our camp, and he himself occupied the whole of the night in going the round of the various outposts. Happily the Sikhs did not execute either of their intended movements, and the next day we arrived unmolested at the English camp, in the vicinity of Kussoor. Gholab Sing with

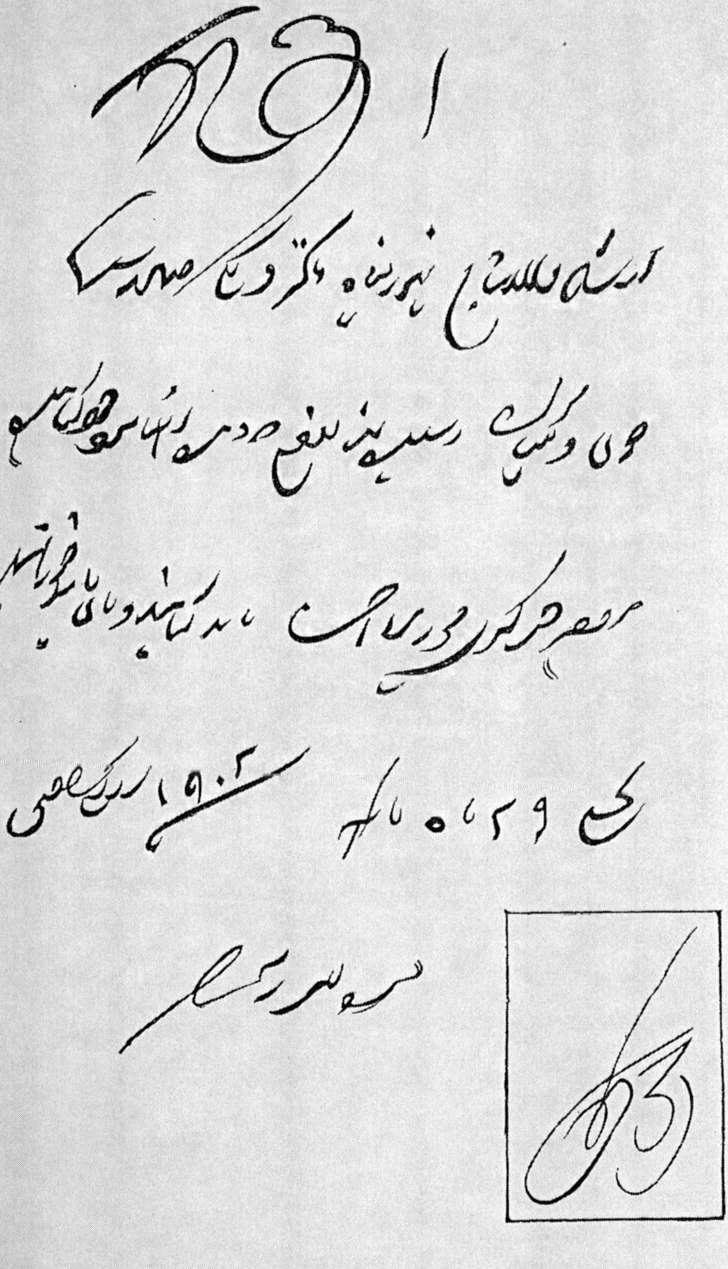

his suite were not received with much apparent cordiality, but when all was settled, and the English had obtained what they desired, the scene changed its aspect ; the young Dulleep Sing was brought from the capital to give his sanction to all the transactions, the English then proceeded to Lahore, and thus ended the independence of the once powerful state founded by Runjeet Sing. The English forces encamped at Meean Meer, about five miles from the city. To enfeeble the country, it was divided into three parts ; one was left to the Sikhs, the second was annexed to the English possessions, and the third, Cashmere, comprising a part of the mountains, was appointed to Gholab Sing, as a reward for the services he had rendered, and also in consideration of a large sum of money he had delivered over to the conquerors. He was promoted to the title of Maharajah of Cashmere, which was made independent of Lahore, but under English protection. Dulleep Sing, after having paid the expenses of the war, remained the ruler of Lahore, and Lall Sing was appointed his wuzeer. Sir H. Lawrence was appointed by the English as Resident, into whose hands the reins of Government were entrusted. One of his first measures was the reduction of the army, and the suspension of several establishments for the manufacture of military stores, including my powder-mill, &c. Instead of these establishments, an hospital was erected in the vicinity of the capital, under the direction of the durbar ; and I was entrusted with the organisation of it. In this hospital, an asylum for lunatics was estabilshed, and I also created another, viz., an hospital for prisoners.

Rajah Lall Sing, who had risen from the rank of muleteer to be minister of state, did not long enjoy the title of wuzeer ; being a crafty Brahmin, of great influence among his partisans, and in possession of immense riches, which he acquired at the time when he was Runjeet Sing's treasurer (he never having rendered any account of the funds under his charge), such a man appeared to the English to be dangerous, and his removal was considered necessary Accordingly he was arrested as a political intriguer, and sent to Agra, with a stipulated pension. Teja Sing succeeded to Lall Sing, and at the same time was appointed Rajah of Seealkote, on account of his treachery to his own country on the Sutlej. At the ceremony of his inauguration, the ranee prohibited her son, Dullep Sing, from making the Tike (saffron sign) on Teja's forehead, being fully persuaded that he had caused the removal of Lall Sing, in order to obtain his post. This inconsiderate behaviour of the ranee, who exercised a great influence on her son, caused the Resident to insure her inoffensiveness by exiling her to the fortress of Sheg-Opur. But not having even there remained inactive (in the revolt at Moultan), Sir Frederick Currie, the then Resident, ordered her to be conveyed into another fortress on the Ganges, her plenipotentiary, Gangaram, and General Khan Sing having previously been hung, as associates in the conspiracy. But the cunning lady knew how to provide herself with means, and to find out a method of escaping from her prison ; and it is reported that she is now living in Katmandoo, the capital of Nepaul, not, however, to the displeasure of the English, who thus effect a considerable saving.

Sir H. Lawrence, perfectly acquainted with all the tricks of the orientals, and knowing well how to treat those people, succeeded in procuring their general esteem and approbation. Nevertheless, a short time after the English had occupied the country, a riot took place at the bazaar at Lahore, which was so serious that the gates of the city were ordered to be shut. The residency was still in the city ; and at this critical moment, the resolute Resident, accompanied by Major Edwardes and a few sowars (mounted soldiers), appeared on the spot where the tumult of the mob was raging, in order to establish tranquillity ; but they were welcomed by the mob with a volley of stones ; Major Edwardes received a slight wound on his forehead, and one of the sowars a sabre wound. On the request of the Resident, Lall Sing caused the ringleaders to be captured ; and one of them, a Brahmin, was hung before the city gate, without ceremony or hesitation.

The principal cause of this by no means insignificant riot, was said to be that an English soldier of the garrison gave a cut with his sword to an ox, which is esteemed by the Brahmins as a sacred animal. Since then, however, oxen are not only killed at Lahore, but at Umritsir, the holy city, and the meat is publicly sold at the bazaars. The Sikhs and Hindoos, who consider the killing of oxen and cows to be a capital sin, can do nothing but grieve at the sacrilege, and weep at their inability to prevent it. Their feelings on this point, however, would sometimes take a more active and dangerous turn; and on one occasion, when the Resident gave an entertainment in the royal gardens, called Shallemar, to which many ladies and gentlemen, and their children were invited, and I also happened to be among the number of the guests, we were near falling victims to the people's vengeance. By good fortune, however, the Resident was apprised of the conspiracy, and all preparations were made for our security, otherwise it would, I am afraid, have gone hardly with us, as the quarters of the troops were at Anarkhali, five miles from the gardens.

Bad health induced the Resident to accompany the Governor-General, Lord Hardinge, to England, and Sir F. Currie replaced him; but as he treated the Sikhs with more indulgence, not being so well acquainted with oriental policy as Sir H. Lawrence, the people soon began to abuse his kindness. Two officers also, named Agnew and Anderson, both of them unacquainted with the manners and customs of the country, and therefore ignorant of the proper method of dealing with such a people, were sent, accompanied by a native, Serdar Kan Sing, to Mooltan, to receive the state accounts from the Mulraj, and to take their posts as governors of that district. Both these officers were barbarously murdered; and the natives, as if by a given signal, rose in revolt against the English. The troops of the provinces Banu-Tank, Hazareh and Peshawur also joined the hostile movement; and a consiracy was detected at Lahore, in which, as before mentioned, the ranee was implicated. Their intention was to carry away Dulleep Sing, and to bring him into the camp of the insurgents. An earnest and bloody struggle arose : Dost Mahomed Khan, of Cabul, whom the English released a few years ago from prison, took the conduct of the Sikhs, and they defeated the English in two battles, at Ramnuggur and Chillianwallah ; and it was not before the return of Sir H. Lawrence that the English recovered their position, by those two deciding battles of Mooltan and Gujerat, on the Chenaub river ; after which—viz., on the 1st of May, 1849—the country was annexed to the English possessions ; the Sikh durbar was abolished ; and my official capacity depending only on the existence of that body, was consequently at its end. I solicited a pension, which I obtained. Dulleep Sing was sent to the interior of India, where he lived upon a pension, derived from the revenue of the same country from which I receive my own ; the only difference between the two pensions being, that I am allowed to expend mine wherever I please. The receipt, however, must be at Lahore ; my agent there presenting a life certificate, signed by an English anthority.

It was in the year 1839 that I had returned to Lahore, after having visited the European continent and my native country. I enjoyed the pleasure, on my return, of being the companion of General Ventura, who was also hastening to India to resume his duties. On our voyage we had many conversations, among which, the events which had happened during my absence from Lahore underwent discussion. On that occasion, the general related to me an occurrence which at first I could scarcely believe, thinking it a pure invention or a mere joke ; but I soon became persuaded that he was in earnest. I give it here with the remark only, that after having arrived at Lahore, I heard it confirmed by other persons, in whose statements I could also place confidence.

Runjeet Sing—thus runs the narative—was told that a saat, or faqueer, living in the mountains, was able to keep himself in a state resembling death, and would allow himself

HARIDAS

to be even buried, without injuring or endangering his life, provided they would remove or release him from the grave after the expiration of a fixed time, he being in the possession of the means of resuscitating himself again. The maharajah thought it impossible. To convince himself of the truth of the assertion, he ordered the faqueer to be brought to court, and caused him to undergo the experiment, assuring him that no precaution should be omitted to discover whether it was a deception. In consequence, the faqueer, in the presence of the court, placed himself in a complete state of asphyxia, having all the appearance of death.

In that state he was wrapped in the linen on which he was sitting, the seal of Runjeet Sing was stamped thereon, and it was placed in a chest, on which the maharajah put a strong lock. The chest was buried in a garden, outside of the city, belonging to the minister, barley was sown on the ground, and the space enclosed with a wall and surrounded by sentinels. On the fortieth day, which was the time fixed for his exhumation, a great number of the authorities of the durbar, with General Ventura, and several Englishmen from the vicinity, one of them a medical man, went to the enclosure. The chest was brought up and opened, and the faqueer was found in the same position as they had left him, cold and stiff. A friend of mine told me, that had I been present when they endeavoured to bring him to life, by applying warmth to the head, injecting air into his ears and mouth, and rubbing the whole of his body to promote circulation, &c., I should certainly not have had the slightest doubt of the reality of the performance. The minister, Rajah Dhyan Sing, assured me, that he himself kept this faqueer (whose name was Haridas) four months under the ground, when he was at Jummoo in the mountains. On the day of his burial, he ordered his beard to be shaved, and at his exhumation his chin was as smooth as on the day of his interment ; thus furnishing a complete proof of the powers of vitality having been suspended during that period. He likewise caused himself to be interred at Jesrota, in the mountains, and at Umritsir, and also by the English in Hindostan. In the "Calcutta Medical Journal" about 1835, there is a full description of the faqueer, and we are there informed, that he preferred having the chest in which he was enclosed, suspended in the air, instead of its being buried beneath the earth, as he feared the possibility of his body being attacked by ants, whilst in that middle state between life and death. Having, however, refused to undergo another trial, several of the English people there doubted the truth of the story, and refused credence in so astonishing a power.* But it is quite certain that had there been any deception as regards the interment of the faqueer, rendering his experiment easy of accomplishment, those engaged or associated with him, and to whom the task of restoring the vital energies was necessarily entrusted, would of necessity be acquainted with the mystery, and able, since his real decease, to emulate his example ; that, however, is not the case. It appears, consequently, that the faqueer was the only one then in possession of that ability ; and as a further corroboration of this view of the case, I may mention that I myself inquired in the Punjab, in the mountains and valleys of Cashmere, and in other parts of India, and used every exertion to find a person possessed of this power, in order to bring him to Europe; or at least to Calcutta, but without success. Several Hindoos told me that such faqueers set no value upon money ; I replied to them however, that at all events they fully appreciated other worldly pleasures. They did not like to hear this statement, implying that the faqueer was a debauchee. Several complaints had, however, been made of him, on which account Runjeet Sing intended to banish him from Lahore. He anticipated the intention, by eloping with a Katrany (woman of a Hindoo caste) to the mountains, where he

* To corroborate the above, my readers can refer to General Ventura (Paris), and also to Colonel Sir C. M. Wade (London), who were present, and assisted at the restoration of the faqueer, some accounts of whom have been published from the Colonel's statement,

died, and was burned according to the custom of the country. His elopement with this woman may serve as a proof (in contradiction to other statements) that he was neither an eunuch nor a hermaphrodite.

Doubtless, it is a difficult task, and not within the power of every one to acquire the skill necessary for the performance of this experiment, and those who do succeed must undergo a long and continual practice of preparatory measures. I was informed that such people have their frœnulum linguœ cut and entirely loosened, and that they get their tongue prominent, drawing and lengthening it by means of rubbing it with butter mixed with some pellitory of Spain, in order that they may be able to lay back the tongue at the time they are about to stop respiration, so as to cover the orifice of the hinder part of the fosses nasales, and thus (with other means for the same purpose, which I shall mention) keep the air shut up in the body and head.* Novices, in trying the experiment, shut their eyes, and press them with their fingers, as also the cavities of the ears and nostrils, because the natural warmth of the body might cause such an expansion of the enclosed gas as otherwise to produce, by the violence of its pressure, a rupture of some of those delicate organs not yet accustomed by practice to endure it. This, I am told, is especially the case with the eyes and the tympan of the ear. For the better acquisition of this power, they are accustomed to practise the holding of the breath for a long period. They swallow a small strip of linen, in order to cleanse the stomach, and by a tube draw a quantity of water through the anus into the intestines to rinse them. This is performed while sitting in a vessel filled with wa er to the height of the arm-pits. It is said that the faqueer in question, a few days previous to his experiments, took some kind of purgative, and subsisted for several days on a coarse milk regimen. On the day of his burial, instead of

* A similar process is explained in some of the *Encyclopædias*, in the article on "Engastrimythe," or the mechanism of the ventriloquists.

food, he slowly swallowed, in the presence of the assembly, a rag of three fingers in breadth and thirty yards in length, and afterwards extracted it, for the purpose of removing all foreign matters from the stomach, having previously rinsed the bowels in the manner I have before mentioned. Ridiculous as this operation may appear to the reader, and as it appears, indeed, to me also, yet these artists must of necessity be complete masters of their body and its organism, and possess a more than ordinary power over the muscles. We are scarcely capable of swallowing a somewhat long piece of maccaroni if it is not well boiled and moistened with butter, &c., to render it palatable. It is probable, however, that they may have lost the sense of taste, and their neck-muscles may be relaxed to such a degree that the long linen strip does not meet with any resistance in the throat. These preparations being nade, the faqueer stopped all the natural openings in the body with plugs of aromatic wax, placed back his tongue in the manner I have before indicated, crossed his arms over his breast, and thus suffocated himself, in the presence of a multitude of spectators. On his exhumation, one of the first operations is to draw his tongue into its natural position ; after this, a warm aromatic paste, made from pulse meal, is placed on his head, and air is injected into his lungs and also through the ears, from which the plugs are withdrawn. By this operation, the pellets in the nostrils are driven out with considerable force and noise, and this is considered the first symptom of his resuscitation. Friction is then strenuously applied all over the body, and at length he begins to breathe naturally, opens his eyes, and is gradually restored to conseiousness. It is related that, two hundred and fifty years ago, in the time of the Gooroo Arjun Sing, a Joghee faqueer was found in his tomb in a sitting posture, at Umritsir, and was restored to life. This faqueer is reported to have been below the ground for one hundred years ; and when he revived, he related many circumstances connected with the times in which he had lived. Whether this tradition be true or false, it is impossible to say ; but

I am of opinion, that he who can pass four months below the ground without becoming a prey to corruption, may also remain there for one year. Granting this, it is impossible to fix a limit to the time during which a suspension of the vital functions may continue, without injury to their subsequent power.

However paradoxical or absurd this statement may appear, and however persuaded I may be that many a reader, believing himself to be a wise man, will smile at the relation, I cannot, nevertheless, avoid confessing freely, that I do not entirely reject all the details given respecting the circumstance, for as Haller observes :—" In the interior of nature no mortal can penetrate ; happy is he who knows a small part, even of its surface." We find much credence given to such phenomena in the most ancient traditions. Who will not remember the history of Epimenides of Creta, who, after a sleep of forty years in a grotto there, is reported to have again re-entered the world from which he had so long been separated ? Who will not remember also the seven holy sleepers, who, according to a Vatican manuscript, were concealed in a grotto near Ephesus, in order to escape the persecutions of the Christians, during the reign of the Emperor Decius ; and who, 155 years subsequently, in the time of Theodosius II, returned to consciousness ? But even rejecting these traditions, have we not also similar examples in the animal kingdom ? Have not animals, especially toads, been detected in rocks, wherein, according to the calculations made, they had been enclosed for several centuries, in a state of sleep or torpor, and which animals, after having been brought into the air, have recovered their vitality ; and it is not necessary to remind the naturalist of the fact, that many species of animals invariably pass the winter season in a kind of sleep, awaking in the spring with renewed and unimpaired energies. Among recent cases, which demonstrate the great endurance of human life, is the follwing relation .—At Vienna, some years since, a Hungarian was, during a period of twelve months, in a comatose state, and his jaw-bones were so firmly closed that it was impossible to open his mouth ; the physicians were consequently obliged to extract some of his teeth, in order to administer some remedies and broth, to preserve life ; he nevertheless at last recovered.

In the Philosophical Transactions for 1705 (Nov. and Dec., Vol. XVII., p. 2177), the history of a case is related, which supports what has been previously mentioned :—" A man of about twenty-five years of age, living in the neighbourhood of Bath, fell suddenly asleep, and continued for nearly a month in that state. Two years afterwards, he was again in a similar condition : his jaw-bones closed themselves ; he was unable to eat, but fell asleep, and continued to be deprived of sensation for seventeen weeks. This occurred at the time when barley was being sown, and when he again awoke it was quite ripe. In the month of August he again fell asleep. He was bled ; stimulating remedies were employed ; and every means of restoration were used which the medical skill of the period could suggest, but in vain ; he did not awake until the month of November." In Plott's Natural History of Oxfordshire (c. 8., sec. 11, p. 196, published in 1677), a case is alluded to, which, not being generally known, I will quote here, it being another evidence of the length of time during which a person may exist without nourishment.

" Rebekah Smith, the servant maid of one Thomas White, of Minster Lovel, being above fifty years of age, and of a robust constitution, though she seldom ate flesh (it scarcely agreeing with her), after she came from the communion on Palm-Sunday, April 16, 1671, was taken with such a dryness in her throat, that she could not swallow her spittle, nor anything else to supply the demands of nature ; and in this state she continued, without eating or drinking, to the amazement of all, for about *ten weeks*, viz., to the 29th of June, being both St. Peter's and Witney fair day ; by which time, being brought very low, her master made inquiry, and found out a person who gave him an amulet (for it was supposed she was bewitched) against this evil ; after the application of this amulet, within two or three days' time (though I dare not suppose there was any connection between the medicine and the disease), she first drank a little water, then warm broths in small quantities at a time, and nothing else till Palm-Sunday again, twelve months after, when she began to eat bread and other food as she had formerly done; and the record states that she was then about the age of sixty, and still living in the same place, ready to testify to the truth of the matter; as were also Thomas White and his wife, who were the only other persons living in the house with her, and who would confidently assert (for they carefully observed), that they did not believe she ever took anything whatever in those *ten weeks'* time, nor anything more than what is before mentioned until the expiration of the year."

The London Medical and Physical Journal, Vol. XXXV., p. 509, states that :—

" An account of the sleeping woman of Dunnibald, near Montrose, was read by the Rev. James Brewster, at the Royal Society of Edinburgh. Her first sleeping fit lasted from the 27th to the 30th of June, 1815. Next morning she again fell into a sleep which lasted seven days, without motion, food, or evacuation. At the end of this time, by moving her hand and pointing to her mouth, it was understood she wanted food, which was given to her; but she remained in her lathargic state till the 8th of August, six weeks in all, without appearing to be awake, except on the 30th of June," &c., &c. This case is well authenticated.

And in J. N. Willam's Miscellaneous Works, published by A. Smith, M. D., p. 339, he states that he had seen many, mostly Jews and other aliens, of a dark, swarthy complexion, sometimes lie six or eight weeks in the torpid insensible condition above described.

After this digression I will return to my own adventures, having first cited a case in which the remedy called Mumiai, and of which mention has been frequently made in this book, proved very efficacious.

In the time of the Maharajah Sheer Sing, it happened that an elephant, in spite of all the caution of the driver, and of the animal itself, during the darkness of the night, fell into a grave in traversing the ruins of old Lahore. Mrs. Van C——was thrown from her howda, and had two of her ribs broken by the fall. I may also mention that she was at that time in the ninth month of her pregnancy. I began my treatment with a copious bleeding from the arm, and afterwards administered to her one grain of mumiai daily, for three successive days, and ordered her to lay quietly on her back, so as not to disturb the bandage. On the fourth day, when I visited her, she endeavoured, but in vain, to make the cracking of the bones audible by moving from one side to the other, the union of the fracture was already effected by the *callus*, and a few days subsequently she was delivered of a fine healthy boy with much ease.

About the same time, under Sheer Sing's administration, a faqueer struck me from behind with a stone, whilst I was passing the bazaar at Lahore; I was told that he was insane, and had already behaved in the same rude manner to some sirdars. On this account I caused him to be imprisoned, placed a chain upon his legs, and had him taken to my powder-mill to work. I gave him good food, administered remedies, and prohibited him from smoking churrus or eating opium, to which habits he was previously addicted. Scarcely was he a few days in the mill when I was informed that he had been bitten by a serpent, and at once sent him some medicaments which I judged likely to prevent the ill effects of the venom. On the same afternoon I visited him, and found him in good spirits. I at first attributed the circumstance to the effect produced by the remedies I had sent, but was surprised on hearing that he had not taken them, he being of opinion that the venom of the serpent was incapable of affecting him, inasmuch as he had often been bitten by serpents without having sustained any injury. The serpent which wounded him on this occasion was a viper, which he had caught and retained in his possession, and he offered to allow himself to be bitten on the tongue, if I would consent to witness it. At that time, Dr. W. Jameson (now superintendent of the botanical garden at Saharunpore) was on a visit to Lahore, and the maharajah showed him great attention, which induced me to inform the maharajah of the offer made by the faqueer, and I requested him to relate the case to Dr. Jameson, as I felt sure he would be interested in it.

As for myself, I doubted the truth of the faqueer's assertion, and was persuaded that no European physician would believe it. Accordingly, I was directed to pressent the faqueer to the doctor, who was at that time stopping at Anarkullee. To test the experiment, I took a fowl with me. The doctor smiled, when I related to him the particulars, and, as I expected, expressed his disbelief of the faqueer's statement. However, the faqueer put his hand over the pot in which the viper was contained, and he was immediately bitten ; he afterwards held the fowl near the pot, which was also bitten ; but the doctor still appeared to think there was some deception in the matter. I took the fowl home, and placed it beneath a basket, where I found it dead on the following morning ; although the faqueer, who was bitten first, was quite well. I then took him, and also the dead fowl, with me, to present them to the maharajah ; and having given him a full account of what had been done, informed him that both the faqueer and the fowl had since been under my surveillance. At his request, the faqueer was presented to him. He was accompanied by a mezur (workman), who had just caught a viper, which the faqueer had put into the same pot in which the former had been, and presented it for the inspection of the assembly. Maharajah Sheer Sing asked him whether he would really allow himself to be bitten by venomous serpents, and whether it was true that he would not thereby sustain injury ? The faqneer answerd in the affirmative, and offered to give immediate proof of it. He uncovered the pot, and was about to present his hand, but the maharajah objected to the serpents which the faqueer had brought with him, and said that he would order some to be procured. He handed to the faqueer seven rupees, which he had just received as nazarana (present), but he immediately gave them to the mezur, saying, " That is a gift of the son of a laundress," and departed. Sheer Sing pretended not to have heard this insulting remark, although it was spoken so loud that every body noticed it ; and I felt much annoyed, having been the cause of the introduction of the insolent faqueer. I reprimanded him, and gave orders for his re-imprisonment as a lunatic. He had not yet given the maharajah a proof of his assertion, and consequently had not deserved the reward of seven rupees. The bad consequences of his unruly tongue, however, did not fail to overtake him ; I did not doubt that Sheer Sing would very soon procure the serpents which he had ordered, and therefore gave instructions to the soldiers who accompanied the faqueer to the mill, to bring him early in the morning to my abode, so that he might be at hand, in case the maharajah should send for us. The next morning the faqueer, on his way to me, met with a friend of his, who inquired where he was going, and why he was fettered ? He replied that he was bound to show to Sheer Sing his ability, and at once, as if in bravado, untied the pot which contained his two vipers, and caused himself to be bitten by one of them. Scarcely had he advanced two steps, when he staggered and fell. But he summoned all his strength, and rose again, in order to proceed, but again fell ; and not being able to rise a second time, a charpai (stretcher) was brought, to convey him from the bazaar to my house. He was followed by a multitude of curious people, and I caused him to be taken into a neighbouring stable, belonging to the faqueer Chirakooddeen, who went immediately to see the patient, as he was then vomiting blood. Chirakooddeen was of opinion that he could never recover, and the injured faqueer being a Brahmin, he wished me to send him to a termsale (an Indian temple), in order to avoid the unpleasant consequences which might attend his death ; but, on mentioning this intention to the patient, he preferred being conveyed to a friend of his, who was living at the tower called Shahburj, where he himself had previously resided; which was accordingly done. I gave him some remedies, and sent him away; but scarcely was he removed from the stable, when the payahs (armed attendants of the durbar) appeared, summoning me to present myself with the faqueer to the durbar. I stated, that he had already received the reward of his insolence, and was not expected to recover; but Sheer Sing, who was probably much annoyed at the epithet, "son of a laundress," despatched several messengers, ordering me to bring him to the durbar on his bed; and I was obliged to obey. I arrived, however, too late, for the assembly had already left the durbar, and Sheer Sing had departed from the Hazooreebagh to the interior of the fortress. On the same day, the faqueer had a swelling on his knee, and diarrhœa but he soon recovered, and afterwards proved very useful to me, when I began to make my experiments with the serpents, which produced so many curious results, that I sacrificed upwards of two hundred fowls in less than six months. At that time poultry was remarkably cheap at Lahore, the English not having yet occupied that country, and four couple could be purchased for one rupee. The faqueer really possessed the secret of preventing his blood being affected by the bites of venomous reptiles; and, having at length succeeded in obtaining his statement of it, I now present it to the public. The faqueer was an arsenic-eater, and to this reason he ascribed the cause of his remaining unaffected by any serpent's venom. Perhaps he was right, because in India arsenic is an ingredient in various compositions which are recommended as remedies against the bite of serpents. He told me, that during his stay under my control, he could not procure the poison, and that that was the reason why the viper's bite affected him, which might possibly have been the case.

On my journey from Cabul to Bokhara, I met with an Affghan physician and horse-dealer, travelling from Bokhara who, it was stated, consumed every day one drachm of arsenic, in order to maintain his appetite, which he lost in the absence of that remedy, and that he had been in the habit of using it since his earliest childhood. He was a thick-set, muscular man, of good intelligence, merry humoured, had a light complexion, and long black hair. The proverb proved true with him :—

> "Quod cibus est aliis, aliis est acre venenum."
> "One man's meat may be another's poison."

In my numerous collection of serpents, I had only three venomous species, namely :—I. The annulated serpent (Aspidoclonion); 2. The cobra di capello (Aspis Naja); 3. Vipers, of different colours and sizes. The first (Aspidoclonion) is reputed to be the most venomous. Its poison affects the throat immediately, whence the Indian name, sungchure (neck-strangler). It is stated that its bite will kill the strongest man in one hour, and that no antidote is yet known. The length of this serpent is about a yard and a half, and it is an inch and a half in diameter. Its back is of a dark-grey colour, the belly white, the head not bigger round than the body, the tail long and pointed. One span below the head, cross-stripes of a white colour commence, similar to rings, each one inch distant from the other, which run down to the end of the tail. It is stated that they live for five hundred years. They cannot easily be excited, and consequently they seldom bite. The man who brought me such a reptile, took it up with a linen rag tied round his hand, opened its mouth with a small stick, introduced the neck of a live fowl, and set them both at liberty. The serpent held the bird for a few seconds, and then released it. The poor animal seemed to be stunned; it did not appear to suffer any pain, but was unable to move, shut its eyes, and sat down. I lifted it up, and examined the bitten part on the neck. It was scarcely to be detected, and looked like the wound from a pin. After the application of some local and interior remedies, it seemed to recover a little; opening its eyes, erecting itself on its legs, and having two watery evacuations of a dark-green colour

A quarter of an hour after the bite, it sat down again, and died. All this lasted about twenty-four minutes. Should not the endermatic application of this virus be the real and true remedy against the hydrophobia? as this poison affects the neck, as well as that of enraged animals. "Extremis morbis, extrema remedia!" It deserves to be tried, if not on man, at least on animals. But many will ask, how can we procure those serpents? to which I reply, that as soon as the efficacy of this substance is proved in a satisfactory manner, it can easily be procured in sufficient quantities from the natives. The reptile can be preserved in Europe as easily as others, especially as its term of life is stated to be of such a long duration. Having found in the slough or cast skin of serpents manifold medicinal virtues, when employed in the way I use them in my system, it is possible that they would also produce a good effect endermatically (introducing them in a prepared state), acting as a substitute for the virus. That is also the case with inoculation; in want of the lymph, the crust dissolved in water, will answer the same purpose. The cobra di capello is less venomous than the annulated serpent, though its venom is stronger than that of the viper. The joghees in Hindostan earn their livelihood by exhibiting the cobra to the public. They carry them in boxes, and when the box is opened, they begin to play on a sort of bagpipe; on hearing which, the serpent erects itself, its neck swells, and it moves its head alternately to the right and left, keeping time to the music as if it were dancing, which affords much amusement to the spectators, and sometimes terror to those who do not know that their venomous fangs have been extracted. The bite of the cobra can, as well as that of the vipers, be cured, for which purpose spirit of sal ammoniac, hartshorn drops, or Eau de Luce, are excellent medicaments; but being seldom at hand when they are wanted, I advise, in all cases of bites from venomous animals, that the poison should be at once vigorously sucked from the wound, which will not be productive of any prejudicial effect on the healthy mouth or the stomach.

It is also advisable immediately to bind a ligature under the wound, until the venom is sucked entirely out. Even if the animal poison is swallowed in considerable quantity, it is quite harmless, as it becomes decomposed by the chyle. The poultry which I killed in the experiments I made, my cook, who was a Mahomedan, would certainly have prepared for the table with great repugnance, owing to their not having been Halal, *i. e.*, killed in the name of God, by letting their blood flow, but had perished whilst the blood was in them; my sweeping man, however, a Bangee of the Pariah caste, eat them with avidity, and grew corpulent upon the fare.

The following case may prove that all large serpents are not dangerous, but on the contrary, sometimes even useful. One day my domestics caught a large one in the surdekhana or teikhana (cellar), which they had killed and thrown it into the street. When I observed its extended stomach, I was desirous of knowing the contents, and having caused it to be opened, we found a rat, which had been swallowed by the serpent whole, and my domestics regretted having destroyed such a brave rat-catcher.

Speaking of serpents, I may mention here a particular disease, which they designate at Lahore, Mar-ashekh (serpent-love), and which, according to their statement, occurs only in the Punjab. I never heard of it in any other place; and I mention it, hoping that the English physicians, particularly those now living in that country, will take the trouble to investigate the subject, and ascertain whether this disease is peculiar to the Punjab, and why it occurs only between the Indus and the Sutlej.

Should the investigation of this curious disease lead to a satisfactory result, and should any one be successful in capturing a real musk-deer in the Punjab, I should be much gratified, and science would be enriched.

The faqueer Noor-oo-Deen, at Lahore, who at present enjoys great respect from the English, for his extended knowledge and eminent merits, was the first who directed my attention to the disease I have mentioned, a short time

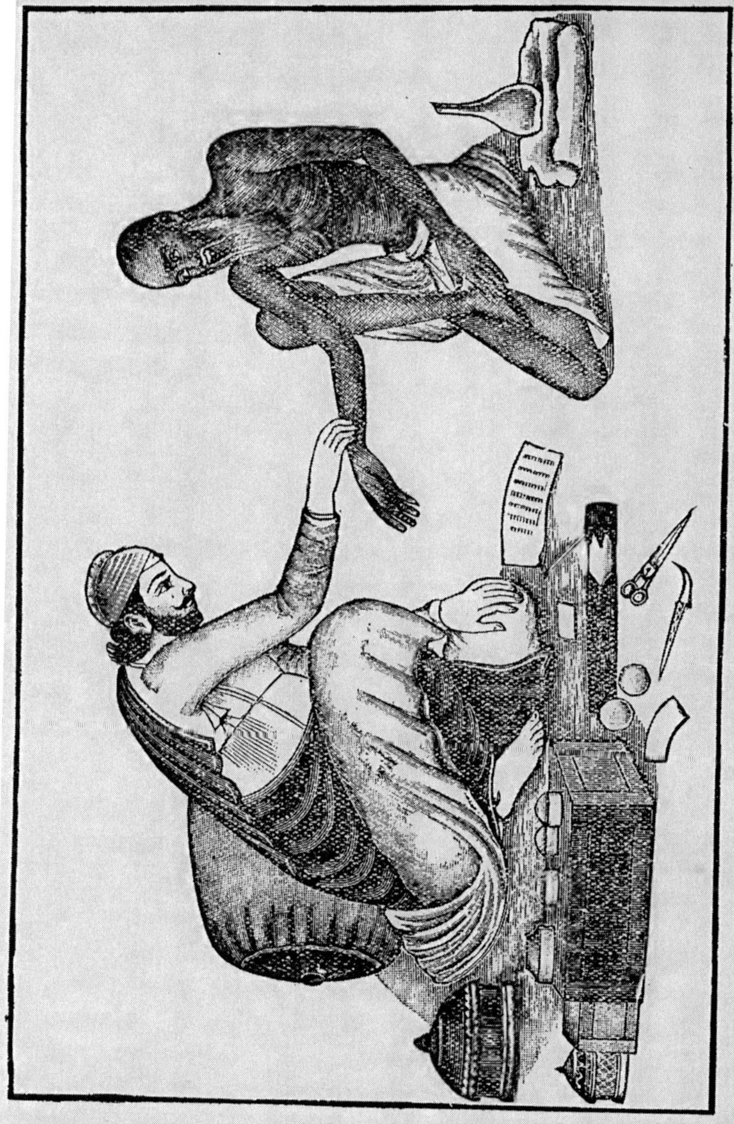

HAKIM

before my first departure from Lahore in the year 1832, and who introduced to me at that time a patient afflicted with it. It was a laundry man, of the age of sixty, although he appeared nearer eighty. He allowed himself to be bitten every month by serpents. He was of short stature, and of a cachectical appearance ; his perspiration, which I perceived at some distance, was peculiarly offensive, and was similar to that of serpents. He told me he had been troubled with that malady upwards of thirty years : that at the commencement he permitted himself to be bitten once a year, afterwards twice, but at that time, once in every month, and that the serpents followed him even into the water. He stated that only four days previously he had been bitten on the upper part of his hand, on which I could perceive a *cicatrix*, and he showed me numerous scars on his hands and feet, so that I could not doubt the truth of his statement. He added, that he had often sucked the venom or poison from the wounds of bitten people. I am of opinion that he, in sucking the poison from others (unless it is neutralized by his saliva) extracts or diminishes it ; but, in their own cases, a similar virus being existent in their system, every time they are bitten the fresh virus neutralizes temporarily the other. *Query*—May not such persons be able to neutralize even hydrophobiac poison ?

The before-mentioned learned faqueer and his four adult sons, as also other native hakims, may give a full explanation of the above case, and procure for the English physicians some such patient, so that they may be able to satisfy themselves of the fact, and investigate the matter. I have seen at least a dozen of them at Lahore, who were all males ; and I am told that the number of such patients in the Punjab is very large. The nature of the disease is, that the patients, at certain periods, have an irresistible inclination to be bitten by serpents ; which they say does them a great deal of good, as for a few days previously they are troubled with fainting and dizziness, nausea, want of appetite, disinclination to work, and heaviness in the limbs. These are the symptoms of the disease in question ;

and at these times the serpents are attracted towards them by the scent, and the patients, looking upon them as their welcome benefactors, willingly stretch out their hand or foot, when the reptile is advancing towards them ; after the serpent has bitten them it retires, and the patient then feels relieved. The greater part of such patients are, once a year, viz., in July or August, visited, wherever they may be, by their reptile friends. I met with only a small number who required to be bitten twice a-year ; and with only one indeed who wanted to be bitten monthly. What I have related is certainly a singular fact, and highly interesting to naturalists. But how is it that this disease is peculiar to the Punjab ? The natives assert, that the bite (when it is with young) of the *Amphisbœna* (erroneously called *Dumuha*, two-mouthed sepent), which is generally believed not to be venomous, is the cause of the disease, and that the virus at certain periods ferments in the human frame. This species of serpent being indigenous in America, it is worth inquiry, whether the disease is not also to be found in that part of the world ? A patient thus afflicted told me, on one occasion, that he was advised as a curative process, to seize the serpent at the moment it approached him, and having previously wrapped a cloth round its head, to bite it off. By neglecting to envelope the serpent's head, he was told that he would lose two of his front teeth.

Some hakims at Lahore recommended as a remedy, the fruit of Crataeva Tapia, mixed with oil, which is used externally as an ointment.

After this digression about serpents, the relation of which may have been of some interest, it will probably not appear superfluous, if I explain the meaning of the expression used by the faqueer who performed the experiments with the vipers, in calling the maharajah, the " son of a laundress."

One of the wives of Runjeet Sing gave birth to a girl, at Vetalah, and in those countries the birth of a female child is not considered as a happy or fortunate event.

By chance a laundress in the neighbourhood brought forth at the same time, a strong boy. The ranee having been apprised of this, and wishing to have a male child at any price, arranged with the laundress to exchange the new-born infants. But nothing beneath the sun can remain concealed, says the proverb ; Runjeet Sing became acquainted with the fact ; but he showed no displeasure at the bargain, and adopted the child as his son. He gave him an excellent education ; and the abilities of the adopted son soon developed themselves, and caused the maharajah to entertain great regard for him, and he was treated with equal respect to the royal prince ; as for instance, he ordered both to be presented with chairs (an honour paid only to the highest rank), whilst the ministers and sirdars were obliged to occupy inferior seats. Ultimately, with the assistance of the minister Dhyan Sing, and that of the troops, after three days' hard struggle, he ascended the throne. Like Runjeet Sing, he was a friend to all Europeans, especially to his neighbours the English, to whom he gave support after the catastrophe at Cabul. The murdered royal prince, No-Nehal Sing, might not have acted in the same manner, and the English may regard his death as a fortunate event. Having thus given a brief account of the political events, &c., of the country in which I spent so considerable a part of my life, I will now present to the reader a more ample detail of the *medium* system to which I alluded in my preface, and also a full account of the incidents which prompted me to adopt that system, feeling persuaded it will prove an interesting subject.

My readers are aware that besides the Allœopathia which I practised for many years, I also tried the Homœopathic method, and my own experience, as well as that of others, brought me to the conclusion that a rational physician may derive successful results from both systems. Nevertheless, I found that the *enormous* doses generally administered by the Allœopaths, and also the *infinitesimal* ones used by the Homœopaths, were both of them far less beneficial than they should be. This observation induced me to investigate the matter with much earnestness ; and in the extensive practice which I had at Lahore, I was induced to adopt the medium between those two extremes. I know well, that in politics the system of *juste milieu* does not enjoy a great degree of credit, especially since Louis Philippe has lost by it the throne of France ; but that which is incongruous and inconsistent in politics, may be otherwise in the empire of science ; and the numerous successful results which I have found this medium system to have effected, have tended most strongly to confirm that opinion. To support my assertion, I may cite the two well-known words of the Greek—*Mydev ayav*—*Ne quid nimis*—" Too much is as bad as too little," as they say in England.

Soon after the death of Runjeet Sing, in the year 1840, I began to experiment upon this new principle ; and five years afterwards, the epidemic cholera raged at Lahore. It proceeded slowly from middle Asia, or Turkistan, through Cabul and Peshawur, as we learned from the "Delhi Gazette", in which it was stated that the epidemic was taking a direction towards the East Indies. I thus had sufficient warning, previously to its arrival at Lahore, to prepare myself for its reception. It was a dreadful spectacle, to witness the fury with which it swept away its victims. At its first appearance, the Hindoos and Sikhs conveyed the bodies of the deceased through the gate called Tunksallee-Derwazeh, because of its being near to the river Ravee, on the banks of which they were accustomed either to burn the corpses or throw them into the river ; but owing to the progress of the cholera, the number of funerals became so great that the passages of the bazaars were interrupted, and the government was obliged to issue an order that the dead should be carried through other gates also ; and thus the Sikhs and Hindoos were, like the Musselmen, carried through the respective twelve gates of the city. When the epidemic had reached its height, there were upwards of eight hundred deaths daily, out of a population of about 70,000. During that fatal period I had the opportunity of making a large number of experiments ; but the six weeks during which the disease raged passed rapidly away ; and, but for the horrible suffering which its longer duration would have entailed upon its victims, I could almost have wished, for the interest of mankind, that my opportunities of observation had been still further extended, in order to enable me to arrive at results which might have been more prolific of benefit to suffering humanity. For instance, I began, during the decrease of the cholera, namely, during the last three weeks, to try the effect of galvano-electric rings as a preventative. I caused a few hundreds to be made, some of copper and zinc, and others of silver and zinc, which I distributed gratis, and observed, that whilst some of those who wore the rings of copper and zinc fell victims to the disease, those who were the silver and zinc rings were all saved. It is true, that some of the latter became infected with the disease, but the attacks were of so slight a nature that, in my opinion, they would have recovered without any medical assistance. But I must repeat, that this was only at the time when the disease was already on the decline; and since that period, I have had no other opportunity of making further observations in that country ; consequently, I cannot assert that this preventative is infallible. However, to ascertain still further the value of these rings for the purpose indicated, I ordered some hundreds of them to be made during my stay at Vienna, in the autumn of 1850, at the period when that Asiatic guest took up its residence in that capital. I presented them gratuitously to many persons, and I have not heard of a single fatal attack attending the wearers. Many medical men and others expressed their opinions upon the subject, and thought the idea a ridiculous one ; but the future will show whether I am mistaken or otherwise. Some of the wearers of these rings at Lahore stated that they diffused warmth in the finger on which they were worn, in fact I observed a sort of rash to break out on the part on which they wore the rings, and they were obliged to discontinue wearing them for a few days, or place them on the other hand. One ring is quite sufficient for one person, although the wearing of several would do no harm. Bracelets, buckles, and chains produce still greater effects, and I am of opinion that such rings, &c., are not only useful during the cholera, but are beneficial in many other respects. I have myself enjoyed the best of health during the last six years, which I attribute in a great measure to the wearing of a ring of this description. I must observe that those who make use of such galvano-electric rings, ought not to be anxious when experiencing any slight indisposition, and should avoid resorting at once to strong remedies, lest the ill effects of those remedies should be attributed to the ring, and thus destroy the confidence of the wearer, and lead to a false conclusion. While advising persons to wear such rings, it is not, however, to be considered that they are talismans or amulets; their virtues are of another character, which I will endeavour to explain. We know well what mighty influence the electric and magnetic fluid exercises on the material world, and that it produces many of those wonderful phenomena, which the wisdom of antiquity was unable to explain; but our modern naturalists have succeeded, if not in absolutely discovering the hitherto hidden secrets of nature, at least in lifting a portion of the veil which conceals them. There is no doubt that an electro-magnetic fluid is diffused through our most subtile nerves, its source or battery is the brain, and it is probable that the wise Creator, for that reason, has there united all the organs of sensation. Through the continual mild and slight stimulation which these rings produce upon the nervous system, in consequence of their affinity with the electric fluid existing in the body, we may believe them to operate in a manner analogus to lightning conductors, and thus to maintain the functions of the nerves in their normal state. I refer the reader, as regards the construction of these rings, to the illustrations of those which I distributed at Lahore and Vienna, as given in the second volume of this work.

In the last year of my sojourn at Lahore, 1849, I observed, in the English medical journals, a description of a galvano-electric apparatus, consisting of one zinc and one silver plate, united by a silver wire, and the statement of its effects, especially upon ulcers and similar cases. This induced me to make some experiments in cases of this description, in which I succeeded ; especially at the prisoners' hospital, where two brothers had on their feet two cancerous ulcers, which were completely eradicated, the one in four, and the other in six weeks. At the same period, it happened that several cases of sporadic cholera occurred ; and, having ascertained the before-mentioned apparatus to be efficacious, and persoaded, as I was, of the benefit of my rings, which are composed of the same materials—silver and zinc—I determined to make an experiment with the apparatus upon these cholera cases, which proved to be of the greatest utility. It was quite natural that when I imagined I had solved that enigmatical question—the positive method of curing cholera—I should endeavour to put my method in practice during the raging of that epidemic in Vienna ; and I accordingly made application to the Minister of the Interior, soliciting him to allow me to attend some of the cholera-patients at the hospital. The Minister consented ; but the interval between my soliciting and obtaining the permission was so long, that the real type of the disease no longer existed : the cases were mere malignant cholera-typhus. Scarcely one of those I saw at the hospital recovered. I only attended three patients. The first removed the apparatus from her body, without any one being cognisant of the fact, and died on the following day ; the second was brought to the hospital in a senseless, dying condition, so that I thought it unnecessary to apply the plates ; and the third patient continued to exist until the eleventh day. As the cholera-patients, however, with or without appetite, were compelled to subsist on meat soups containing parsley, celery, onions, &c. ; and the medicines which were administered were prepared by their own apothecary ; and as the disease was on the decline ; I discontinued my attendance, without arriving at any definite conclusion.

At Lahore, I performed some operations while the patients were under the influence of chloroform ; and among these were two boys who were troubled with stone in the bladder. Both were operated on with the apparatus altus, with the assistance of Dr. Hathway, the surgeon to the Residency. But the operation on one of them, the most healthy-looking lad, terminated fatally, which may be attributed to the stone being attached to the mucous membrane of the bladder, The mother of this boy gave him secretly, shortly after the operation, a quantity of butter with sugar, believing it would strengthen the patient. The boy began to vomit in a violent manner, felt oppressed, and started from his sleep; and this may possibly have accelerated his death. The other boy recovered. A year previously, assisted by Dr. A. Hening, I operated on a boy labouring under the same disease; the operation was effected after he had inhaled the vapour of ether, and he remained drowsy for three days. The cure, however, was speedily effected, although two large stones had to be extracted from the neck of the bladder, which were with great difficulty withdrawn. My colleague began to doubt, whilst I was operating, whether any stone at all existed. But instead of one, there were, as I have already mentioned, two large ones.

As regards these anæsthetic agents, I prefer the inhaling of ether to the application of chloroform, although I must confess, that much depends on its being properly prepared and skilfully administered. Dr. Hathway performed, in my presence, many successful operations with chloroform. We procured ours from Kanpore. I also performed, assisted by Dr. Hathway, two amputations at the gaol hospital, whilst the patients were under the influence of ether, without either of them uttering a word; nevertheless, I adhere to the opinion of those who assert that the tenth part of chloroform mixed with ether makes a preferable composition.

At Lahore I made the acquaintance of a native Mahomedan stone-operator, who, like the other native surgeons of the east, extract the stone through the perineum, according to the old method of Celsus. Two fingers of the left hand are oiled, and introduced as far as possible into the rectum, whilst the operator presses with his right hand somewhat

JERAH

above the navel downwards. Thus the stone is felt with the finger in the rectum, when it is drawn down and cut out of the bladder through the middle flesh. But if they are not able to bring it down, which is often the case with adults, they are compelled to leave it, being ignorant of the use of European surgical instruments, or the lateral operation. They cure the wounds *per primam intentionem* ; fatal cases seldom occur, but a fistula frequently ensues. There are also native oculists at Lahore, who are Musselmen. They sit in the streets, operating with rude instruments ; but in spite of their theoretical knowledge, which cannot be deniedr, they blind more patients than they cure. They contract they depress by means of two instruments, a lancet and an awl.

The three jerahs (native surgeons), also Mahomedans, whom the durbar appointed to be my assistants at the hospitals, did not possess much skill, and besides their ointment boxes they had only some razors, lancets, pincers for drawing teeth, and cupping-apparatus. Of operations with other instruments they had no conception. They did not even know how to bind an artery, and amputation was a process of which they had never heard. My operations for the extraction of the stone seemed to them a miracle ; they soon, however, became proficient in the operations of tapping and vaccination, for both of which they had a strong inclination.

In the Punjab, the inhabitants practise a sort of animal-magnetism, which they call *jara*, or *manter*. It is employed for inflammatory, rheumatic and nervous pains, especially in the eyes, ears, teeth, &c. The operator, a man or woman, places himself opposite the patient, holding a green branch or a small stick in his hand ; with this he drives, according to his assertion, the evil spirit from the affected parts, by striking the patient's body occasionally with his instrument, in a downward direction. With that he mixes a little hocus-pocus, by murmuring odd-sounding words, and at intervals blowing upon the affected parts.

The pulse is considered of very great importance in the east ; and they believe the doctors are able to investigate by it the most latent diseases. Uroscopy is also in credit among the natives. Sometimes I could not forbear laughing, when at consultations with the hakims ; but I thought that when among wolves one must howl also. On one occasion, we deliberated about curing a chronic gonorrhœa, on which occasion a hakim proposed the local balneum cucurbitae citrulli : a water-melon was proposed to be procured and opened, the contents of it to be crushed, and the membrum virile una cum scroto introduced. Another, boasting of his ability, brought a still better remedy on the carpet,recomending it as a *probatum est.* This highly praised remedy consisted in roasting a sugar-melon, wrapped in dough, and while lukewarm making a hole therein per quod foramen penis erectus inserendus et semen virile injiciendum esset. Risum teneatis amici !—But we did not employ either, a hakim of Peshawur prescribing pills of camphor, convolvolus argenteus, opium, pyrethrum and zedoaria ; these, together with some injections of solution of sulphates of zinc and copper which I administered, produced the desired result, and the patient was cured within a month.

These consultations were generally held in the presence of the patient, so that he might choose whichever remedy he preferred. In the assembly of the hakims, the Persian language was spoken, and the technical terms used were Arabic, which no patient could understand ; but if there were present any Hindoo physicians or pundits (astrolgers), which was always the case when consultations were held at respectable houses, then the Indian language was spoken, because generally the Indians are not versed in the Persian.

Alms are given on every occasion of illness, but mostly at the time when the patient's last hour seems to be near ; and consequently large numbers of poor faqueers and Brahmins assemble on these occasions at the entrance to the houses, especially of those inhabited by wealthy people.

Chronic diseases are temporarily treated with a composition of myrobalons ; and in the following spring china-root decoctions are employed. This is their last resource ; which corresponds with the "change of air" recommended by our

ATTAR

European physicians, that being the panacea invariably resorted to by the latter, when they are at a loss what to do with their patients.

I have already mentioned the asylum for lunatics which I established at Lahore, and will now inform the reader of the origin of that establishment.

Major Mac Gregor, the director of the police at Lahore, on passsing the bazaar on horseback, was one day stopped by a woman, who was believed to be insane. On account of this accident, the Resident issued an order that the durbar should establish an asylum for such persons. I was consulted upon the subject, and it was resolved that such patients should be received into my hospital. Accordingly, many lunatics were brought there, and they were generally followed by a great many curious spectators. I succeeded in curing, in the course of two months, the first five individuals under my superintendence, which fact I communicated to the Rajah Teja Sing, and he ordered me to present them to the assembly at the Residency of Anarkullee: which I did. But they manifested no desire to see them, and looked upon the matter with indifference, by which I began to perceive that my stay at Lahore was near its end, and that the best thing I could do was to return to Europe. Neither did I think it necessary to wait for the arrival of my assistants, whom I had, with the permission of the government, requested to come over; namely, an apothecary and a surgeon, from Europe. Both of these gentlemen had received from me 3,000 florins for the expenses of their journey, and I intended also to pay their salaries from my own private purse; for as my health was on the decline, in consequence of the many affairs to which I had to attend, I was really longing for some relief.

The indifference shown to me, however, in the Residency, did not prevent me from presenting the restored lunatics to the native durbar at the fortress, and I was ordered to send them to their respective homes. The woman who stopped the police director at the bazaar I presented to Major Mac Gregor when he was in the Kotchery (office). They had committed her to me in a most miserable state, nearly naked, and fettered like a wild beast; now she was dressed in a white gown, and looking quite genteel. Without having been invited to sit down, she took her seat modestly between the Sherishtedars, or clerks, and behaved with great decorum. The people looked first at one another, and then at the woman, as if, though conscious of her identity, they could scarcely credit the evidence of their own senses. Even Major Mac Gregor was astonished, and asked me what I had done to make her behave so well? My answer was, "by cleanliness, some physic, douche-baths, decent dress, good food, amusements, occupation, presents, promises, &c., &c.; all this, connected with good treatment, scarcely ever fails to bring back such poor creatures to a state of reason. I never beat them, never ill-treat them, but I prevent them from doing any mischief to others or to themselves." This reply highly pleased the Major. The woman in question was about forty years of age, and when she was committed to my care, she was so furious that every one feared her. She was jumping about, beating all whom she met, and would have flung stones and other projectiles at any one near her, if she had not been prevented; but her fury soon subsided, she became as quiet as she had formerly been boisterous, and was scarcely able to walk. On an examination, I found her suffering from the syphilitic disease. I asked her how long she had had that disorder; she answered, a long time. Probably she had a *lues occulta*, which might have been the cause of her mental complaint, only when the *lues* broke out again she got rid of the disorder. I regret having neglected that opportunity of trying what effect syphilitic inoculation might have produced. This woman gave me a curious relation of what had occurred to her, and which she stated to have been the primitive cause of her madness. She told me that she had sometime since spent all she was worth on the occasion of the marriage of her only son, but no sooner had the bride arrived than she discovered her to be an hermaphrodite. She made her complaint to the kardar (magistrate) of the village without obtaining any satisfaction, because the judge inclined to that side where the money was in greater abundance. This fact induced her to go to Lahore and apply to the English for redress. On this occasion she lost her reason. Nevertheless, she stopped the right person at the bazaar—the director of police, he having probably been pointed out to her as the superior judge, to whom she should apply. At Lahore, I had the opportunity of seeing several hermaphrodites, who enjoyed the privilege of being admitted at all births and nuptial festivals, to congratulate the parties and get presents, this being, in fact, their sole means of subsistence. The birth solemnities, however, only take place when the child is of the male sex, never, on any occasion, at the birth of a female. They go so far in this matter as to conceal the latter event ; and the greatest part of the inhabitants of the Punjab, whether Musselmen, Sikhs, or Hindoos, are all quite happy when a new-born female departs this life. They would consider it an insult, should any one congratulate the parents on the birth of a female. I am sorry to have to relate a fact which is so very uncomplimentary to the ladies, but the first duty of an historian is to tell the truth. If the fair sex in Europe are desirous of knowing why such little regard is paid to their charms, they need only ask the first Hindoo they may meet with, and he will give them the ungallant answer, that a son brings money into the house, whilst a daughter carries it away.

One of the before-mentioned lunatics, whom I cured, was a brother-in-law of the Maharajah Runjeet Sing, namely, Mirza, brother of the famous Goolbegum. He was fond of smoking churrus, and used to quarrel, when intoxicated, with his brother and sister (Nobab and Goolbegum), about the estates which Runjeet Sing gave them. He again became insane, and they committed him once more to my care, where he remained until he promised them in writing never thenceforth to smoke churrus, or quarrel with them. On account of this, Goolbegum took him to her abode in the fortress, so that he might be properly watched. I met him there several months afterwards in perfect health.

Having mentioned the habit of smoking churrus, I will make the reader acquainted with some other intoxicating materials that are used by the natives. An agreeable intoxicating beverage is prepared by the inhabitants of the Punjab from the hemp plant. It is especially indulged in by the Nahungs, faqueers, and the poorer classes, as they are unable to procure more expensive spirits. Those who abstain from opium and poppy-heads, also make use of a draught of this hemp liquor; for it is notorious, that those who are addicted to opium must daily get their accustomed draught, otherwise they suffer pain in all their limbs. This, however, does not occur in using the hemp plant, as they can abstain from it without any unpleasant effects; and in my opinion it is the least prejudicial of all the intoxicating beverages generally used. The longing for this drink, especially among the lower classes of the population, induced the late government at Lahore to devote a certain sum for its preparation and distribution. Not far from the outside of the Delhi gate, near the road to Umritsir, close by my hospital, there was an establishment called Seid Gunge, where this beverage was delivered gratuitously. As might be expected, the Nahungs flocked there in hordes, and this munificence was greatly abused. I made several trials on myself, my friends, and my domestics, to ascertain its effects; and I found that inebriation commenced about half-an-hour after taking it, and lasted about three hours, upon which a sound sleep ensued. Those who have partaken of it, feel no ill effects on the following day; there is none of that headache, giddiness, or nausea, &c., which generally follows inebriation from wine or spirits. The intoxication is accompanied by a good appetite, and the imbibers become excessively jovial; laughing, joking, and talking, often without control. Even if the stomach is surfeited, no ill effect is experienced; the digestion is not thereby impaired, and no costiveness is to be feared. In the Bengal Dispensatory, p. 584, it is stated that the composition of *cannabis indica*, called majoon, is most fascinating in its effects, producing extatic happiness, a persuasion of high rank, a sensation

Page 158

BHANGEE

CHURSEE BHISTEE

FAQUEER POSTEE

x

of flying, voracious appetite, and intense aphrodisiac desire. In the same Dispensatory, p. 594, it is mentioned that in several cases of acute and chronic rheumatism, half-grain doses of the resin were given, producing unequivocal aphrodisia, and great mental cheerfulness ; alleviation of pain in most instances, and remarkable increase of appetite in all.

Disorders of the mind, occasioned by continual inebriation from the hemp plant, have been cured by blisters placed on the nape, leeches on the temples, and exciting nausea by very small doses of tartar emetic or salt purgatives. The preparation of the hemp plant beverage is as follows :—Any quantity of the dried hemp plant is washed in a vessel with cold water, to cleanse it from the seeds, stalks, earth, and other impurities ; it is afterwards pressed, dried in the sun, and kept for use. A portion of this clean dried hemp herb, mixed with a few kernels of pepper, is put into a saucer, and crushed with a wooden rubber, pouring thereon occasionally a little water ; when it is completely crushed, and becomes a pap, more water is then gradually added ; it is then filtered through a piece of coarse linen, that the fine particles of the herb may flow equally through, and the liquor must be drunk before it makes any sediment, the effect being principally produced by the resinous particles of the herb, which are not very soluble in water. For beginners, one or two scruples of the dried plant will produce intoxication ; those who are confirmed in the habit can take from two to four drachms, and a few inveterate drinkers can take even an ounce. If the hemp herb is mixed with almonds, melon or pumpkin seeds, sugar, spirits, &c., or if milk is used instead of water in its preparation, the beverage is of course more agreeable.

Majoon is an aromatic confection of *cannabis indica*, and is used in Turkey, Arabia, Persia, India, and Egypt. Some people adulterate the majoon with the seeds of *datura stramonii*, which increases the intoxicating effect. Sometimes, instead of using the hemp plant beverage, they use a butter containing the effective parts of the plant. In the preparation of this, they take equal parts of cleansed hemp herb and of butter, to which is added some water, and they are boiled together until the water becomes entirely absorbed. Whilst warm, it is pressed through a loosely woven linen, into a vessel filled with cold water; and this butter, which is of a green colour, may be washed again, either with pure water or rose-water. They sometimes boil a certain quantity of cleaned hemp herb in half water and half milk, till half of it is evaporated; it is then strained and curdled. The butter is afterwards, in the usual manner, separated from the coagulation, and contains the effective (*i. e.*, the resinous) part of the herb. Five to ten grains of this composition is a sufficient dose. It can be flavoured with spices, such as pepper, cinnamon, saffron, ginger, &c., and sweetened with sugar; and by means of isinglass or gum tragacanth, it can also be converted into lozenges, which I used as *bon-bons* at Lahore. It is true, I could administer them only to Musselmen; the Sikhs and Hindoos being unwilling to take any medicines prepared with liquids by European hands, but invariably obtaining them from us in a dry state, mixing them in their own vessels, and using water procured by themselves. This difficulty, however, was afterwards removed, when the hospital was established; for as patients of every nation met with a liberal reception, the Sikh government, aware of the religious restrictions in that country, appointed a certain number of Hindoo attendants by whom the remedies were prepared, and took care also to provide me with some water from the river Ganges for the preparation of the medicines. The intoxicating drug called *churrus*, used for smoking, is prepared as follows:— the fresh and ripe hemp plant is held over a mild fire to soften it, and afterwards bruised in a mortar till it becomes a compact mass. Another very curious method of obtaining it is, by persons wearing leather breeches passing through the hemp-fields, so that they come in contact with the hemp plant, by which a quantity of the resinous substance attaches itself to the leather garments and other parts of the body, which they afterwards scrape off and collect. But the best way is to gather the resinous parts by rubbing the plant in

KAR-KHANA ABKAREE

its growing state with the hands. In the bazaars of India, the different sorts of churrus are sold under various names, as Bokharian, Jarkandian and Cashmerian ; but the best is called churrus mumiai, *i. e.*, wax-like churrus.

Churrus is never used as an interior remedy. I have made different trials with it, and refer for a further description of its qualities to the second volume of this work.

The general use of churrus consists in mixing it with tobacco, and smoking it in the hooka (water pipe), and the natives sometimes place themselves in a circle around the hooka, each taking a few inhalations, and then passing the tube to another. The inebriating power of churrus manifests itself immediately, but also ceases very speedily. Its immoderate use frequently produces mental derangement.

The Sikhs are forbidden smoking tobacco, and consequently from smoking churrus also, inasmuch as it is always mixed with tobacco. As a compensation for this deprivation they are permitted to use opium and spirituous liquors to any extent, whence the great number of opium-eaters among those people, both males and females, in all classes of society.

The cannabis indica, has a similar appearance to our cannabis sativa, but they are very different in their properties, and it is remarkable that the former loses its effective virtue when transmitted to Europe. It is asserted that even the resinous extract which was prepared at Calcutta, was less energetic at London than in India. If that be the case, I ascribe the circumstance to the difference of the climate, or its conveyance over the sea, having myself experienced that several medicaments, which I had brought with me from those countries, lost their virtue during my six months' voyage down the Ganges and across the ocean. It has yet to be ascertained whether our cannabis sativa would be of the same effective nature in India as in Europe. The apparent difference between those two plants consists only in the size of their seeds, those of the cannabis indica being smaller than those of the European plant.

Opium, as I have already mentioned, is also extensively

used in India, and is still more detrimental than the other intoxicating drugs whose preparation and use I have been describing ; ample particulars respecting the effects produced by it will be found in the second volume. The abuse which the inhabitants of India make of this poisonous drug is freqeuntly carried to such an extent that all medical assistance proves vain and futile. As an example, I will mention the case of a lady who poisoned herself by the excessive use of this drug, a short time previously to the annexation of the Punjab. This lady took poppy juice mixed with oil, which is the usual method adopted when they wish to baffle medical assistance. Her motive for committing suicide, was jealousy, her husband having another wife, whom she believed to enjoy the love of her consort in a higher degree than herself. The magistrate, on hearing of the circumstance, requested me to attend her. An hour had passed since she had taken the opium, and I found her in the full possession of her senses, which she retained up to her last moment. She was sitting on her bed, and related to me calmly what she had done. In order to lose no time, I began to administer some remedies, and ordered her to be conveyed to my hospital. But she was past all remedy, and after having been for twenty-four hours in a sitting posture she fell back dead, as if struck by apoplexy ; she had previously complained of feeling severe pains in her limbs, and requested her son to pinch them continually.

Those who desire to abstain from the habit of taking opium, or drinking the cold infusion of poppy-heads, are recommended to take a large quince, and having cut away a portion, and made a cavity in the centre, to weigh it, and then to put in the tenth part of its weight of opium ; the opening is then to be filled up with the piece of quince ; and, enclosed in a paste, it is placed amidst hot embers, and left until the paste has become charred. The quince is then to be taken out, cleaned from its burnt coat, and the remains of the opium thrown away, the effective part of it having been absorbed by the quince. Of this preparation they should take daily the same quantity as they had been accustomed to take of opium. At Bokhara I saw a hakim of Kashgar, who acquired some reputation for his skill in curing opium-eating, which he performed in the course of three days. On the first day, he gave one drachm of a powder, probably *smilax china*, mixed with water ; on the second, he ordered four other smaller powders, (probably cortex radicis daturœ stramonii, with sugar) to be taken at intervals of three hours, each of them weighing 10 grains, which produced a stupor. On the third day, he gave a drastic purgative, the principal ingredients of which was semen crotonis tiglii, after which he gave them a decoction of liquorice root *ad libitum*. On this critical day the patient was allowed no food, and during the three days of that treatment he was carefully watched, lest he should taste brandy or other intoxicating beverages, which would produce injurious consequences to the patient. On the fourth day the patient was set free, and felt no desire to take either spirits or opium, the effect of the cure having been to produce an aversion to them. In Europe also, spirit drinkers are weaned from their bad habits by mixing some spirits with all their provisions, which has the effect of disgusting them with the flavour. In a Persian book, the following remedy for the above-mentioned abuses is recommended, and which professes to have the advantage of effecting the cure in one day ; namely, the before-mentioned bark of the thorn-apple root, mixed with water ; this is administered until it produces intoxication almost to madness ; when the patient is in that state, his body is to be rubbed with warm oil, and continued till he falls asleep. In that state he remains generally nine hours. On his awaking he appears like a drunken man, but on continuing to rub the body with oil for about two hours after his awaking, he becomes perfectly cured. His first drink must be milk and water. It is said that the decoction of China-root is efficacious in preventing the pain in the muscles which is experienced after abstaining from opium, and in curing those which owe their origin to the immoderate use of it. It would, perhaps, be worth while to try the effect of rubbing the body with warm oil, either with or without the administration of the bark of the thorn-apple, or China-root, &c., in cases of intoxication, or poisoning by opium. The following experiment by Magendie proves that narcotin may produce different effects, according to the different combinations in which it is administered. One grain of narcotin, dissolved in olive oil, killed a dog in twenty-four hours, but 24 grains, dissolved in acetic acid, were administered to another without any prejudicial effect. In its natural state it is still less energetic, and 129 grains did not do the least harm. From these experiments, it may be conceived how easily medical skill may be baffled by the combination of the drug with oil, as in the case of the lady whose suicide I have already mentioned. I cited a receipt of a Kashgar physician, and another taken from a Persian book, and I could cite a still greater number of similar receipts, which however, are all possessed of some peculiarity or oddity. It is true, that we cannot deny the utility of some, but most of them are of such a nature, that it is scarcely conceivable how the human brain could invent such ridiculous imaginations. The following may serve as an example of Persian wisdom, and I mention it for the benefit of our accoucheurs, who may make use of it if they choose. It is nothing less than a method of replacing an abortion of two months, and of carrying it to maturity. For that purpose they say, the embryo must be wrapped in some raw yellow silk, bestrewed with sugar and *semen sisymbrii irionis*, and then swallowed by a wife or girl, which will produce the desired result. It is quite indifferent whether it is swallowed by the mother or any other female, only that when a girl is to undergo this operation she must be of the age of puberty. When the child is born, it will come forth with the silk on its feet! I hope the reader will feel much edified at the recital of this new revelation of medical science; but we must remember that this outrageous operation is described in a dingy manuscript of very ancient date. But what shall we say when, in the year of grace

1850, in the most civilised part of Europe, viz., in the city of Weimar, in Germany, there was a work published which surpasses in its absurdities all the oriental manuscripts with which we are acquainted. The book in question was probably written for the mere purpose of making money, and bears as its title, "The Wonders of Sympathy and Magnetism, &c., by Gerstenbergk."

In India, where the palm, *cocos nucifera*, grows, the bakers use the juice of it, which is called toddy, to leaven the dough. At Lahore, where toddy cannot be procured, they employ in place of it a mixture of different spices; and, as the ladies at Lahore would probably like to know what spices they are daily eating in their bread and pastry, I therefore take the liberty of giving them the recipe of my Hindostanee baker. It is true the mixture is composed only of innocent drugs, which are taken in such minute quantities that they can never injure health, and that most of them evaporate during baking. The recipe runs thus:—Musk, nutmegs, cloves, mace, cinnamon, saffron, cardamum seeds (lesser), ginger, fennel seeds, root of the betel plant, bind-weed (convolvulus argent.), mild inderjuo seeds, shell of the cuttlefish, sugar of bamboo, gum-tragacanth, mastic, and liquorice-root ; of each, one scruple. Some people take also the kernel of the cotton-seed, or the flowers of euryale ferox (a water plant). These different materials are pounded and mixed together, and kept in a small box. When required for use, a small portion is mixed with pollard, or wheaten flour, and made into a paste with sour milk, in the proportion of one scruple of spices to three ounces of the meal. The paste is then enclosed in a cloth, and in summer the leaven is ready for use on the next day, but in winter not till the third day. To this they add three pounds of flour, and, with water, in which a little salt is dissolved, make it into a hard dough, which they knead on a board for half an hour, and then put some sugar into it. Instead of the latter, I used some sweet potatoes (convolvulus batatas), when they were in season, boiling, peeling, crushing, and mixing them with the dough.

These potatoes communicate to the bread an excellent flavour, and keep it for a longer time soft and elastic. The bread is made in loaves of about the third of a pound in weight, and is put to leaven on the leaves of *butea frondosa*, and afterwards baked. How strange a mixture to replace the toddy, and the office of which is performed in our own country by simple yeast.

In Ainsli's *Materia Indica*, we read :—" Toddy is a sweet, aperient, most delicious drink. Taken fresh from the tree, early in the morning, before the sun is up, it is certainly a luscious and most pleasant beverage, cooling, refreshing, and nourishing ; it is besides employed for making the best kind of Indian arrack, and yields a great deal of sugar. Europeans, especially delicate females, in India, who are apt to suffer much from constipation, find a cupful of this toddy, drank every morning at five o'clock, one of the simplest and best remedies they can employ."

It may, perhaps, be of some interest to my readers to cite here a passage from a scientific work, unknown to the greater part of the public, which may serve as a comment on the above subject. This passage is taken from Smith's *Encyclopœdia*, Vol. III., p. 332 :—"There is no food which may not be made a medicine in one form or another. Water, bread crumbs, eggs, gelatine, and osmazome (brown soup), are thus used. And we find, also, that food, taken improperly or immoderately, may become poisonous ; for instance, flour and sugar, to persons affected with diabetes ; bread and potatoes, in scrofula ; meat, in cases of fever, &c., &c. Again, as civilisation has progressed, several medicaments and poisons have been discovered to be valuable for habitual use as dietetics, spices, stimulants, or cosmetics. In fact, there is scarcely any class of medicines which does not afford some aid to our culinary operations, even resins, acrid poisons, and narcotics not excepted (asafœtida, Peruvian balsam, capsicum, saffron, cherry-laurel, &c.) A certain Tyrolean peasant took arsenic as a stomachic, for which it has also for a long period been used in veterinary medicines.* We enjoy beverages

* This circumstance confirms the probability of the story of the

containing poison or narcotics, as tea, hops, alcohol, and carbonic acid. The Russian soldiers drank even nitric acid instead of whiskey. Empyreumatic substances, which contain, according to the opinion of Reichenbach, the strongest poisons, as creosote, picamar, and kapnomar, we enjoy in roasted and smoked meats, and in empyreumatical beverages, as coffee, rum, whiskey, &c. The porter and ale drinkers swallow, according to parliamentary reports, an incredible quantity of coculus menispermum, nux vomica, capsicum, ledum palustre, &c. We smoke tobacco (which contains one of the most formidable poisons), or take it for snuff; many even chew it, and the Portuguese flavour their melons with it. The natives of the east intoxicate themselves with opium and hemp plant. Lead, bismuth, and even arsenic (in rusma), and other metals, are found on the toilettes of the ladies. Prussic acid and veratrum are cosmetics. Manganese, copper, and other poisonous metals are found in a normal state in the food which composes our daily fare : for example, in the various kinds of cereals, &c."

The before-mentioned tree *butea frondosa*, yields the well-known gum called Bengal Kino, which, with copperas affords a good ink ; and it bears yellow-reddish flowers, which are recommended for use in hip baths, by the native physicians, in urinal disorders. They are used also by the poorer classes for dyeing or colouring their clothes on the *Holy* (carnival) and *Besanti* (yellow feast). The light powders called *altah*, which they throw over each other, during the Holy, and which are of variegated colours, are prepared from rice and water-nuts (*trapa bispinosa*) ; the yellow one is tinted with the same colouring substance. The water too, which they throw on each other during the Holy, is coloured with the same flower, because of its fugitive nature. The dried leaves of the above tree are also in requisition among the natives for a variety of purposes, and are sold at the bazaar at Lahore

Affghan physician, whom I mentioned as habitually using arsenic; and, it will be recollected, that he was also a horse-dealer, and therefore likely to be acquainted with its use in veterinary medicine.

in bundles. The grocers wrap their spices and other articles in these leaves instead of paper, and the confectioners and curd sellers do the same ; the latter knit two or three of the leaves together, either with wooden pins or with thorns, so that they have the shape of a cup, in which they exhibit the curds for sale ; and the Hindoo mountaineers, who are not permitted to use glass or china, employ them as plates in which they serve their food. The rajahs Dhyan Sing, Soochet Sing and Heera Sing were accustomed to take their repasts from similar cups and dishes, sitting with their retinue on white cloths, spread upon the ground. Every guest has one or more of these cups placed before him, and they only employ their fingers in eating, as forks, knives or spoons are not used by the native inhabitants. The Maharajah Gholab Sing, however, does not dine in company, but invariably takes his meals alone, in the kitchen where the dishes are prepared, having previously passed an hour or two in performing his ablutions, and repeating his poojah (prayers). It is a common custom in India for every Hindoo to prepare his own dinner. He makes a circle, washing the hearth within it, beyond which no person, even of his own caste, is allowed to pass ; and if any stranger, ignorant of the custom, should place his foot beyond this sacred circle, the dish he has been preparing is considered as polluted, and is thrown away untouched, no matter how expensive the ingredients may have been. There are a large number of Hindoo castes, and much diversity prevails in their habits and customs. In some of these, a person will not eat of a dish prepared even by his own brother ; and should he be dangerously ill, would rather confine his diet to dried fruits than take any food which another person had touched. This extreme peculiarity, however, attaches only to a few of the Hindoo castes, as by far the larger number resemble in this respect the Sikhs (reformed Hindoos), who do not object to eat of any dish which has been prepared by a Brahmin. One of my orderlies, *i. e.*, attendant of my house, who was a Brahmin, had eaten of a cake which had been bought at the bazaar, but which by accident had been touched by one of his companions who was a Mussel-man, and in consequence, he was looked upon by those of his caste as being polluted. In order to purify himself, he was, by way of penitence, obliged to give a splendid dinner to the Brahmins of the neighbourhood, the cost of which absorbed about a month's wages ; and to eat a sugared paste compounded of milk, butter, urine, and excrement, the four being derived from the sacred animal of the Brahmins ; which, although he knew its disgusting composition, he devoured with great devotional avidity, and which completely effected his restoration to purity in the eyes of his fellow Brahmins.

In the hot season, ginger beer is a great favourite in India as a beverage, especially when cooled by immersion in a freezing mixture of ice and saltpetre. It is prepared much in the same manner as in this country. Milk-punch and grog are also extensively used, as well as cooled soda-water (with a small quantity of wine), lemonade, orgeat, &c. These beverages, however, are used mostly by Europeans ; the natives prepare a variety of cooling drinks from almonds, the seeds of melons, pumpkins, cucumbers, &c. ; adding to them arkh-e-goolab, arkh-e-keora and *bedemusk*, *i. e.*, the distilled waters of roses, sweet scented pandan, and the flowers of the Egyptian willow. They use also a syrup made from the berries of the *grewia asiatica* ; a vinegar syrup flavoured with mint ; buttermilk ; milk-and-water ; and curdled milk with salt and water ; those who can afford to incur the expense of artificially cooling these beverages, use, when ice connot be obtained, a mixture of water and saltpetre, agitating in it the vessel containing the liquid to be cooled. It is not always, however, that cold drinks are the most effective for quenching the violent thirst experienced in the hot season ; on the contrary, my own experience teaches me that the more of these which are taken, the more the thirst increases ; whilst a cup of warm tea or coffee with milk, produces a contrary result, and should therefore be used in preference to cold beverages in such cases.

Cold baths are much used in India, both by Europeans and natives; but especially by the latter; in fact, it is almost impossible to over-estimate the benefits arising from them. I have myself experienced the restoring influence of cold-bathing, and from the commencement of April till the end of August, I refreshed myself with at least two cold douche-baths daily; and sometimes took one even during those intensely hot nights, which so often deprive the European of sleep. The wealthy can afford to employ servants day and night in fanning and otherwise administering to their comfort in these hot climates, but the poorer classes must perform the ventilating or cooling processes for themselves as they can. But besides the inconveniences arising from the heat of an Indian summer, there are other annoyances to be experienced or prevented; such as the prickly heat (as it is called), the attacks of mosquitoes, and those troublesome dust-storms which occur regularly in the Punjab about the middle of June. These dust-storms are sometimes so thick that, in broad daylight, they will occasionally, for a few minutes, produce as great a darkness as that of night. Another disagreeable Indian visitor is the simoom (hot winds), which ordinarily continue for six weeks, during which the inhabitants of India, native and European, are compelled to pass their time during the day in cellars beneath the ground, or else they must cover every aperture to their dwellings with *tattis* (mats made from the root of the *andropogon muriaticum*), which they keep constantly sprinkled with water. The douche-baths I used were produced by causing a goat-skin to be filled with fresh well-water, and poured over my head. Besides the cleanliness and cooling effect which these baths afford, they exercise a beneficial influence on the skin and nervous system, as also on the lungs, stomach, kidneys, and even on the remotest parts of the body, by stimulating their action. It is necessary, however, to be careful in the use of the cold bath, and to avoid taking one when the body is in a perspiration, which in India, I need scarcely say, is often the case. The same rule also holds good as regards warm bathing in winter ; and it is highly dangerous to leave the bath too suddenly, and expose the body to the influence of the cold air. The natives, both Moslems and Hindoos—male or female—whether winter or summer—hot or cold—whether in the Ravee or the Ganges—by drenching themselves at the wells, or washing in their own homes—are, figuratively speaking, always in the water. Their simple and favorite beverage is—not beer, wine or brandy, but sherbet, *i.e.*, water sweetened with raw sugar, and therefore they generally enjoy good health. They make great use also of gymnastic exercises, in which *tshapi* and *muti* are special favorites when they are fatigued, and assist materially in promoting the circulation ; the former may be described as pinching, and the latter is a process of striking with both fists on the body. The natives of India have also a peculiar way of rinsing the mouth and cleansing the teeth, which is generally done when they perform their religious exercises, of which ablution is an essential part. They use for this purpose the twigs or branches of various trees and shrubs ; but as each nation uses a different kind of twig, &c., it would occupy too much space to detail the numerous plants employed ; it is sufficient to observe, that they are generally of an astringent nature, and whilst cleansing and strengthening the gums, have a beneficial effect on the stomach also.

The Sikhs generally employ an hour or two in the operations of the toilet ; and before ablution they rub their hair (which in most cases is long and black) with curds. When the hair has become silvered by age, they dare not dye it, being strictly forbidden by their religious tenets. The Musselmen, however, are very fond of dyeing the hair, and for that purpose make use of a great variety of compositions containing oxide of iron, myrobolans, *Lawsonia inermis*, *Indigofera Anil*, &c. They also darken the eyelashes with black sulphurets of lead or antimony.

The following are the recipes for two of the hair dyes which are principally in request :—Of Lawsonia inermis and Indigofera Anil, take each two parts, and of dried myrtle leaves and emblic myrobolans, each one part; these are made into powder and mixed with water to the consistency of a soft poultice, which is applied to the hair. It is stated that this composition stimulates the growth of the hair, blackens that which is grey, and presents its splitting. The second recipe is one which I have myself used in earlier years, in India and in Persia, for colouring my beard; and is generally recognised by the orientals (who are extremely fond of possessing fine long black hair), as the best preparation for the purpose. The powdered Lawsonia inermis is made by water into a soft pap, and applied in that state to the hair, taking care that all the hair is completely overspread to the roots. It is then covered, and fastened up with leaves, or by a piece of waxcloth or oilskin, and having been suffered to remain for from half-an-hour to an hour, the preparation is then washed off. The effect of this is to dye the hair a bright red colour; which colour, by the next process, is converted into a beautiful black. The second application is a paste prepared with water from the powder of the indigo plant which I have before mentioned; it is used in a similar manner to the first, but must be allowed to remain on the hair for three hours; being then washed off, the operation of dying is completed, and the hair is rubbed with oil or pomatum, to give it lustre and suppleness. The only inconvenience of the processes I have described, which are so cheap in the east, is that they require to be repeated about once a week, for, as the hair grows from the roots, it would otherwise, after a few days, show at that part the natural colour of the hair, and consequently present a very unsightly appearance. These operations are generally performed at noon, a time when every one is at home, either for rest or indoor occupation.

A weak solution of nitrate of silver is sometimes used in Europe for dying the hair, but if this be used after the preparations which I have just described, instead of darkening, it will convert the colour into a grey like that of ashes;—this fact I learned from the Nabob, Jubber Khan, at Cabul, who, having admired the colour of my beard, and ascertained it to be produced by nitrate of silver, forthwith applied it to his own hair, which had been previously dyed with the compositions I have described. The result was as indicated, and the nabob became for some time the laughing stock of the community.

Besides the solution of nitrate of silver, they use in Europe a compound powder of litharge, soap, chalk, starch, and a little sulphuric acid, &c. This is also well-known in the east, but is not in esteem, inasmuch as it is productive of noxious effects as regards health, and also renders the hair stiff and rough.

With regard to this digression on medical and domestic matters, I may, before I return to my narrative, mention to my readers, that at the end of this volume they will find a short rhythmical essay by the well-known Dr. Triller (which I have translated from the German), on the means of ensuring a merry old age, and although it does not evince much poetical fervor, is nervertheless valuable for the advice it contains.

The maharajah Sheer Sing, was, in his private character, extremely polite and amiable ; he had an intense desire for knowledge, and devoted great attention to European skill, industry and learning. In these matters, he could, of course, only acquire information from Europeans, and would enter freely into conversation with them, without the slightest observance of the etiquette which his position might have commanded. On one occasion, in the course of our conference, he inquired whether I had any relations in Europe ; and learning that I had a younger brother at Kronstadt, who had formerly been in the military service, but was at that time exercising the profession of a watchmaker, the maharajah inquired whether he could repair machinery of that description which was out of order ; and, on my replying in the affirmative, he asked whether I thought my brother would make up his mind to leave Kronstadt and come to Lahore, if he should send for him. His reason for asking this was, that (being a patron of the fine arts) he had in his possession a large number of English musical boxes, clocks, watches, and other similar machines, many of which were damaged or broken. I assured him I had no doubt my brother would willingly respond to his invitation, and that I would myself provide for his family, which would remain in Europe. The maharajah at once requested me to send for my brother, and to take the necessary steps for his voyage, &c., and several times subsequently made many inquiries as to whether I had sent, and if he would come, whether he was on his way, and whether he might soon expect to see him. The urgency of these reiterated requests was such, that I strongly solicited my brother to accede to the maharajah's desire; and he accordingly set out on his journey from Kronstadt to Lahore. Arrived at the isthmus of Suez, he heard, to his consternation, of the murder of the maharajah and his wuzeer, and of the other horrid massacres in the capital, which I have before described. He continued his journey, however, and arrived at Ferozepore, on the boundary of the Punjab, in the beginning of February, 1814; which, as the reader may recollect, was the epoch when Heera Sing was the powerful wuzeer of the young maharajah Dulleep Sing, and the time when all Europeans were dismissed from the service of the Sikhs and sent from the country. I was myself at that time severely ill; and the minister, having heard that no hope of my recovery was entertained, permitted my brother to pass the frontier and visit me at Lahore; thus verifying the proverb, that "out of evil, good cometh." On the very day on which my brother arrived at Lahore, my recovery commenced; but whether this was due to the pleasure I derived from his arrival, or a new remedy I had employed on that day, I am unable to say; both causes, possibly, assisted in producing that result. My illness had probably been for some time slumbering in the system, for I had previously been using, as a beverage, a wine made from Cabul raisins and sugar, which had not been properly fermented; and this may very likely have laid the foundation of the disease I am about to describe. After having exposed my sight to the powerful rays of an Indian sun for some hours, the stomach being empty, one of my eyes became very much inflamed. Not having properly attended to this circumstance, and, as was necessary, immediately applied leeches or bleeding, I found myself on the following morning totally blind ; an *Amaurosis* being formed, so that I was unable to seek for any of my medicines. No European physician being at Lahore, I was obliged to have recourse to the native drugs, and consult with native doctors. Leeches, blisters, collyriums, &c., later employed, seemed of no avail, and for a whole fortnight I was unable to sleep night or day, and was without food of any kind ; for on my attempting to take the slightest nourishment, even pure water, the stomach rejected it again immediately ; and from the circumstance of an acrid fluid sometimes rising to my mouth, and an unnatural feeling of heaviness in the stomach, I was led to conclude that there was an ulceration there. Erratic swellings in the joints, accompanied by dysentery, followed ; and I was so weakened, that on the morning of the day when my brother arrived, I was in a piteous state of blindness and exhaustion. On that day I commenced using that simple remedy which contributed to my restoration from the very dangerous illness at Kheirpore, on the Indus (as the reader may remember), viz., masticating some of those large raisins, called there *monaka*, which I found to act as a balm to the stomach, or rather, perhaps, to the ulceration there. From that moment I grew visibly better, my appetite and strength gradually increased, and I was at length restored to health.

As regards my brother, it soon became evident, that in the altered state of political affairs in the Punjab, there could be no probability of his obtaining any engagement which would justify him in remaining ; he therefore returned again to Europe, accompanied by Colonel Steinbach.

As an instance of the fanaticism of the Nahungs (the robber-pack I have before mentioned), I may relate an occurrence which took place at Umritsir, in which a German friend of mine, Herr August Schofft, was near losing his life by their fury. This gentleman is an artist of some celebrity (at this time in St. Petersburg), and he, accompanied by his lady, visited the East Indian Presidencies shortly before my severe illness ; and having met with great success in consequence of his skill in oil painting, he came to visit me at Lahore. At this time the court happened to be at Umritsir, and I received an order from Sheer Sing to present myself at that place with my guest. On our arrival, it happened that one of the principal Sikh priests, named Baii Goormuck Sing, was present, and the maharajah desired Herr Schofft to furnish him with a specimen of his abilities, by sketching a portrait of the Baii ; which he accordingly did, in pencil, and the likeness was a striking one. The result was, that the maharajah and several of the principal persons of the court sat to him for their portraits, and Herr Schofft accordingly met with great respect and consideration.

I may mention here, that Herr Schofft had kept copies of these portraits, and that on his return to Europe he painted, from these and other sketches which he had taken, a large picture of the Durbar of Lahore, which is considered to be his masterpiece, and which was purchased from him by Louis Phillipe, and is still, I believe, at Paris.

In the centre of the city of Umritsir is a gigantic reservoir of water, from the midst of which rises a magnificent temple, where the *Grunth* (the holy book of the Sikhs) is read day and night. Around this sheet of water are the houses of the maharajah, the ministers, sirdars, and other wealthy inhabitants. The square itself is called *Durbar Saheb.* At the time of Runjeet Sing and Sheer Sing, the scene which presented itself at this temple, when the court was at Umritsir, was of the most brilliant description, and at certain periods all the notabilities of the Punjab were to be seen collected together in all the splendour of oriental pageantry. During our stay at Umritsir it happened that the inhabitants gave an invitation to the court to visit the sacred temple at night time, when it was gorgeously illuminated; and Sheer Sing honoured me with his commands that we should accompany him, sending us a richly caparisoned elephant for our accommodation. Sheer Sing inquired of my friend, Herr Schofft, if he could take for him a drawing of that brilliant scene. He answered in the affirmative, but proposed to the maharajah that it would be better if the scene was sketched under the effect of daylight instead of the imperfect one of the illumination. He was accordingly ordered to adopt that suggestion. On the following morning we went to the house of the Baii Goormuck Sing, who had promised, on the previous evening, to send a servant to point out to us the most elevated terrace in the square (which was in the mansion of Runjeet Sing), from which Herr Schofft could get a view of the temple and the surrounding buildings; on this place he prepared his atelier. He occupied the whole of the day in sketching the scene, and on the following day he also went there, but alone, to continue his work. About noon, having that morning received some newspapers from my native place, Kronstadt, I went to him, and he desired me to read to him the news whilst he was painting. About an hour before sunset, his work was nearly finished, and as the court had already departed for Lahore, whither we wished also to proceed immediately, he requested me to go to our quarters and to procure some boxes in which he could enclose his paintings. Our quarters were outside the city, in a garden formerly belonging to the prince No-Nehal Sing. When I reached home I immediately forwarded to him a horse and servants, as he had told me he should finish his painting within an hour after I had left him.

Herr Schofft was a great smoker, and attracted attention in Umritsir from his scarcely ever being seen abroad without having a cigar in his mouth. Now smoking is considered by the Nahungs and the Sikhs as sinful, or rather criminal; more especially in or near such a holy place as their chief sanctuary; Herr Schofft was aware of this, and therefore studiously avoided smoking whilst engaged in taking this sketch. It happened however, that, as is customary with painters, he now and then in the course of the work placed one of his pencils in his mouth, in order to keep it separate from those in the left hand, whilst using another with the right. This was observed by those who stood watching his operations from beneath the terrace, and they imagined, in consequence, that he was smoking. The rumour first spread about in whispers one to another, and as the impression became confirmed, a general indignation manifested itself ; and loud exclamations were soon heard, that the feringhee (frank) was committing sacrilege by smoking in their sacred place. The people speedily increased in numbers, and a clamorous mob soon surrounded the palace. The artist was at first unconscious of the cause of the gathering, but he soon became aware by their shouts and threats, that he was in some way the object of their fury, and that he was consequently in a dangerous position. He had no sooner, however, made up his mind that his best policy would be to effect his escape, if possible, unperceived ; when some of the ringleaders of the mob, who had made their way through the palace, rushed upon the terrace, and attempted to seize him. Being a strong and vigorous man, he succeeded in wrenching himself from their grasp, and made his way to the staircase, which to his dismay he found crowded by the mob, who were making their way up. Knowing that his only chance lay in breaking through them as quickly as possible, he struck out right and left, and having the advantage of being always uppermost of those who attempted to stay his progress, he succeeded in reaching the bottom with some few bruises. Here, however, the affair presented a still more formidable aspect ; for no sooner had he reached the foot of the staircase, then he was seized by the collar and other parts of his coat by half-a-dozen of the mob, and saw at a little distance the glittering of several of their weapons. He gave himself up for lost, and in the energy of despair threw open his coat, and taking advantage of a slight confusion at the moment (caused by a struggle to get possession of the gold watch which he had held in his hand, and had at the same instant relinquished to them), he slipped from the coat, which was held on all sides, and pushing away those in front of him, he succeeded in reaching the street; here his nether garments fell, in some unaccountable manner, about his feet, and he stumbled and fell into a miry puddle which was immediately before him : he instantly sprang to his feet, and rushed to the entrance of a dark stable close adjacent. The mob concluded they had now secured their prey, but they were mistaken ; for Schofft had, fortunately, whilst passing this stable on a previous occasion in my company, entered it, and noticed its back entrance, which led into the bazaar ; through this back door he then gained the bazaar, and from thence (the mob all the way at his heels), reached the house of his protector, Baii Goormukh Sing. The door was immediately shut, and Schofft was saved.

He there met with a kind reception, and on cleansing himself from the mire and blood with which he was covered, it was found that he had not only received several contusions on the head from the iron knobs on the shields of the Nahungs, with which they had struck at him ; but also a sword wound on the back, by which his braces had been cut through, which at once explained to him the cause of his fall into the mire at so critical a moment. The mob not evincing any inclination to disperse, the police interfered, and compelled them to retire.

During all this time I was at home, expecting his arrival every moment ; and at length, when it was quite dark, some of the persons whom I had sent with the horse, came back to me with the news of the riot, and informed me that he was in the hands of the mob. This filled me with consternation, and I immediately sent to the commander of the fortress (a friend of mine), soliciting him to assist and endeavour to save the unfortunate painter. With great promptitude, he despatched a whole company of regular troops to the city, and on their way they met Schofft on his road home ; he having been disguised in an oriental costume, and sent on horseback accompanied by an escort of police. My first care was to dress his wounds ; and early on the following morning we left Umritsir for Lahore. I may add that the watch, and the plate, &c., which I had sent with his luncheon, were of course lost ; but the painting was subsequently recovered.

It was a fortunate circumstance for me that the ranee, during the war with the English on the Sutlej, in consequence of the many abortions she had experienced, was affected with ophthalmia, and had not consented to the demands of the Commander-in-Chief, Teja Sing, who was also suffering from fever (or from fright), and wished my attendance in the camp. I had, therefore, the advantage of remaining in the city (avoiding the inconvenience of compromising myself with the English, by becoming an *attache* of the hostile Sikh camp, which subsequently caused the dismissal of Colonels Mouton and Hurbon), and also of becoming personally acquainted with the ranee, whose portrait I have presented to my readers.

The result of the war on the Sutlej, I have already mentioned ; and, as my office at Lahore was almost annihilated on the annexation of the Punjab by the English, I made up my mind to return to Europe ; but the season not being favorable for the homeward voyage, I determined to employ my leisure in visiting the valley of Cashmere, which is rich in historical, physical, and industrial interest, hoping not only to obtain a collection of the plants of that country, and thus enrich botanical science ; but also, at the same time, by excursions into the surrounding mountains, to improve my health, which had been sensibly impaired by the duties and unceasing exertions of the past two years.

Having obtained the necessary permission from the English government at Lahore, and also from the maharajah of Cashmere, Gholab Sing, I departed from Lahore, and reached the valley of Cashmere in three weeks, without the occurrence of any incident worth noting. Arrived there, I entered into communication with the maharajah, and he proposed that I should enter his service. This, however, I declined, more especially as it would interfere with my proposed journey to Europe ; but I promised him

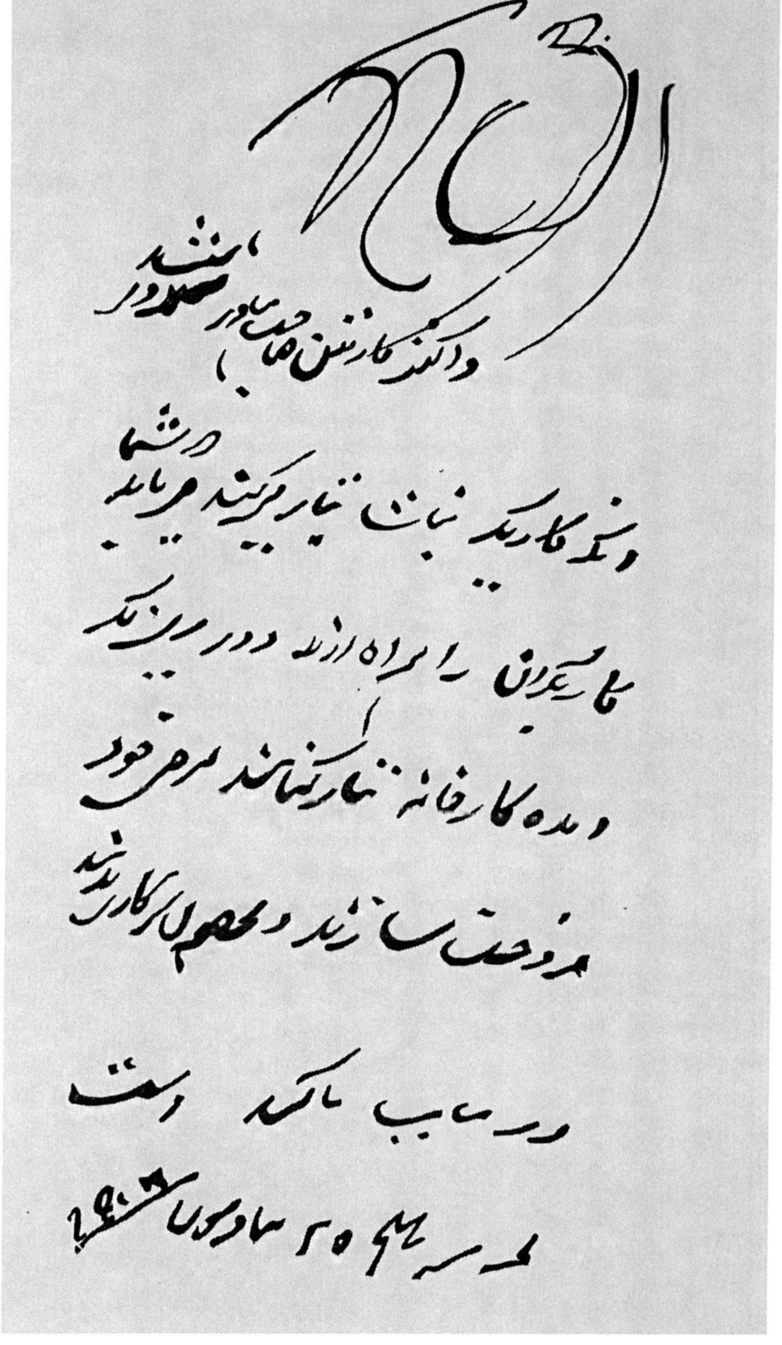

that I would hasten my return to India, and pass a few years in his country, not only in cultivating ground on my own private account, but also according to his desire, in attending to his personal service. The maharajah was anxious to know what sort of farming I intended to adopt in Cashmere, when I informed him that I had observed that, notwithstanding the great consumption of tea and sugar in his dominions, the cultivation of them had never been attempted, and that they were consequently imported from foreign countries. The sugar used in Cashmere is imported from India, and is conveyed with much difficulty over steep mountains through almost impracticable passes, the journey occupying three weeks; and the tea is brought from Thibet, in the shape of cakes, and is very much inferior to that which is produced in India. I explained to the maharajah, to his great astonishment, that the soil of Cashmere was favourable to the production of both these articles; and also that the sugarcane (which will not grow there) was not essential for the production of sugar, as it could be prepared of equal quality from a kind of beet-root, for the cultivation of which that soil was eminently adapted; and informed him that I should therefore solicit permission to establish a sugar manufactory, both land and labour there being exceedingly cheap. The maharajah agreed entirely with my plan, and gave me an order for the purpose of enabling me to carry it out, which will be found among the plates to this volume. God willing, I shall endeavour to carry that intention into effect.

As I have acquainted my readers, my hopes were to re-establish my health in these hilly countries; but I had reckoned without my host; for the greater part of my domestics being natives of Cashmere, and aware of my activity and zeal in assisting the suffering part of mankind, they did not fail to trumpet my medical success at Lahore to their countrymen, who flocked to my abode with patients from morning till night. For two months, there were not less than a hundred persons daily, to solicit my assistance: I accorded it to them gratuitously; and from their incessant attendance, I was not only compelled to expend the whole of the day in distributing medicaments, which were administered in the form of lozenges, but was also obliged to devote my evenings to the preparation of those which were to be used on the day following. In fact, it frequently happened that whole families came from some of the more distant villages, and bringing their provision with them, they encamped in my garden, and remained there for two or three days, until I was able to furnish them with the requisite medicines and advice.

I was, however, to a great extent, repaid for the labour to which I was thus subjected, by being able to make many experiments, and thus practically convince myself of the medicinal efficacy of the plants and drugs of Cashmere, which were those I principally tried there. I had also the opportunity of introducing operations which had been hitherto unknown in that country; as for instance, tapping in a case of dropsy, which I performed in the presence of the maharajah and several others, who were completely amazed at the quantity of liquid drawn from the patient.

At the time I am now writing, the news has just arrived from India, that the maharajah Gholab Sing is himself suffering from dropsy; and had the arrangements which I had made respecting this work permitted, I should certainly have returned to India before this, and have probably been able to have rendered him some assistance. I have, however, forwarded to him (if not too late) some medical advice, and also instructions for the preparation of medicines which can be procured on the spot, and administered by his own people; for the Hindoos, as I have before mentioned, will not take anything which has been prepared or even touched by a stranger.

At the period when I was at Cashmere, the maharajah had several English visitors, whom he treated with the greatest hospitality. Some of them had come from Simla *via* Thibet. At that time, and previously, it was the custom for every European, of whatever nation he might be, who visited the valley of Cashmere, to be received as a guest, and entertained as such, from the instant of his entering the country to the moment of his departure; even the hill-porters who carried the baggage (for it is impossible to employ animals heavily laden, on account of the badness of the roads in that hilly country) were by the officials of the maharajah placed at the disposal of the visitors. In a conversation, however, which I had with the maharajah, he complained that many of the servants of the European visitors had abused the hospitality displayed towards them, for they had frequently taken with them very large quantities of saffron, and other products of the country, much beyond what they could really use during their sojourn. This circumstance, I believe, has led to an alteration in the custom.

The most eminent of the visitors at that time, were Lord Gifford, brother-in-law of the Governor-General of India, and the unfortunate Colonel King, who afterwards (in consequence of imagining that imputations were thrown upon his courage and ability) committed suicide. We sometimes dined together at the maharajah's ; and it may, perhaps, appear very ridiculous to those who are unacquainted with oriental customs, to be informed, that on these occasions, we were obliged to send our own cooks, our own wines, and our own plate, and other culinary, or, gastronomic apparatus. The maharajah would make his appearance during dinner, but, of course, would never partake of our repast ; and, to show us particular attention, he ordered preserves, fruit, ice, and sweetmeats, to be sent to us from his own kitchen. Besides this kind of hospitality, he would frequently minister to our entertainment in other ways, as by exhibitions of fireworks, illuminations on the river, music, dancing-girls (bayaderes), &c.

The kings of France professed to cure the king's-evil, by laying the hand upon the patient ; and the kings of England to cure epilepsy, by blowing thrice upon the person affected with that disease—the maharajh emulates their example, by professing to cure all cases of paralysis, although he adopts a more substantial and effective method of operation. He administers, for this purpose, a *maioon* (electuary) the ingredients of which, as he informed me, are cinnabar, *anacardium orientale*, and nux vomica, with thirty-five spices. It is prepared as follows—The cinnabar is boiled in butter, and the nux vomica, anacardium, and spices, are then added ; these ingredients are then ground, or, rubbed together, with a sufficient quantity of honey, in order to form an electuary, a process which occupies three days. The dose (twice a day) is from five to ten grains. The electuarium nucis vomicæ of Timur Shah, which the Hakims still consider a valuable remedy, is a similar compound, the preparation of which I now give—Any quantity of nux vomica is macerated or immersed in warm milk, the milk being poured off, and fresh milk substituted every day, for seven consecutive days ; on the eighth day the nux vomica is suspended by inclosing it in a linen cloth, in a stewpan filled with new milk, and boiled ; the nuts are then peeled and split, and the internal germ removed and thrown away (the latter being considered poisonous) they are then washed, dried, and rasped to powder, which is afterwards boiled in honey. The following spices, mixed with twice their weight of honey, are then added to complete the electuary, *viz.*—white, black, and long peppers, cinnamon, nutmeg, betel-nut, mastic, English galangale, Emblic myrobalon, India spikenard, cardamoms, cumin seeds, fennel seeds, small fennel-flower seeds, saffron, ginger, cloves, aloes wood, guiacum wood, sandal wood, and *Xylobalsam.* The dose of this medicine is half a drachm to one drachm ; and it is recommended as an anodyne, hypnotic, and aphrodisise ; also, as being valuable in removing palsy, curing gout, stopping catarrh, strengthening the stomach, &c.

I could introduce a great variety of anecdotes illustrative of the manners, customs, &c., of the inhabitants of Cashmere, and the peculiarities of their country, which have never yet been published, did the object of my work permit. I may, however, mention a curious species of theft which is sometimes perpetrated there. On the lakes in Cashmere are large numbers of floating gardens, or, masses of weeds, upon which earth is thrown, and they serve as beds for cultivating melons, cucumbers, turnips, carrots, cabbages, egg-plant-apples, and different other culinary vegetables. If, however, the gardener does not keep a watch over this moveable property, he may perhaps find, that during the night, the garden itself has been cut from its fastenings and removed ; and as, in these cases, the thief joins the stolen mass to a similar one of his own (thus completely altering its shape, postion, &c.) it is rarely possible to identify the garden, or, discover the perpetrator of the robbery.

During my stay at Cashmere, I did not neglect any opportunity of acquiring a knowledge of its botanical treasures, or, of collecting such plants as appeared likely to be of any service for medicinal purposes ; I thus gathered a considerable herbarium vivum : The drawings of those which I considered as most valuable in medical botany, may be seen in the second volume, and their properties and effects (as far as I was able to discover) are also detailed in the pages of that volume. Besides the Flora Medica Cashmereana, there are also descriptions of other plants, which I collected in the plains of the Punjab, the virtues of which I tested, and now communicate. Many of them are, probably, already known to European physicians, but, as I have written not for Europe alone, but also for the East, I have introduced them, because many of the Indian physicians are not thoroughly acquainted with them—not even with their forms or properties. It would have been easy for me to have doubled or tripled the number, had the limits of this work permitted.

Many of my readers may possibly question the utility of these descriptions, on the ground, that, even supposing the efficacy of the plants to be established, and their utility in medicine practically and successfully proved, the knowledge of them cannot be of any service to European physicians, as they will not be able to procure supplies. This, however, is not the case ; for, although their principal use may be in India, the shawl merchants of Cashmere, who are in constant communication with France and England, would willingly forward whatever might be required, to any part of India or Europe. On this point, I have only to observe, that their transport should not be by the long route round the Cape of Good Hope, but by the Red Sea and the Mediterranean ; or, if possible, entirely overland ; because, unless they are in hermetically-sealed packages, they invariably suffer by a sea passage. I may further mention, that my catalogue of Cashmerean plants is not by any means complete, and that, should Heaven permit me to fulfil my intention, of again visiting that country for a couple of years, and then of returning to Europe, I shall publish a Supplement to this work, in order to supply the deficiencies, and therein state any occurrences of interest which my happen.

Having passed the months of July and August in Cashmere, I left that beautiful country, on my way to Europe, in the month of September, taking with me a quantity of Cashmerean produce. After calling at Lahore, where I stayed till the end of October, I passed the Sutlej, and went, *via* Ferozepore, Loodiana, Umballa, Saharunpore, and Rajpore, again to the hills, *viz.*, to Mussoorie, in order to visit my two daughters, whom I had placed at an educational institution there, which is under the direction of some French ladies. I spent three days at that place, and then continued my journey, passing from Meerut to Goormuckteesur, on the Ganges; where I had previously engaged a small vessel to convey me to Calcutta. The voyage down the Ganges was an exceedingly pleasant one, in many respects, and lasted two months. Among the incidents which excited my attention on the river, the relation of which may interest the reader, was that, as we approached Bengal, I observed, on both banks of the Ganges, a gradually increasing number of cane-mats, coverlets, drinking vessels, &c., and also many sick persons lying upon mats, &c. On inquiring the cause, I found that it was the custom of the country, among the poorer classes, that when a patient was supposed to be past all hope of recovery, his relations conveyed him to the banks of the Ganges, so that he might die in the vicinity of the sacred river. The relations or friends of the patients, visit the spot, to ascertain whether they are still living ; when death ensues, they purchase a sufficiency of wood to make a funeral-pile, and commit the body to the flam es ; when their means do not afford the expense of doing this, they merely burn a portion of the face, and then push the body into the sacred river. When a patient, thus situated, happens to recover, he considers that he has, as it were, acquired a new life, and thenceforth all his former relations and friends are treated as strangers ; he never returns to the dwelling in which he had formerly resided, but wanders down the Ganges, until he arrives at Santipore, near Calcutta, where he settles himself ; and it is a curious fact, that nearly the whole population of Santipore is composed of such persons. These people never again hold any communication with those who had been nearest and dearest to them ; and they contract marriages amongst themselves only. This town or colony, the only one, perhaps, of its kind in the world, may be called the "Colony of Convalescents." The Ganges teems with crocodiles, and wild geese are found in great abundance.

When I arrived at Calcutta, I found that one of the finest merchant vessels, called the "Prince of Wales," belonging to Messieurs Green and Compy. was about to sail for England. I made arrangements for my passage homeward, and after a week's stay only in Calcutta, went on board. This short stay at the capital of Bengal, prevented my observing any of the operations of the celebrated Dr. James Esdaile (now in Scotland) whose cases of amputation, &c., performed without pain, and without the use of chloroform, &c., while the patient was under mesmeric influence, were then attracting considerable attention. The *Delhi Gazette* of India observed—" Though Dr. Esdaile's performances are not yet countenanced by the faculty, let us hope that he possesses moral courage sufficient to prosecute his measures."

We enjoyed the most delightful weather during the voyage ; the only annoyance being the frequent calms, which caused us to be two months in reaching the Cape of Good Hope. In the beginning of April we reached Cape

Town, the aspect of which, at the foot of the Table Mountain, is exceedingly picturesque. The town is constructed with much regularity, and the houses are very comfortable dwellings, principally of one flat only. Almost every European comfort is to be found there; they have good hotels, elegant shops, handsome public buildings, an exchange, a theatre, and several others, and the town is well lighted with gas; I was surprised at not being pestered at the Cape by beggars, a peculiarity I do not recollect to have met with in any other place I visited in my travels.

On our arrival at the Cape, the harvest season was just over, and we were able, on our walks through the town, or in country excursions, to refresh ourselves with some of the most delicious grapes I ever tasted. To some of my readers, it may, at first, appear strange, that the harvest season should be over so early in the year as April; but, be it remembered, the Cape is in the southern hemisphere, where the seasons are precisely the reverse of ours; January being the hottest, and July the coldest month of the year. After a stay of four days, we again put to sea, having, during that time, taken in a supply of fresh water, poultry, &c., but we had not long been out of sight of land, when our poultry were attacked by an epizootic, and destroyed, so that we were obliged to call at St. Helena, to procure fresh provisions. There were a few cases of death on board, *viz.*, some invalids and a sailor who had been notorious for his immoderate drinking. The bodies were, according to the custom of mariners, wrapped in linen cloths, and weights having been attached, they were committed to the deep, accompanied with prayers.

Besides these cases of disease, which terminated fatally, there were a few others, with regard to the treatment of which I was consulted. I may mention two of them, as the diseases frequently occur, and I had the good fortune to extricate the ship's surgeon from an embarrassment respecting them. The first was that of a testy old colonel, who, according to his own assertion, was troubled with severe rheumatic pains to such a degree, that he was on the verge of despair. In this perplexity he addressed himself to me, with the avowal, that the medicines he got from the surgeon were not worth a penny, and that if I could not assist him, he must die. I asked him, whether he had ever been affected with syphilitic disease, which he admitted to have been the case many years before. I, therefore, acquainted the surgeon with this circumstance, and advised him to administer decoction of sarsaparilla to the patient. There was none on board, however, at that time, but, when we reached the Cape, the surgeon procured a supply, and began to administer it. The impatient colonel, not finding instant relief, again gave vent to his exclamations, telling me that the beverage was of no service ; I persuaded him, however, to persevere : after a fortnight, he acknowledged himself to be considerably better ; and, in a month, he was completely restored to health. The second case was that of a child of twelve months, which, from difficulty in cutting its teeth, was afflicted with convulsions, could not enjoy any food, became visibly weak, and every one felt certain that the child could not live many days. Leeches, scarification of the gums, warm baths, lenitives, and purgatives, had all been used, to no purpose. On perceiving the desperate state of the child, I inquired of the surgeon whether he had tried blistering, and on finding he had not, advised him to do so ; he accordingly applied two (one behind each ear) and from that moment the spasms ceased, the teething began, and the child grew better.

Divine service was regularly performed on board the ship, the captain performing it every Sunday, morning and evening. There were about two hundred persons on board, but, we nevertheless had plenty of provisions ; in fact, we may be said to have fared luxuriously ; for, besides an abundance of necessary food, we had pastry of some kind or other daily, as well as delicious cakes for dessert, and many sorts of wines, malt liquor, and spirits. Twice a-week champagne was served at our table. One day we met with not fewer than nine ships, with some of which we entered into communication, inquiring the name of the vessel, whence it came, whither it was bound, what was its cargo, how long it had been on the voyage, and what other vessels it had spoken with on its way. These communications, unless the ship be within speaking distance, are all made by flag-signals, of which every vessel possesses a book, or index. Previously to the day on which we met with the vessels just mentioned, we had not come in sight of any during several weeks, when a sail was reported to be visible on the horizon ; the passengers immediately went on deck to behold the sight. It was an American whaler, and many of the sailors were sitting on the tops of the masts to get a distant view of the ocean. On the coast of Africa, near the Equator, we encountered a vessel, which, from the account given us by the captain, was coming from Bombay, bound for Calcutta, and had been driven by adverse gales into this part of the Atlantic! The crew and passengers were sorely distressed for want of provisions, and, without knowing even the name of the captain, we supplied them with rice, potatoes, beer, &c., gratis.

At various periods of the day, even when the sun was but slightly visible, the captain and officers took observations with their nautical instruments ; and, after making their calculations, would point out to us, on the map, the exact spot on the watery plain which we were then traversing. In the early part of our voyage, as we approached the southern hemisphere, we gradually lost sight of the northern constellations, and when we reached the Equator, we could not any longer descry the polar star ; but, we were compensated for this, by the appearance of other constellations in the south, which were gradually manifested within our horizon, among which that of the Cross is the most magnificent, the others being considerably inferior to the northern. These incidents may probably appear superfluous to those who have made the voyage ; but, to numbers who have not crossed the waste of mighty waters, they may possibly afford some interest.

The various events which I have described in this volume, have all been written from memory ; as the only time which I could spare for committing any observations to paper, was fully engrossed in noting down those which related to medical subjects; therefore, it can easily be imagined, that some of the minor details may be slightly inaccurate, and that many an important fact, which would have been worth recording, may have escaped my remembrance. I can, however, assure my readers, that, as far as my memory serves me, I have presented to them a faithful record, and that I never have, in any instance, wilfully swerved from truth.

In conclusion, I now insert (in a Translation by a professed literary character) Dr. TRILLER'S *Rules of Health.* This reputable author flourished towards the close of the 17th century, and published a highly esteemed series of Epic poems, entitled, *The Abduction of a Saxon Prince.*

RULES OF HEALTH.

I.

There is a charm in health and length of days,
Which all men covet, and which most might gain;
And I shall now attempt, in humble lays,
To tell how I my aged-life did gain.
However man the debt of nature pays,
He may, at least, longevity obtain;
Learn how I lived, and note what I advise,
As proper means to win so rich and rare a prize.

II.

'Tis to divine beneficence we owe
Not only life, but that great blessing—health;
Yet, man must ever carefully bestow
Attention on himself, to aid the wealth
Which nature has bestowed, as though,
Without our will, she would do good by stealth;
Nor should we treat her rudely, lest we feel
That nerves and muscles are not made of stone nor steel.

III.

This lesson have I learned in nature's school—
  To act as she dictates. A calm, contented mind
I sought; took food and exercise by rule;
  And hence, was able year to year to bind.
Our delicate construction, man's misrule
  Too oft destroys body, and, with it, mind.
It was not by the aid of drug, nor herb, nor charm,
I reached old-age, and kept life free from harm.

IV.

The curing virtues which in med'cines dwell,
  Should in disease alone be in request;
If you resort to them when you are well,
  You may expect them to disturb your rest.
Besides, you rob them of their power disease to quell,
  If in your service they are idly pressed;
They who would not medicaments forestall,
Should take in health no medicines at all.

V.

By tinctures, powders, mixtures, draughts, and pills,
  A hale man always undermines his strength;
Lays the foundation for a host of ills,
  Which take away from life degrees of length:
Medicine not needed, many a person kills,
  Which, kept till wanted, might give health and strength;
He who a sink-hole of his body makes,
Decided steps for its destruction takes.

VI.

Those are mistaken who in every Spring
  And Autumn fancy that they physic need;
Nature relieves herself: both man and thing
  Are subject to her laws; to purge and bleed
For custom's sake, what is it but to fling
  Health, strength, and life away? Blockhead indeed
Is he, who swallows med'cines he does not require;
Long ere his time, shall such a dunce expire.

VII.

He who would spend an aged life in ease,
Must, in his habits, keep within due measure;
In labor, food, and sleep, the medium seize,
In wine and women take not too much pleasure.
Such was the counsel of Hippocrates,
Who thought good health was an important treasure:
And, at the age of six score years, expired,
Loved, honored, reverenced, and much admired.

VIII.

Night into day let no man think of turning,
Nor sleep by day to wake up when 'tis night;
A brain confused, or with strong potions burning,
Cannot conceive of men or things aright:
Let me remark, such feasting folks concerning,
They are not wise; but act as if in spite
Of sense and reason; for, surely, every one
Requires some rest after hard labor done.

IX.

Why should we, glutton like, our bodies feed
As if we wished grim Death to cast his dart?
Why should we hasten to the grave with speed,
As if from all our friends we longed to part?
Of temperance every man on earth has need,
To save him from affliction's direful smart;
Then why use food as if it held the germs
Which make ourselves rich nourishment for worms?

X.

Suppose that we should wish our lamp to burn,
We trim it, nicely, with sufficient oil;
But, if we overcharge the feeding urn,
Of course, the brilliancy of light we spoil,
Or, put it wholly out: hence, we may learn,
Without much labor or fatiguing toil,
If man his "feeding urn" (his body) surfeit,
The darkness of the grave must prove the forfeit.

XI.

A little generous wine makes glad the heart ;
  Unbends the mind o'er which dull sorrow reigns ;
Lightens sad melancholy of its smart,
  And makes infirmity forget its pains ;
Invigorates the blood ; performs its part
  In quickening circulation through the veins ;
It prompts digestion, and the stomach braces,
Languor dispels, depression, too, displaces.

XII.

If you a recipe for Death require—
  Drink, when o'erheated, ice-cold water ;
The effect of which, when freely you perspire,
  Is, to produce of health a complete slaughter :
Should this not fully act to your desire,
  It will to comfort leave but little quarter ;
And a consuming, slow, yet sure decay,
Will take, midst sufferings, life, at length, away.

XIII.

But above all things, let us never fail
  To seek the freshest and the purest air ;
The richest blessing in the world's vast pale,
  Either for peasants, courtiers, or the fair ;
Without it, all creation would grow stale,
  And Death usurp dominion everywhere ;
All animated nature through its aid
Is vivified, and from destruction stayed :

XIV.

'Tis the balsamic stay of human life,
  Increasing strength, and general health bestowing ;
All those who slight it, set themselves at strife
  With the Creator's aim, with good o'erflowing
Enjoy the bracing air when Spring is rife
  With balmy odors, gentle zephyr's blowing ;
They are rich stores of nature's vital wealth,
Producing length of days and perfect health.

XV.

Therefore I say to those who age admire,
In the free air gaily yourselves disport ;
And of its virtues full supply acquire,
By vigorous exercise and merry sport ;
So may each one most healthfully respire,
And strengthen every outwork of life's fort ;
By air and exercise the body thrives,
And men of sense thus lengthen out their lives.

XVI.

But, while I thus commend the bracing air,
I must enjoin, in terms not less emphatic,
That you avoid all drafts ; for they prepare
The way, and bring on pains rheumatic,
Which to remove may baffle all your care,
And leave, for years, those twinges so erratic ;
Air is of use, but drafts are dangerous things,
And spare not peasants, merchants, bankers, kings.

XVII.

Also avoid, as you would shun the pest,
Air that is foul, no matter how created ;
In crowded rooms be not a frequent guest,
Nor sit for hours with wine or grog elated ;
Foul-air and drinking will disturb your rest,
And bring on pains not easily abated ;
And should you feel such fumes affect your brain,
Rush to fresh-air to make you well again.

XVIII.

Cleanliness is next to Godliness, says Paul ;
And common-sense corroborates his saying ;
Some wash but seldom, others not all—
Yet, washing is as needful, oft, as praying :
If once you into filthy habits fall,
You are from prudence and religion straying ;
Keep pure your body by such free ablutions
As may preserve you from unclean pollutions.

XIX.

Neglect not bathing, as too many do,
For, thereby, you may ward off many an ill;
Sometimes a warm-bath may your strength renew;
But, of the cold, be sure to take your fill.
The Easterns, old and young, this course pursue,
Nor shun the water though it should be chill;
Hence, such diseases as fell gout and stone,
To Indians and to Persians are scarce known.

XX.

Clean linen as a comfort we esteem,
And frequent changes of our underdress;
These as essential to our health, I deem,
And therefore urge them on you with some stress:
Tis of importance, trifling though it seem,
What I would now upon your minds impress—
Forget not that whene'er you are attiring,
Not to put on cold garments, while perspiring.

XXI.

Do not neglect the sea, nor flowing river,
But, in due season, go to beach or brink;
Yet, do not stand undressed, to shake and shiver,
Nor from the healthy plunge affrighted shrink;
Lave well your limbs, e'en though muscles quiver,
And learn to swim, nor be afraid to sink;
Swimming invigorates all the limbs and breast,
Makes the day cheerful, and at night brings rest.

XXII.

But, above all, let Diet have your care,
For, therein healthy action most depends;
Of after-efforts you may well despair
For past imprudences to make amends:
To this point, therefore, I again repair,
As frequent repetition sometimes tends
To impress a truth more strongly on the mind,
And its observance to our practice bind.

XXIII.

A few words more, and then, I shall have done—
  Let man consider well our nature's laws ;
In every mortal underneath the sun,
  Effects are consequent upon some cause ;
Body and mind united are in one,
  And each affects the other ; therefore, pause
Before intemperance blasts the body's healty
And robs the mind of intellectual wealth.

XXIV.

All who these Rules will wisely lay to heart,
  May hope to reach a venerable age,
Nor wish to stay, nor fear hence to depart ;
  For what is Death but *freedom* to the sage ?
Death has no terrors that can make them start ;
  And when they quit, at length, this mortal stage,
Pleased with the life of prudence that is past,
In hope they quietly shall breathe their last !

I.

To Dr. Triller's *Rules of Health*, I add one more,
  Though at the hazard of your condemnation ;
For, there are thousands now, as heretofore,
  Who will not thank me for my observation :
I also know, that you may quote from lore
  Of ancient days, of some consideration,
To show the error of the Rule I want
To give, regarding the Tobacco-plant.

II.

Poisons (as arsenic, opium) may, from use,
  Lose much of their intrinsic, mortal power ;
Yet, they are *poisons* still : 'tis the abuse
  Of the pernicious weed (on which I shower
The censures of great men—whether as *juice*,
  Or *leaf*, or *dust*) that at this hour,
Many conceive it innocent ; but, know
It is to health a deleterious foe.

III.

Urban the Eighth, we read in history's page,
  Passed on *snuff-takers* ex-communication.
The Czar of Russia, in a former age,
  Punished the crime of this abomination
By cutting off the nose. The still more sage
  Senate of Berne, on due deliberation,
Forbade the Swiss to *smoke* Tobacco, as a crime
Great as was *theft* or *murder* in the code divine.

IV.

In Canton Valois, I have read or heard,
  Exists a prohibition of its use in Youth;
A man must wait until he gets a beard
  Before he *smokes.* And 'tis a well-known truth
That James the First, of England ("the absurd")
  Tried force, to put Tobacco down; forsooth,
A silly trick, in that pedantic king;
As Englishmen, *by force,* will not do anything.

V.

Sultan Amurad the Fourth, to death condemned
  All *smokers* of Tobacco. And that great man
Baba Nanuk, whose conduct I commend,
  By a religious obligation, formed a plan
To keep it from the Sikhs; he did forefend
  That poisonous weed, and through the nation ran
His interdiction; e'en as a remedy for pain,
All efforts to administer the weed, prove vain.

VI.

The so-called *barbarous* Sikh, preserves his race
  Against the noxious plant; while boasting Europe tries
To increase its filthy use; Governments have the face,
  In spite of health, to form monopolies
Of this most baneful weed—What a disgrace!
  E'en England's Rulers common-sense defies,
Bartering (by Acts of Parliament) the health
Of a whole people, for a little wealth!

VII.

Able physicians often have asserted,
  By *snuffing* up Tobacco, also *smoking*;
The plant is from its *true use* much perverted.
  In the fair-sex it ever is provoking
Sensations of disgust—in short, it is diverted
  From Nature's purpose ! and I end, invoking
The Genius of the British Isles, to banish hence
  Customs so contrary to Common-sense !

J M H.

EXPLANATIONS OF THE PLATES.

:o:

The lithographic engravings in this, the first volume, are faithful copies of Portraits and Sketches, taken by a native at Lahore—excepting only the likeness of the Faqueer Haridas, which I had from Captain Gardner; and though I never saw Haridas, I rely no the resemblance; for, on showing it to several natives, who knew him well, as also to General Ventura and Colonel Sir C. M. Wade, who were present at the restoration of the Faqueer, they recognised the likeness.

Before entering upon the Explanations of the Plates, I shall give some account of the manners and customs of the Sikhs and Hindoos, in addition to the communications already made.

Sikh, *Sing*, *Singh*, *Khalsa*, are names of that people known to the English by the appellation *Sikhs*. *Sikh* is a derivation from *Sikhna*, to learn; hence, the Sikhs are disciples (pupils) of Baba Nanuk, the Reformer. *Sing*, signifies a *lion*, or *hero*; the Sikhs conceiving themselves to be a powerful race, a nation of warriors.

In their religious principles, they are Reformed Indians. Formerly, the Sikhs inhabited the Punjab only, but, are now to be met with in various parts of Hindostan; as in Cashmere, Thibet, in the North; in the South, at Moultan and Scinde; as far as Calcutta, in the East; and, in the West, at Pishawur and Cabul. Notwithstanding their Reformation, the Shikhs, like the Hindoos, burn their dead; and were they not prohibited by the English, they would burn living beings also with the dead. Their hair, as elsewhere stated, is long; it is wound up in a knot, placed on the fore-part of the head, around which, beginning at the knot, they wind a long and narrow muslin of fine texture, which they denominate *Destar*, *i. e.* head-dress, bearing the appearance of a helmet. The more opulent add to this head-dress pieces of silk, embroidered with silver and gold; also hooks and clasps, with projecting feathers, and a variety of pearls and precious stones. They wear earings of gold and gems; armlets and bracelets, and a profusion of neck ornaments—as exhibited in the male and female portraits in Plates 1, 2, 3, 4.

The Hindoos wear their hair short, which may be seen below the head-dress, as in Plate 4. Every morning, after ablution, during their rites, they tattoo themselves on the nose between the eyes, with saffron, sandalwood, &c. by which their different Castes may be distinguished, and whence the performance of ablution is visible. In Plates 1, 2, 3, the head is engloried; being the sign of majestic eminence.

PLATE. I.	Maharajh, or, Maharajah (King) Runjeet Sing	*v.* page	94
	Maharajh (King) Kurruck Sing,	„	
	Konwar (Heir-apparent) No-Nehal Sing, ...	„	
	Maharajh (King) Shere, or, Sheer Sing, ...	„	
PLATE. II.	Ranee (Queen) Chunda,* ...	„	111.
	Maharajh (King) Dulleep, or, Dhulleep Sing, ...	„	
	Sirdar (Nobleman) Jewahir, or, Jowahar Sing, ...	„	
	Rajah (Prince) Lall Sing, ...	„	
PLATE III.	Maharajh (King) Goolab, or, Gholab Sing, ...	„	119.
	Rajah (Prince) Dhyan, or, Dehan Sing, ...	„	

* This is a distinct personage from Maha-Ranee Chund Kour, wife of Kurruck Sing, mother of No-Nehal, who for a short period was Queen; and was murdered by her female slaves, as related on page 108. Though employed under her government, I never saw her; much less was she visible to any painter; consequently, I have not obtained a likeness; but, in her stead, I give the portrait of Ranee Chunda.

Rajah (Prince) Soochet, or, Suchet Sing, ... *v.* page 119,
Rajah (Prince) Heerah, or, Heera Sing, ... „

PLATE IV. Rajah (Prince) Teja Sing, ... „ 123.
Rajah (Prince) Deena-Nauth, or, Deenanath, ... „
Faqueer or Fakeer (Devotee) Noor-oo-Deen, or, Noorudeen, or, Nouredden, ... „
Sirdar (Nobleman) Dost, or, Dhost Mohamed,* ... ... „

PLATE V. Charaina Sowar (a Cuirassier) „ 124
Nahung, or, Akalee (Immortal) fanatic Sikh, ... „

PLATE VI. Sing Sipahee (Sepoy) ... „ 100.
Mooselman, or, Mussulman Sipahee (Mahomedan Sepoy) „
Gorekhee Sipahee (Napaulese Sepoy) ... ... „

PLATE VII. Haridas ... ... „ 131

PLATE VIII. Hakim, or, Hakeem (Mohamedan or Mahomedan Doctor) „ 145.

The Doctor is feeling the pulse of his patient, behind whom is a urinal bottle. A medicine chest, containing simply electuaries and pills (in wooden boxes) is beside him ; before him lies his notebook, and near it his inkstand, with a cane-pen sticking in it, together with penknife, scissors, recipes, and a couple of pomegranates.

PLATE IX. Attar, or, Uttar (Druggist) ... *v.* page 154.

The Druggist is sitting on the outside of his shop, serving a customer. A very small and simple distilling apparatus, with a refrigerator (cooling vessel) is before him. It is worthy of remark, that not any names or labels are to be

* This present Regent of Cabul does not strictly belong to this series of portaits ; but, as he is notorious in the history of the last Sikh war, and having obtained a striking likeness of him, I present it to my readers.

seen on any of the bottles or jars ; probably, to keep their contents a secret from others.

PLATE X. B'hangee (Hemp-plant Drinker) *v.* page 158.

Chursee Bhistee, or Mushkee (a Mahomedan watercarrier) smoking Churrus. In his hand, he holds a hooka, which he is lighting with a coal taken from the fire before him. On his back, is the goat-skin in which he carries water.

Faqueer Postee (Poppy-head Drinker) smoking his hooka, while rubbing poppy-heads with his hands in a vessel with water, which he afterwards strains through a cloth and drinks. He is tattooed on the arm. Behind him may be seen the goat-skin containing water.

PLATE XI. Kar-Khana Abkaree (Stillatory) page 161. The Distiller, as well as the Drinker, is a Mahomedan. This mode of distilling is, however, very imperfect.

PLATE XII. *Fac smile* of the *Badela* (document) re-appointing the Author of this work Physician to the Court of Lahore, also, Superintendent to the Gunpowder and to the Gunstock Manufactories, delivered by the Vizier (Wuzeer) Jowahar Sing, under Dulleep Sing's government. A copy of the document is exhibited on account of its peculiarities. It is headed with the Signature of the Vizier, and stamped with three seals ; the innermost of which, like the document itself, is in the Persian language ; the other two, together with the Vizier's signature, are in the Goormukee character, similar to the *Grunth* (holy-book) of the Sikhs; and which characters are already known in Europe. On the margin of the page is a Signature, which may serve as a specimen of the many signatures with which the back of the document is covered ... ... *v.* page 117.

PLATE XIII. Copy of a document, in Persian, authorizing the writer of these volumes to establish, for his own account, a Beet-root Sugar manufactory, at Cashmere. It is headed with the signature of Maharajh Gholab Sing ... ... *v.* page 181.

PLATE XIV. Copy of an Order, issued by the late Sikh-government, to the author of this work, to receive and entertain as Guests, the eighteen English prisoners taken at Aliwal, and forwarded from Philoor, by Runjoor Sing. This Order; also, is headed with the Signature of Gholab Sing, who, in the absence of Lall Sing, was then temporary Vizier of the State of Lahore ... ... *v.* page 126.

The reason for presenting these Copies to the public, is as follows—In the course of last year, I was informed by the Chief Director of the Imperial Government Printing Office at Vienna, that there were 500 different species of native, and 104 foreign types, in that establishment ; among which I observed the Goormukee characters of the Sikhs, mentioned in the explanation of Plate XII : yet, amid that vast collection, the character of the signature of Maharajh Gholab Sing, as exhibited on this and the preceding document, is not to be found—a curiosity worthy of observation—and, at the request of the Director of that famous establishment, the writer hereof has undertaken, on his return to the East, to furnish that hitherto unknown character in Europe, to the Imperial Printing Office, after having ascertained the reality of the existence of such a *Character*, and that it is not merely a *Monogram* belonging to this family of the Rajahs of the Hills.

In a corner of this Plate, is added a similar Signature of the late Rajah Heera Sing, nephew of Gholab Sing.

PLATE XV. Omitted ; and consequently the explanations have been left out.—*Ed.*

PLATE XVI. Jerah, or Jerrah, or Jurrah (Surgeon) or Nai (Barber) or Hajam (Cupper) ... ... *v.* page 153.

The Barber is represented shaving the head. His apparatus near him.

Led by sagacious taste, the ruthless king
Of beasts, on blood and slaughter only lives;
The tiger, formed alike to cruel meals,
Would at the manager starve; of milder seeds
The generous horse to herbage and to grain
Confines his wish—though fabling Greece resound
The Thracian steeds with human-carnage wild;
Prompted by instinct's never-erring power,
Each creature knows its proper aliment;
But man, the inhabitant of every clime,
With all the commoners of Nature feeds!
Directed, bounded, by this power within,
Their cravings are well aimed: vouptuous man,
Is by superior faculties misled;
Misled from pleasure e'en in quest of joy,
Sated with Nature's boons, what thousands seek,
With dishes tortured from their native taste,
And mad variety, to spur beyond
Its wiser will, the jaded appetite!
Is this for pleasure? Learn a juster taste;
And know, that *temperance* is true *luxury*.

INDEX

PAGE.

Introduction - - - - - - - i.
Alloepathia and Homœopathia - - - - iv.
Tea and Coffee not pernicious - - - - vii.
Medical knowledge, the result of Experience - - ix.
Agreeable form in which Medicines may be administered - - - - - - - - x.
The grand Rule to be observed by all Medical men - xi.
Nostrums—Morrison's and Holloway's Pills, Warburg's Drops, &c. - - - - - xii.
Arsenic recommended, as a Medicine - - - xii.
The Science of Medicine—Stationary - - - xiii.
Advice on the Preparations of Medicines - - xiv.
Monopolies of Churrus, Saffron, and Putchuk-root, by the Cashmerean Government - - - xv.
Object of this work - - - - - xvi.
Recommendation to the faculty in India - - xvii.
The Author's return to Lahore, in 1839 - xviii.
Letter from the late Wm. Stinner, to the Author - xxii.
Fatal power of Prejudice - - - xxiii.
Sydenham, &c - - - - - - - xxiv
How the properties of Medicines may be ascertained - xxv.
Minute doses alone, can produce real medicinal action xxvi
A pocket-book recommended to Physicians and Families - - - - - - xxvii
ADVENTURES, DISCOVERIES, EXPERIMENTS AND HISTORICAL SKETCHES - - - - - 1
The Author leaves Home (Kronstadt in Transylvania) in 1815 - - - - - - - 1
Voyage to Constantinople - - - - - 1
Travels towards Jerusalem, 1817—1819 - - 4
The Author introduces Vaccination into Syria, in 1822 7

PAGE.
Barber, Governor of Tripoly, in Syria - - 18, 8
Lady Esther Stanhope, at Araba, in Syria - - 9
Kannobin not a Town, but a Convent - - - 10
Tapeworm, 52 yards in length - - - - 12
The Author's agreeable abode in Palestine during several years - - - . - - 13
The Cæsarian operation thwarted by the Greek Bishop 17
Wolff, the wide-world known Missionary - - 19
The Author present at the Siege of Acre - - 19
Voyage to Alexandria - - - - - - 19
The Author visits Mr. Reynolds, at Cyprus, in 1823 - 20
Attanas Keptenak, at Alexandria - - - 20
Doctors Hemprich and Ehrenberg - - 81, 21
Padre Tomaso - - - - - - - 21
Mr. Henri De Turck - - - - - - 23
The Author accompanies the Pacha of Damascus to the Fair at Muzerib - - - - - 23
Journey through the Desert, to Bagdad - - 23
Made of Healing practised by the Arabs - - 24
The Agha of Hit - - - - - - 25
Kind reception by Mr. Swoboda at Bagdad - - 31
Deserted by the Guide, in the Desert - - - 35
Embarked for Bender-Bushir, in Persia - - 27
Famine at Mosul, in 1828 - - - - - 40
The Author at the point of death, at Heirpore, in Scinde - - - - - - 41
From Bagdad to Lahore, the Author travels four months ;. two on land, and two on water - - 45
The first patient in Lahore, the adopted Son of General Allard - - - - - - 45
.The Author attended Rajah Suchet Sing into the mountains - - - - - - 46
The Author's treatment of Hydrophobia - - 48
Colonel Sir C. M. Wade - - - 49, 48
New Nose made by the native of India - - 49
Milk-Sugar made by Order of Runjeet Sing - - 51
Coffee unknown at Lahore, in 1832 - - - 52

PAGE.

The Author struck by a *Coup-de-Soceil* - - 53
Glanders cured by the Author - - - - - 54
General Avitabile very fond of Hanging, as a Punishment - - - - - - - 55
A Musk-deer caught, in the Plains of India - - 56
Runjeet Sing - - - - - - 57, 58
The Author appointed Superintendent of a Gunpowder and Gunstock Manufactory, at Lahore - - 57
The Author's return from India to Europe, in 1833-1834 - - - - - - - 59
Vaccination introduced, at Dhera-Ghasi-Khan, by the Author - - - - - - - 59
Vaccination unknown at Cabul, in 1833 - - - 60
The Author's collections of Plants and Antiquities - 61
Loss of the Bactrian Scroll! - - - - - 62
Opening of the Tombs, at Cabul, by the Author - 62
Hospbegi, the Minister of State, at Bokhara 69, 68, 66, 65
Fatal operation on a Student, at Bokhara - - 66
Cure of a chronic Asthma, at Bokhara - - - 69
Efficacy of Wax-oil - - - - - 71
Two unfortunate Armenians from Astrakhan, at Bokhara 72
Horse-milk (*Kumiss*) a nutritious beverage - - 74
The Author's speculation in Sable-skins, at Nishni-Nowgorod - - - - - - - 76
The Author's excursion to St. Petersburgh, in 1834 - 79
The Author's conversation with the Grand Duchess Helene, at St. Petersburgh - - - 79
Trip to Kronstadt, the Port of St. Petersburgh - - 80
Encounter with a Chimney-sweeper - - - 81
Arrival at Kronstadt, in Transylvania, on Christmas-eve, 1834 - - - - - - - 81
Narrow escape of the Author from falling down a Precipice - - - - - - 81
Visit to Vienna, passing through Hungary, in 1835 - 83
A visit to Dr. Hahnemann, at Paris, 1835 - - 83
Voyage from London to Hamburgh, in 1835 - - 84
Homœopathic Medicaments of Dr. Lehman, at Kothen 84

	PAGE.
The Author returns to Kronstadt, his native place, in 1835 - - - - - -	84
Sojourns at Vienna, from Spring to Autumn, in 1836 -	84
Second voyage to Constantinople - - -	85
The Plague not contagious - - - -	86
The Author's success in the Plague-hospital, at Pera -	86
Success of Homœopathic doses at Constantinople, during 1836-1838. - - - - -	88
Cure of the Sultan's son (the present Sultan) by an Armenian lady - - - - -	90
The Author leaves Constantinople for Lahore, in 1838 -	90
An account of the Plague at Palee - - -	92
The Author's recovery from the Plague, caught at Palee - - - - - - -	93
Arrival at Lahore (by the Overland route) in the Spring of 1839 - - - - -	94
Doctors Murray, Steel, and Macgregor - - -	96
Administration of Homœopathic doses to Runjeet Sing - - - - - - -	96
The Author's recompence, by Runjeet Sing - -	97
An account of the Suttee—the burning of Wives, &c. -	101
Colonel Henry Steinbach - - - -	101
Ascension of Kurruck Sing to the throne - -	104
Commencement of the bloody Scenes in the Punjab -	105
No-Nehal, Kurruck Sing's only Son, usurps the throne	105
Deaths of Kurruck Sing, No-Nehal Sing, and Meean Oottum Sing (eldest Son of Gholab Sing) on one day - - - - - - -	106
Ascension of the Ranee Chund Kour, Mother of No-Nehal Sing, to the throne - - - - -	108
Sheer Sing's ascension to the throne - - -	109
Assassination of Sheer Sing, by Ajeet Sing - -	111
The royal prince Pertaub Sing, twelve years of age, assassinated by Lena Sing, uncle to Ajeet Sing -	111
Ascension of Dulleep Sing, youngest son of Runjeet Sing - - - - - - -	112
Jellah Pundit, a fanatical Brahmin - - -	112

PAGE.
Massacre of Heera Sing, and all his Retinue - - 113
The Author's escape, when Sheer Sing was assassinated 114
Dismissal of the Author from the Court of Lahore, in 1844 - - - - - - - 114
The Author re-instated, by Jewahir Sing, in 1844 - 117
Jewahir Sing shot, by the Soldiery - - - 118
Cholera-morbus at Lahore, in 1845 - - - 119
Runjoor Sing, Commander of the Sikhs at Aliwal - 119
Robbery committed by Runjoor Sing's soldiers - 119
Lall Sing, appointed Prime Minister - - - 121
Teja Sing proclaimed Commender-in-Chief of the forces - - - - - - - 122
Prince Waldemar of Prussia, in the English ranks - 123
Decisive Battle of Sobraon, on 10th February, 1846 - 123
Death of the Baba Beer Sing - - - - 124
Utter Sing, brother to Lena Sing the murderer of the Prince - - - - - - - 124
Gholab Sing remained neutral, at Jummoo - - 125
The Author's conversation with Gholab Sing - - 126
English prisoners at Philoor, sent as Guests to the Author's house, by Gholab Sing - - 126
The Author accompanies Gholab Sing, as private Counsellor, to the English Camp - - - 126
End of the Independent State founded by Runjeet Sing - - - - - - - 127
Sir Henry Lawrence, appointed to the English Residentship, at Lahore, in 1846 - - - 127
Lall Sing removed, by the English, to Agra, and pensioned - - - - - - - 128
Tejah Sing created Rajah of Seealkot - - - 128
The Ranee exiled, by the English, to the Fortress of Sheg-Opur, and afterwards to anothor Fortress on the Ganges, whence she contrived to escape - 128
Sir Frederick Currie Resident of Lahore, during the absence of Sir Henry Lawrence, who accompanied Lord Hardinge to England - - - 128
Murder of Agnew and Anderson, at Mooltan - - 129

PAGE.

Decisive Battles of Mooltan and Gujerat, in 1849 - 130
End of the Author's official post, as Physician to the Court - - - - - - 130
Suspension of Life, in the person of Haridas - - 131
A Faqueer uninjured by the bite of venomous Serpents 138
Dr. W. Jameson - - - - - 139
Arsenic Eaters - - - - - - 141
The Author's collection of Serpents - - - 142
Advice in all cases of Bites from venomous creatures - 143
Serpent-love (said to be restricted to the Punjab) - 144
Sheer Sing, "The Son of a Laundress," explained - 147
The Author's adoption of the Medium-system, in Medicine - - - - - - 147
In 1845, upwards of 800 deaths daily from Cholera, at Lahore - - - - - - 148
Galvano-electric Rings - - - - - 149
Zinc and Silver plates, united by a silver wire - - 150
Operations, whilst patients were under the influence of Chloroform - - - - - - 151
Ether and Chloroform mixed, preferable - - 152
Mahomedan Stone-operator - - - - 152
Native Oculists at Lahore - - - - 153
Amputation unknown at Lahore, until introduced by the Author - - - - - - 153
A sort of Animal-magnetism practised in the Punjab - 153
The pulse considered of high importance, in the East - 153
Alms given, in the East, on every occasion of Illness - 154
Major Mac Gregor, director of Police, at Lahore - 155
The Author sends for Assistants, to Europe - - 155
Many Hermaphorodites at Lahore - - - 157
Natives of the Punjab rejoice at the demise of Female infants - - - - - - 157
Intoxicating beverage prepared from the Hemp-plant - 158
Churrus, smoked in the pipe, very intoxicating - 161
The Sikhs and Hindoos refuse Medicines prepared with Liquids, by the hands of Europeans - 160

PAGE.

The Sikhs forbidden to smoke Tobacco, but permitted to take Opium and Spirituous liquors - - 161
Cure for Opium-eaters, Drinkers of the infusion of Poppy-heads, &c. - - - - - - 163
Magendie's Experiment - - - - 164
"Wonders of Sympathy and Magnetism, &c. by Gerstenbergk" - - - - - 165
There is no food which may not serve as Medicine - 166
It is common for every Hindoo to prepare his own dinner - - - - - - - 168
Cold beverages sometimes increase Thirst in the hot season - - - - - - - 169
Beneficial effects produced by Cold-baths - - 170
Two Recipes for Hair-dyes - - - - 171
Sheer Sing extremely polite and amiable - - 173
In 1844 all Europeans dismissed by the Sikhs - - 174
The Author visited, at Lahore, by his Brother - - 174
Herr August Schofft's adventure at Umritsir - - 175
Colonels Mouton and Hurbon dismissed - - 180
The Author's intention and object in again returning to Cashmere - - - - - - 180
Tapping for Dropsy, unknown in Cashmere, in 1849 - 182
Europeans, up to 1849, received and entertained as Guests in Cashmere - - - - - 183
Lord Gifford and the unfortunate Colonel King visited Cashmere - - - - - 183
The Maharajah of Cashmere (Gholab Sing) pretends to cure all cases of Paralysis - - - 183
Curious species of theft, practised in Cashmere - 184
Cashmerean Plants may be obtained by Doctors in Europe - - - - - - - 185
In September 1849, the Author leaves Cashmere for Europe - - - - - - - 186
The Author visits his two Daughters at Mussoorie - 186
Pleasant passage down the Ganges to Calcutta - 186
Inhabitants of Santipore, on the Ganges - - 187

PAGE.

Dr. James Esdaile's operations at Calcutta, upon patients under Mesmeric influence - - 187
No Beggars seen by the Author, at the Cape of Good Hope - - - - - - - 188
Dr. Triller's *Rules of Health* - - - - 191
The Author's addition, on the abuse of Tobacco - 197
Explanation of the Plates - - - - 201
Index - - - - - - - - 207